Praise for Becoming Gandhi

Perry Garfinkel's engaging and delightfully funny *Becoming Gandhi* shows us how the Mahatma's message can matter in our lives. Brilliant. Highly recommended.

—Daniel Goleman, author of *Emotional Intelligence* and most recently *Why We Meditate*, with Tsoknyi Rinpoche

It is beautiful to be inspired by Gandhi. It is even more amazing to learn to embody his love and freedom, honesty, and blessings in our own lives. Perry shows us how this is possible.

—Jack Kornfield, author *A Path with Heart* and cofounder of Insight Meditation Society

In this timely book, Perry Garfinkel writes, "Truth is elusive and mercurial." What is not elusive or mercurial is the brilliance of this book, rich with anecdotes, humor, and wisdom. Perry takes us on a journey with Gandhi, almost literally step by step. As a memoir of spiritual travel, this is the medicine we all need in these times—truly an inspiration. And that's the truth.

—Nancy Slonim Aronie, author of *Writing from the Heart* and *Memoir as Medicine*

Engaging and insightful, *Becoming Gandhi* is one man's quest to follow the footsteps of Gandhi and rediscover the moral compass that has been abandoned by today's culture of me-centered instant gratification. In reading, we are inspired to reflect on our own journey and what it means to align our life with our heart.

—Tara Brach, author of *Radical Acceptance* and *Trusting the Gold*

Gandhi was truly one of the last figures of the European historic colonial period and all that was linked to it. As a Brit of Bangladeshi (and therefore historic Indian) descent, I still struggle to find our colonial past in our education system. I welcome writers like Perry who are able to transcend cultural barriers. As he writes, "All I need to do is take the blinders off and look for the clues along the way." Writing about historic events or persons is nothing new but what is important is that Perry makes Gandhi relevant today!

—Munsur Ali, Chairman, Culture, Heritage and Libraries,
City of London; and film producer

What would it be like to live like Gandhi? Garfinkel finds out, not just by reading Gandhi's words but by living Gandhi's truths. Garfinkel's struggle to abide by Gandhi's morality becomes a complex meditation on the struggle to be good, and what 'good' even means in our own troubled times. By engaging with Gandhi's personal code of ethics, Garfinkel makes Gandhi come alive and challenges us to think seriously about what principles we cherish.

—Andy Rotman, Professor of Religion, Buddhist Studies,
and South Asian Studies, Smith College

An integrated view of Mahatma Gandhi's life and thought based on a careful analysis of some of his guiding principles, *Becoming Gandhi* illuminates areas that usually get ignored and offers a theoretically insightful and practically rich view of how to lead a Gandhian, or Gandhi-like, life in the modern world. The book also uses Gandhi to understand the nature of religious faith and to mark a moving personal journey from Judaism to Buddhism via Hinduism.

—Bhikhu Chotalal Parekh, British House of Lords,
and author of *Rethinking Multiculturalism*

BECOMING GANDHI

Living the Mahatma's 6 Morals Truths in Immoral Times

PERRY GARFINKEL

SIMON & SCHUSTER

London · New York · Sydney · Toronto · New Delhi

PARAMOUNT

First published in India by Simon & Schuster India, 2023

1 3 5 7 9 10 8 6 4 2

Simon & Schuster India
818, Indraprakash Building,
21, Barakhamba Road,
New Delhi 110001.

www.simonandschuster.co.in

Hardback ISBN: 978-93-92099-85-4
eBook ISBN: 978-93-92099-86-1

Typeset in India by SŪRYA, New Delhi
Printed and bound in India by Replika Press Pvt. Ltd.

FSC
www.fsc.org
MIX
Paper from responsible sources
FSC® C016779

Simon & Schuster India is committed to sourcing paper that is made from wood grown in sustainable forests and support the Forest Stewardship Council, the leading international forest certification organisation. Our books displaying the FSC logo are printed on FSC certified paper.

To Sue Mattison

You've shown me what true strength and commitment are in the face of all adversity. I knew you had it in you, my dearest Big Sis.

THE DALAI LAMA

FOREWORD

I have always believed that the best way to preserve the legacy of the great statesmen of the past is to try to abide by the values they upheld and to apply them in our contemporary situation. I am glad to see that writer Perry Garfinkel has done precisely that with Mahatma Gandhi and shares his experiences in this book.

In the last century, Gandhi ji showed how the long-standing Indian tradition of non-violence (*Ahimsa*) could be applied in practical terms. His achievements were admired and emulated by such figures as Martin Luther King Jr, Nelson Mandela and Archbishop Desmond Tutu. Being non-violent and doing no harm are not only morally correct, they are practically appropriate too.

I also try to be a follower of Gandhi ji's message. Ever since I was a small boy growing up in Tibet, I had heard about him. As I began to know more about his life I was deeply inspired by his adoption of non-violence in India's freedom struggle. Indeed, I have put this into practice in my own efforts to restore the fundamental human rights and freedoms of the Tibetan people.

I also admired the simplicity and discipline of Gandhi-ji's way of life. Although he received a thorough, modern education, well versed in western ways of living, he returned to his Indian heritage and deliberately cultivated a simple, wholesome life in accordance with Indian tradition. He dedicated his life for the welfare of the common people, who everywhere constitute the majority.

In this book Perry Garfinkel explores six of Gandhi ji's principles to see not only if they can still be applied today, but also whether he could put them into practice himself. The non-violence that Gandhi ji advocated was not the mere absence of violence. To him, nonviolence was a way of life that was needed to be adopted for the broader wellbeing of humanity.

Cultivating non-violence and compassion is part of my own daily practice. It is of practical benefit. It brings satisfaction and peace of mind that is a sound basis for maintaining genuine, kind relationships with other people. This is important since our own successful and happy future is so interlinked with that of others.

In this book, the author provides readers with an opportunity to discover the many ways in which Gandhi ji contributed to making the world a better place and what each of us may learn from his example.

17 June 2023

Preface

Bapu, my great grandfather, Gandhi, used to say with amusement that he was like a magnet attracting all the faddists and nutcases of the world! When Perry approached me with his idea of living like Gandhi, the first thought that came to my mind was "Thar she blows!" Here's a nutcase who believes that in today's time he can live the simple, frugal and abstemious life that Bapu lived, that too an American! As he talked to me of his idea, I began getting scared, I started realizing the guy was serious! "Does he even know what it entails? Should I dissuade him?" Then I thought this was a fad and would soon pass. Well, Perry proved me wrong.

His journey was three folds—discovering and understanding Gandhi, not just the man but his belief; discovering the land and people of Gandhi's India; and most important, testing himself by taking on the challenge of living according to the tenets of Gandhi, as many as he could. The other search was also to see where Gandhi was at present, in the land he helped liberate, was he at all there? Was he relevant? Did he matter?

This book is the story of Perry's experiments with Gandhi. In writing it Perry has imbibed Bapu's wry sense of humour too in that he has definitely lived Gandhi!

The other quality I have come to admire in Perry is his

tenacity. He never gives up. He faced so many hurdles in his path to accomplish, first his experiment and then get this book published. He never gave up. Over the years I grew accustomed to missives from Perry popping up in my inbox after long gaps of silence informing me that he was closer to his objective. This book is the result of Perry's adventurous spirit, to go where not many dare to go. His die-hard spirit, never giving up. And above all, because he is a nut case! Who else would have done what he has in today's time?

For me, there is a sense of loss with this experiment by Perry. Perry met my cousin Satish and became friends with him. He met my father Arun in Rochester and interviewed him. We lost Satish almost two years ago and my father on 2nd May. They were both eager to read about Perry's adventure.

The book is definitely a must read. Sail on, my dear friend.

TUSHAR GANDHI, socio-political activist,
and author of *The Lost Diary of Kastur, My Ba,*
and *Let's Kill Gandhi!*

CONTENTS

A Day in the Life of Mahatma Gandhi

How did Mahatma Gandhi get so much done? Discipline, focus, commitment, obsessiveness, the desire to make every day count—and count for the good of others. He kept to his daily schedule almost religiously. In fact, I believe adhering to this agenda every day became part of his spiritual ritual, his sadhana. The Sanskrit translation of sadhana is "realization." In Hinduism and Buddhism, it's a spiritual exercise that evokes a divinity, identifying and absorbing it into himself.

4 a.m.—Wake up call. Gandhi believed rising 90 minutes before sunrise, which Hindus call Brahmamuhurta, is the auspicious time to meditate, do yoga and other spiritual practices.

4:20 a.m.—Community prayers including one of his favourite bhajans, "Vaishnav Jan To" and Prabhatiya (morning bhajan), accompanied by others. Also begins writing, work or short rest.

7 a.m.—Breakfast, followed by 5 km morning walk. Helps in ashram kitchen, cleaning utensils and latrines, cutting vegetables, grinding wheat, etc.

8.30 a.m.—Meets visitors, begins writing or reading. He wrote many letters; the collected works of his written documents includes more than 30,000 letters. (On Monday he kept a day of silence.)

9.30 a.m.—Oil massage in the sun and a bath plus shave. He used minimum water to save the precious liquid. Cleanliness was also a part of his discipline; he often carried a broom around the ashram to clean whenever he got a chance.

11.00 a.m.—Lunch of vegetarian diet of fresh vegetables and fruits, with low intake of sugars, salt, and fats.

1 p.m.—More correspondence, more visitors. Often there would be a line of people waiting to meet him, to discuss pressing issues of the time.

4.30 p.m.—Spinning his charkha (hand spinning wheel), which was his meditation and became a revolutionary tool encouraging Indians to forego British clothing made with Indian cotton.

5 p.m.—Evening dinner.

6 p.m.—Evening prayers, with community bhajans. Sometimes he would sing along with the people at the ashram, followed by a short prayer and speech, reflecting on current issues.

6.30 p.m.—Evening walk.

9 p.m.—Bedtime.

Timeline of the Life of Gandhi

October 2, 1869—Birth in Porbandar.

May 1883—Married at age 13 to Kasturbai.

September 29, 1888—Reached Southampton, England for law school.

May 27, 1891—Called to the Bar—Returned to India to practice law.

May 25, 1893—Reached Durban (Natal), South Africa.

August 22, 1894—Founded the Natal Indian Congress.

September 11, 1906—Organized the Advent of Satyagraha at Empire Theatre, Johannesburg, where attendees vowed to oppose the Black Act by noncooperation with registration laws.

January 10, 1908—First of three arrests, sentenced to imprisonment at Transvaal in South Africa for failure to register.

May 20, 1915—Back in India, established Satyagraha Ashram, Kochrab.

March 18, 1922—Trial at Ahmedabad Circuit House where Gandhi received a sentence of six years' imprisonment for sedition.

May 5, 1930—After leading the Salt March, arrested and sent to Yeravda Prison for breaking the salt law.

September 20, 1932—The fast commenced for the treatment of untouchables.

December 14, 1934—All India Village Industries Association established.

August 8, 1942—Quit India resolution adopted; gave the call "Do or Die."

February 22, 1944—Death of Kasturbai; cremated at Aga Khan Palace.

August 15, 1947—Spent the day in fast and prayer. (Day of India's independence)

January 30, 1948—Nathuram Godse assassinated Gandhi.

INTRODUCTION

Let the Journey Begin

By reading this Preface, you have just joined what will hopefully be the experiment of a lifetime that changes both of our lives. Let me set the ground rules, parameters, frameworks, timelines, caveats, excuses, permissions and other details that will help you navigate your way—if not to be Gandhi, then to become a person who leads a more ethical, principled, spiritually and morally based truth-full life.

As you will read in Chapter One, I first thought to undertake this effort more than a decade ago. It took me another 12 years to build up the confidence, belief in my commitment to this and, frankly, the funding to actually begin this arduous journey, both inner and outer, including travel to three countries plus my own United States. Little did I know how much it would change me, how many miles I would travel, how many inspirational people I would meet, and some disappointments I would encounter, both in the world and in myself.

I took it seriously in the summer of 2019. That was when I started finding and contacting knowledgeable sources in each country. As a dogged reporter who prides himself in finding the email and phone number for anyone anywhere in the world, that deep dive, which necessarily required a lot of reading and googling, was a relatively easy and a very enjoyable and informative exercise. You may also want to research anything additional to what I write here, and experiment with your own ways to follow the 6 principles. I can't speak for Gandhi, but you have my wholehearted permission and encouragement to think outside the box and off this page.

The Big Goal is to see if, in the face of a sociocultural climate that appears bereft of moral integrity, one could follow Gandhi's moral compass, on the one hand; and on the other, to travel to countries where he spent considerable time to see how much had changed in the years since he left them. In other words, did he leave an enduring footprint that others followed or were Gandhi's tracks swept away and forgotten by time and human nature? In these times of questionable ethical values, of increased violence and rampant lying, I was prepared to admit such evidence might be hard to find. In fact, in one too current example of the failure of the nonviolent movement, which was one of Gandhi's primary pillars, as I'm writing now, CNN just reported that 39 mass shootings have taken place in the United States in the first three weeks of 2023, killing more than 60 people, per the Gun Violence Archives.

The hard part, then, would be living these principles day in and day out on a personal level. There will be a lot of inner work, mental adjustments, a veritable paradigmatic shift of attitude. I will have to change my mind in the most fundamental ways. Change my habits, modes of thinking, daily actions.

The ground rules are simple: try to rigorously follow the 6 principles on a daily basis, keeping them in mind through the day, whether hanging out with friends and family, alone in my apartment, or out there in the world. But also to give myself some slack. If I "fall off the wagon," forgive myself quickly and get right back on it. The latter would happen with frequency, as you will read. But I realized very soon that once engaged in this experiment, even when I fell off, there would be no turning back. Once the veil is lifted, it's hard not to see the world for what it is, and see yourself for who you are, who you are not, and who you aspire to be.

How long would this experiment last then? People started asking me when or if, for example, I would drop vegetarianism and return to eating meat as soon as it ended. I planned to dedicate one full year to this project. It expanded to some 18 months of strict adherence to all of the principles, and even some that Gandhi didn't consider in the course of things. I admit I slacked after that but, as I said, once you know which way the compass is pointing, you can't completely turn back; you always return to your True North. You find the balance that suits you best, or at least better than before you started.

I frame this journey and this book around the six principles. Some sources list up to eleven Gandhian principles. I chose only six; already you can call me lazy.

- **Truth.** In practice, truth is simply telling the truth but Gandhi meant it to mean more. He said, "God is Truth," and later changing it to "Truth is God." He coined the term Satyagraha—loosely translated as "insistence on and holding firm to truth"—as a form of nonviolent resistance. I take this on, first focusing on practicing truth in thoughts, words and actions, with particular attention to lies I tell myself. I look at how society views truth now.

- **Non-violence.** Although Gandhi was not the originator of non-violence, he was the first to apply it as a strategy to move the dial in the direction of justice, as a peaceful weapon to protest social wrongdoings. His motto: "An eye for an eye makes the whole world blind." Taking it from the political to the personal, I look at how we all act out psychological violence—in passive aggressive behaviors, in road rage, clenched jaws, in couched (and not so couched) language—that sabotage our best interests. I myself am guilty: I was once a featured guest on *The Phil Donahue Show* speaking about my own passive aggressive behavior in my previous marriage.
- **Vegetarianism.** Vegetarianism is deeply ingrained in Hindu and Jain traditions, the setting in which Gandhi was raised. In his London years as a law student, he embraced it more seriously to not only satisfy the requirements of the body and his religious beliefs but also to save money by not buying expensive meats. His book, *The Moral Basis of Vegetarianism,* and articles he wrote for the London Vegetarian Society's publication become my personal diet book. I was a meat-and-potatoes kind of kid, just like my father. I became a macrobiotic many years ago, have defaulted to meat in recent years, but an ayurveda diet I went on last fall convinced me I need to clean up my eating habits. Don't we all?
- **Simplicity.** Giving up unnecessary spending is the simple maxim Gandhi had in mind. But it also has ramifications in our glutinous nature, in thinking that more of anything is more. Today that concept flies in the face of conspicuous consumers on spending sprees

in shopping malls. But Gandhi had a political motive in his so-called Swadeshi movement: by making their own clothes using a spinning wheel (*charkha*), Indians would deal an economic blow to the British establishment in India. These days consumers boycott various brands and stores to protest their company policy, a Gandhian spin. The contemporary "voluntary simplicity movement" draws directly from this Gandhian principle. I will closely examine my spending patterns and make budget slashes. Gandhi called it "reducing himself to zero."

- **Faith.** Gandhi meant belief in a Higher Power, no matter what religion. He wrote: "Mine is a broad faith which does not oppose Christians...not even the most fanatical *Mussalman*. I refuse to abuse a man for his fanatical deeds, because I try to see them from his point of view." It's the ability to see things from the point of view of someone from another faith that tests the faith of Mankind. How are we doing with that? Not so good: the majority of wars in the world are religious wars. My challenge will be to find some balance between my practice of Buddhism, the religion of no God, and Judaism, the religion that invented the One God. I will test the boundaries of my belief in faiths I don't believe in.
- **Celibacy.** Called *Brahmacharya*, sexual abstinence was a spiritual path to achieving purity, according to Gandhi, who took the vow of chastity at the age of 38. Some people question whether Gandhi himself adhered to this, with stories and allegations he slept next to teenage girls to test his restraint. Celibacy is not for everyone. Is it for me? I will endeavor to find out, keeping copious notes on

> my fallings in and out. With my luck, the woman of my dreams will walk into my life and fall in love with me at this very point in my life. What will I do...or, more precisely, not do?

I never intended this to be categorized in the how-to or self-help genre. I think or hope you can help yourself without my telling you how. Nonetheless, as I made my way around the world, around my mind, and finally around this book, I realized it would be helpful to at least sum up each chapter with what I learned, some tips for your (and my own) benefit. I call these end-of-chapter sections "How to Gandhi."

With these guidelines and to-do's and with no further ado, here we go. Next stop: becoming the change.

1

WHY GANDHI? WHY NOW? WHY ME?

"I call him religious who understands the suffering of others."
—Mahatma Gandhi

"And the God of all grace, who called you to His eternal glory in Christ, after you have suffered a little while, will Himself restore you and make you strong, firm and steadfast."
—1 Peter 5:10, King James Version of the Bible

I cry more, often triggered by the gravity of the human condition.

But I also laugh more, often triggered by the inherent humor in the human condition.

I feel more.

I empathize more.

Emotion researchers generally define empathy as the ability to sense other people's emotions. One of the last notes Gandhi left behind before his death in 1948 was later published in "Mahatma Gandhi: The Last Phase." Gandhi wrote something that demonstrates his level of empathy and how pivotal it is to his philosophy of life: "I will give you a talisman. Whenever you are in doubt, or when the self becomes too much for you, try the following expedient: Recall the face of the poorest and the most helpless man whom you may have seen and ask yourself, if the step you contemplate is going to be of any use to him [or her]. Will he [or she] be able to gain anything by it? Will it restore him [or her] to a control over his [or her] own life and destiny? ... Then you will find your doubts...melting away."

This talisman—any object ascribed with religious or magical powers intended to protect, heal, or harm individuals for whom they are made—came to be known as "Gandhi's talisman," a moral compass pointing the way toward how people should consider the viewpoint of others, to make ethical decisions then ensure their actions benefit fellow humans in some way.

While I've always thought I am an empathic person, with Gandhi's direction, I now look more closely at the impact of my words and actions.

Nowadays the word "empathy" is bandied about as an important component of emotional intelligence, and as a quality that distinguishes good leaders. There are already books that show how following the Gandhi code of ethics makes for good business, such as *Gandhi, The Eternal Management Guru: How Mahatma's principles are relevant for modern day business*, by Pratik Surana (Notion Press, 2017); and *A Higher Standard of Leadership: Lessons from the Life of Gandhi*, by Keshavan Nair (Berrett-Koehler Publishers, 1996).

Empathy is a quality I admire in others, and one I have hoped to embody more. So, on that count, I can declare this experiment a small success. In the past, I often took the me-first approach. How does what you're feeling affect me? Now I try to remember others' needs. On a more practical level, like Gandhi himself, I have made strides toward changes that I learned or adapted from following Gandhi's regimens:

I now eat oatmeal for breakfast—me, the kid who felt oatmeal was a punishment when my mother did not let me have my favorite Frosted Flakes, Trix or Fruit Loops.

I am now a pescatarian—not vegetarian like Gandhi but a big step toward better health for me who, like my father and his father and other would-be macho men, took great pride in declaring themselves a "meat-and-potatoes man." (Side note: my grandfather died of a heart attack; my father had two heart "events," so certainly there were some life-and-death motivations for me if I wanted to live a long and healthy life).

I fast regularly, long ones, short ones. I have been intermittently fasting, an approach I only recently heard of, often skipping two meals in a row from time to time.

If these relatively mundane and superficial changes suggest that I'm asking you to go *only* on a self-improvement mission, you are wrong—though that will surely be a byproduct. The goal here is to imagine a world, albeit a utopian world, in which people act, think and speak with the highest moral sensibilities and aspirations, as Gandhi had hoped of all human beings. And then I'm asking you to assess your life and values, and behaviors mental and actual, as I have here, to see how they align with and fit into this Utopia. Finally, then, to make adjustments personally if this is indeed of interest to you, as I posit they should be, if you want to live in a place free of violence, free of lies and deceits, where faith, integrity, compassion and empathy can thrive...rather than just simply survive. So far I do not see evidence that enough people have jumped on the moral bandwagon. And I confess this from the start: I have tendencies that preclude me from living in that utopian society. Thus this experiment in change.

Empathy would be one of the last lessons I'd learn by looking at the world and myself through the prism of Mahatma Gandhi. Not that I wanted to be Gandhi. I found the man to be almost inhumanly perfect in his discipline and idealism, not my style. My research also showed me he was not a saint or avatar or even mahatma, "great soul," the honorific poet Rabindranath Tagore gave Mohandas Gandhi in 1915.

Mahatma Gandhi fascinated me on almost too many levels. The breadth and depth of the man's interests are daunting.

He was at the forefront of more movements than people know him for: namely, the nonviolent fighter for India's independence from its colonial ruler, England. That independence was achieved in 1947; a year later he was assassinated by a zealot right-wing Hindu.

At feet 5 feet 5 inches (167.6 centimeters) and weighing approximately 102 pounds (46.7 kg), Gandhi nonetheless cast a long shadow as precursor to a number of intersecting social and cultural trends: of living lightly on the Earth, a.k.a. minimalism or voluntary simplicity; of vegetarianism and animal rights; of using natural and homegrown fabrics, a.k.a. artisanal products; of innovative educational initiatives; and on and on. A Who's Who of Brilliance cutting a huge swath across a wide spectrum, some 20 renowned world leaders and thinkers claimed Gandhi as a major influence.

He innovated, motivated, masterminded, mobilized, moralized, energized. He inspired many millions and not just in India but throughout the world. There are hundreds, if not thousands, of streets and squares in India named after him. The same holds true of streets, avenues and boulevards in some 30 other countries. A statue of him appears in virtually every Indian city and village. Gandhi statues also have been erected in more than 70 other countries, with the United States having the largest number of Gandhi statues, memorials and busts. He was a writing machine, a prolific author whose works in books, newspaper articles, treatises and letters fill 100 volumes. Equally, he was a voracious reader, having read close to 400 books in his lifetime.

I was fascinated as much by what Gandhi had achieved as by what he had not. He never held a title other than as a barrister. He was never elected to or held a political post; he never even campaigned for one. He never held a government position. He never served in the military. He never had an actual fulltime salaried job. He never amassed a fortune; his only possessions were so minimal as to be negligible. He never was ordained as a spiritual leader. Yet, his face graces every Indian paper currency, to the exclusion of any other leader in India past or present. And despite all the "nevers," he is one of a very few people in history called "The Father of the Nation" without having been a military leader or president of his or her country.

The degree to which the odds were stacked against me to attain anything close to being Gandhi were made clear when I read about a 2012 poll called The Greatest Indian, conducted by *Outlook* magazine in partnership with CNN-IBN and The History Channel. The judges decided to disallow Gandhi as a candidate since, as they put it, "it is impossible for anyone to come close to the father of the nation when it comes to leadership, impact and contribution." So what chance would I ever have of approaching anywhere near the Mahatma?

I simply (simply?) wanted to see if any ordinary person living in the early 21st century could follow six of the principles on which Gandhi built the foundations of his morally driven game plan. What drove me to explore this question? Because I saw myself and society moving further away from a moral point of view.

I knew it would be an arduous task. Turns out it was more arduous than I had ever imagined.

The endeavor was so difficult that while the original title of this book was "Being Gandhi," I surrendered to the reality that the best I could hope for was to eternally strive to *become* closer to what Gandhi stood for. I figured that if I remained always in the state of becoming Gandhi, then each act, thought and word throughout my days would be enough. The gerundial form implies perpetually seeking, a good place to be. The folk singer Bob Dylan knew this. As he told Martin Scorsese in "No Direction Home," the filmmaker's documentary about the singer: "An artist has got to be careful never really to arrive at a place where he thinks he's at somewhere. You always have to realize that you're constantly in a state of becoming. As long as you can stay in that realm, you'll sort of be alright."

If it was good enough for Dylan, it was good enough for me. As the chorus of the Jewish ceremonial Passover seder song repeats after the accounting of each of the many blessings God has bestowed on Jews: "Dayenu"—it would have sufficed.

Like swimming in an infinity pool, there was no finish line; there would just be endless laps of realization and hopefully self-realization.

Gandhi himself implied he felt uncomfortable with being the object of some sort of goal in itself when he addressed the term "Gandhian," which many of those who had followed his ideals began to use. As he told a gathering of the Gandhi Seva Sangh in 1936: "There is no such thing as 'Gandhism,' and I do not want to leave any sect after me. I do not claim to have originated any new principle or doctrine. I have simply tried in my own way to apply the eternal truths to our daily life and problems...The opinions I have formed and the conclusions I have arrived at are not final. I may change them tomorrow. I have nothing new to teach the world. Truth and nonviolence are as old as the hills."

Suffice to say that being Gandhi would turn out to be unattainable—but the journey of becoming him was an effort that will continue to engage me as long as I live. How about you?

The idea to undertake this experiment first came to me when Barack Obama began campaigning for the United States President in 2007. Here was the first black man elected to that office, whose campaign slogan echoed the famous line that Mahatma Gandhi was credited with saying (later we will expose who really said it):

"Be the change you want to see in the world."

Obama had adapted it: "Change will not come if we wait for some other person, or if we wait for some other time. We are the ones we've been waiting for. We are the change that we seek."

When I read that Obama said he was more influenced by Gandhi than he was by Martin Luther King Jr., I thought that would surprise many, especially young black Americans who may never have heard of the skinny little man from India with wire-rimmed John Lennon glasses.

In his book *A Promised Land*, Obama wrote: "Gandhi had profoundly influenced my thinking. As a young man, I'd studied his writings and found him giving voice to some of my deepest instincts. His notion of 'satyagraha,' or devotion to truth, and the power of non-violent resistance to stir the conscience; his insistence on our common humanity and the essential oneness of all religions; and his belief in every society's obligation, through its political, economic, and social arrangements, to recognize the equal worth and dignity of all people—each of these ideas resonated with me. Gandhi's actions had stirred me even more than his words; he'd put his beliefs to the test by risking his life, going to prison, and throwing himself fully into the struggles of his people. Gandhi's non-violent campaign for Indian independence from Britain, which began in 1915 and continued for more than 30 years, hadn't just helped overcome an empire and liberate much of the subcontinent, it had set off a moral charge that pulsed around the globe.

"It became a beacon for other dispossessed, marginalized groups—including black Americans in the Jim Crow South—intent on securing their freedom," wrote Obama.

I thought that there would be millions of all races who also knew little or nothing about Gandhi, other than perhaps seeing Richard Attenborough's multiple Academy Award-winning film *Gandhi*. (It actually surprised me as I traveled in three countries how many times people said that film was the source of their knowledge about the man.)

Failing to identify anyone on the landscape in the last 100 years who impressed me with a vision of what a moral compass would even look like, I turned to Mr. Gandhi.

There is one other person, a living icon of moral impeccability, who I (and almost every other human being) hold in highest regard and with whom I actually had a most auspicious meeting years back: His Holiness the 14th Dalai Lama of Tibet. I had interviewed him at his home in McLeod Ganj, India, the seat of the Tibetan Government in Exile, while I was on assignment for *National Geographic* magazine. It was my most unforgettable experience as a journalist, and as a sentient being. I flatter myself to think it was memorable to him as well, even some 20 years later. In a rare moment of brilliance, in the middle of interviewing his nephew in Tibet which I'd toured before I went to McLeod Ganj, I asked him to leave his uncle a message on my tape recorder that I would take to His Holiness a few weeks later. The message was, "Uncle, every day we Tibetans hope and pray you will come back to your homeland." It was a poignant yet hopeless hope. When I played that tape for His Holiness six weeks later, the head of the Tibetan Government in Exile knew the futility of that happening better than anyone. His brow furrowed in sadness as he listened. I could feel he was deeply moved by his nephew's desire—a ripple of desire that ran through anyone with a sense of justice. The interview that followed took a sharply different turn, much more intimate and personal than I had imagined.

Thinking that meeting might be stored in his memory, perhaps I could have had an in to follow this living moral compass of exemplary character, now 87 years young as I write this.

But I did not choose him to build this experiment around because, for one thing, such a busy man with so many important people grabbing at his robes for the simple honor of having some of his karma rub off on them would barely have time for lowly me. More so, though, he was a man literally born to such greatness—by virtue of the time-honored selection process of reincarnation that took a 2-year-old named Tenzin Gyatso from a nondescript village called Takster, in the Tibetan Plateau of Qinghai province, China, and elevated him to the exalted leader of a country and a figure held in highest esteem around the world, no matter what their religious affiliation—that it would be difficult to relate to his life.

Mohandas Gandhi, by contrast, showed little to no potential for greatness as a young student, even as a young lawyer. He had human flaws. He was at times divisive; not everyone loved him. He was, in short, relatable, especially to me.

But the Dalai Lama himself held Gandhi in highest regard, as clearly evidenced by his many comments in interviews and in his own writing. To wit: this piece he wrote for *India Today* in August 2021:

"For me Mahatma Gandhi symbolizes Ahimsa, or non-violence, as well as Karuna, or compassion. One of my main commitments today is to promote these two principles, and I believe that India is the only country with the potential to combine its ancient knowledge with modern education. Gandhiji exemplified both Ahimsa and Karuna, and I think of him as my teacher...To me, he remains the model politician, a man who put his belief in altruism above all personal considerations and consistently maintained respect for all great spiritual traditions... Today, in a world where bullying and killing still take place, we need compassion and non-violence more than ever. I am firmly committed to combining these ideals with the best of modern education."

So what was good for His Holiness, was good enough for me.

While Obama brought Gandhi back into my consciousness (having traveled on many assignments in India since 2004, of course I saw his face and image all over the place, but he remained a distant figure to me), it was when I hit rock bottom, morally speaking, that I realized I needed to make some changes myself. That came when I could not have found myself in a less than Gandhian moment: I was in Colombia's gorgeous coastal city of Cartagena, as historic as it is hedonistic, on an assignment.

One night, wandering the city looking for adventure, I met a woman 30 years my junior at a bar. We danced for hours with intermittent breaks to do shots of tequila which we washed down with beer. She did things with her hips while doing the salsa that I did not know were humanly possible, smoothly and sensually suggestive, in perfectly syncopated rhythms that spoke to my soul.

Hot and sweaty, we stumbled back to my hotel, quickly turned on the AC, stripped naked, and jumped into the cool shower together. Her hips continued to do wonderful things. After that, all I remember is sliding into the chilled 1,000-thread Egyptian cotton sheets and falling asleep before my head hit the pillow. It was as decadent a night as a bachelor could want. Yet, I woke up feeling empty, sad and unfulfilled. The pain I felt was palpable within my soul.

Despite all I could and should be grateful for in my life, I still felt like I wanted and deserved more. It was an insatiable desire. I had become what Buddhists call the Hungry Ghost, a craving for something eternally out of reach... yet we keep reaching, even as we have no idea what that is.

As is often the case, when you think you've hit rock bottom, there is another bottom below that bottom, which is where the mind takes over. Mine took a downward spiral into the abyss, a bottomless hell realm of self-doubt, self-loathing and worthlessness, where even my self-effacing charm could not deflect the mistakes I've made and failures in my life. And then came an avalanche of thoughts and self-inquiries for which I had no answers. Who am I? Why am I? How many people had I fooled to get here? How many people had I inadvertently hurt by my own insecurities? When did I display stubborn conviction, all under the guise of my self-righteousness? When will my come-uppance finally crash in my face? How many times have I sabotaged my own opportunities for happiness?

There is great pain associated with taking a cold hard look in the mirror with unblinking eyes. It's a kind of self-inflicted pain that can bring some surcease of suffering—but only when you've reached your threshold and are ready to change. I had reached my limit and hoped this journey could ease my pain.

Dehydrated, recovering from a headache and nursing pains in my hip muscle (how do Latinos not hurt themselves thrusting like that on the dance floor?), over strong Colombian coffee I took stock of myself. My life was headed in the wrong direction, if I aspired to any semblance of a righteous path. That was Day One of my decision to transform according to Gandhi's principles.

My first thought as I surveyed my current environment was that the difference between Gandhi and me could not be more apparent. It was going to be an uphill struggle just to follow the basic principles, let alone presume to attain any kind of Gandhian equivalency.

Really? I'm going to *what*? Give up the way I have been living since consciousness woke me from the depths of blissful ignorance? Detach from indulgences, addictions, rabid consumerism, violent thoughts, selfishness, and plain old mean actions? Tell the truth 24/7, giving up little white lies or big fat falsehoods? Including self-deception, those lies big and small we tell ourselves, those "stories" of unworthiness and inability that become fact in the repetition of them? Give up meat? SEX!? My life as I knew it?

Would I be able to go as deep as the Mahatma did to break the cycle of attachment to *me,* to abstain from my everyday reality? To free myself, not, as in Gandhi's case, from the chains that tied India to the colonial British Empire, but from the very things I think make me who I am?

Indeed, could anyone living a rich and full life in the 21st century adhere to the principles Mahatma Gandhi set forth in his writings and in life? And why would they want to do so anyway, swimming against the strong tide of immoral behavior? And with what desired results?

For my part, it had been 12 years since I wrote my last book. In that time, I had gone from rags to riches to rags, from being basically homeless, living out of my car, couch surfing at friends' houses, interspersed with weeks at a time at my mother's assisted living complex in New Jersey and the occasional assignment at 5-star hotels; to finally settling at a modest apartment in Berkeley, California. I'd gone from a healthy specimen to the diagnosis of an autoimmune dysfunction whose name it took weeks to pronounce (polymyalgia rheumatica) to the bionic man with two new titanium hips.

So was I ready to "be the change?" You bet. Any change would be better than my perception of my reality. I needed to hit the delete button and reset, reboot, reinvent myself. On the verge of entering another momentous decade of my spin around this Glorified Star, I wanted to prove to myself that my own change was possible, that I could reverse counterproductive personal trends, and overcome my own decaying body. Who among us wouldn't want to?

Change. Such a simple, succinct word, eloquent in its monosyllabic elegance. If only it was that simple to actually change from bad habits to good, from counterproductive to positive thoughts, from self-sabotage to self-realization.

Yet, all of these personal trials pale compared to what our dear planet is suffering, and what our society is enduring, with multiple crises shaking our world's proverbial paradigm to its very core. Violence, a.k.a. terrorism, is rampant. Mass shootings are a regular occurrence. Government and corporate corruption are simply business as usual. Politicians turn away from true leadership, filibuster their way out of committing to laws that could help people but award lucrative contracts to cronies. Racism remains a perennial blemish on humankind. Women and LGBTQ+ people must fight constant attempts at disenfranchisement. Conspicuous consumption is on the rise, tempered only by shrinking paychecks, if not by whole companies going down. Environmental protections are disappearing or being violated. Mental health issues are of increasing concern; suicide rates are up. Physical health is not looking good either; obesity, diabetes, and heart disease are ever on the rise.

On top of that—likely perhaps because of all that—our moral benchmark has dropped precipitously, as social science studies suggest. Or you can just read today's headlines. We lie, we cheat, we have affairs, we make heroes of people who bilk the system or celebrities famous only for being famous. For starters.

But you know all of this. Why would I be the right guy to take it on? Fair question. Even before undertaking this endeavor, I was already getting flack. Publishers in India were extremely wary that, having read some of my earlier stuff, I would joke about Gandhi, which would not be tolerated or favored by Indian readers. Gandhi, I was quickly made aware, was sacrosanct. Humor at the expense of Gandhi was off limits.

An Indian friend who runs a marketing and communications company from his New Delhi offices, well-connected up and down the roster of fascinating people, took to calling me Gandhi Lite. I could not refute it.

Another friend, a writer born in India who has lived in the

United States since attending an American University, wondered what gives a white Jewish American the audacity to write a book about Gandhi? How often had I even been to India, she challenged me? Her response also suggested that for a Caucasian to try to "be like Gandhi" was committing cultural appropriation.

Was I? I took her observations to heart. With respect and humility, I replied that this is not a book *about Gandhi.* It's a look inside myself, a straight white American male who I hope is still evolving. As a world-travelled journalist, parent and grandparent, I consider it my responsibility to carry knowledge and traditions from one group of people to the next. This is how we progress as a global community.

I keep staring at this phrase—"Be the change that you want to see in the world"—as though it contains some special elixir. And that if I fully imbibed it, it will magically transform me. I just need to unravel it to discern any sort of clue that will aid my metamorphosis. Countless NGOs, organizations, companies and groups have adopted this phrase as their name or their slogan. A quick check reveals: Be the Change, a women-of-color-owned and operated consulting business, in Oakland, California; Be the Change Foundation, a nonprofit founded "to support young generations to reach their fullest potential," based in Santa Clara, California; the United States Men's National Soccer Team adopted it following the death of George Floyd in support of the Black Lives Matter movement; a nonprofit collective of "positive, conscious artists" called Be the Change; Milaan Foundation, a charitable organization registered as "Milaan–Be the Change," based in New Delhi, which "envisions an inclusive and equal world, where every girl has the knowledge, skills and social environment to pursue her dreams and explore her full potential"; Nike shifted its slogan from "Just do it" to "Let's all be part of the change"; Let's Be The Change, based in Bangalore, India, a non-profit organization which "aims to build a cleaner, healthier and more sustainable society by working in synergy with the citizens and the Government"; there's even a Be the Change Tarot reader on YouTube, with 35,000 subscribers.

When I asked that tarot reader, Jess Young, what she knew about Gandhi and why she chose it, she wrote to me with her poignant story of why she chose that handle:

"Yes, I was aware it was from Gandhi when I chose it. For me, it was a very personal reason for choosing it as the name of my channel. I have experienced a chaotic childhood, rape, drug addiction, and prison. I found sobriety, my spirituality, my gifts, healing, and a beautiful new life. I like to think that my experiences allow me to understand and be compassionate to others, and that I am able to help through my channel, as well as through living by example. Be the Change is the reminder to myself that just by living my life as my best self, I can show others that regardless of where they are coming from in life, they can overcome and experience a beautiful new life too."

She signed it with "Love and Light."

I especially liked this one too: James Madison University, a public research university in Harrisonburg, Virginia, had adopted the slogan "Be the Change" in 2006 "designed to encapsulate the Madison experience for students," according to its website. Then I bumped into an article that a decade later the university had conducted a survey to ascertain from students how effective the line was in affirming the school's ethos. The word that caught my attention in that article was that the institution was looking to "rebrand" itself via this Gandhian line. I wondered if Gandhi ever would have thought to use "branding" in his own...branding. Andy Perrine, JMU associate vice president for communications and marketing, launched a campus-wide study to see how it could make—and be—a change. That change became "Being the Change." This intrigued me so much I called Andy, who corroborated all this and added a fact I would not have anticipated. The university trademarked the line "Being the Change," officially registered with the federal United States Patent and Trademark Office, thus putting it in the same category as Subway's "Eat Fresh," Allstate's "You're in good hands" and Kentucky Fried Chicken's "Finger lickin' good."

This is all to suggest that the phrase has renowned status, resonating with so many people these days. Yet, I suspect that none of the groups using "Be the change" know that Gandhi did not actually say it quite that way. And while it's fine to say it's the thought that counts, what is that thought? Let's deconstruct.

Be. One of the most complicated action words in the English language, "to be" is the most protean English verb, the most irregular and constantly changing forms. I am, you are, they were, we've been, etc. And that's just for starters. In any tense, it connotes a state of being. To simply be. It sounds easy until you try it. Be in the moment; be the moment. Be fully present and accounted for. Be accountable; be responsible for your actions. Come into your being-ness. Be *somebody*. Not just anybody. Certainly don't fall into actress/comedienne extraordinaire Lily Tomlin's mistake: "I always wanted to be somebody, but now I realize I should have been more specific," she advised in her award-winning 1985 one-woman Broadway show "The Search for Signs of Intelligent Life in the Universe."

Be yourself; after all, that's the only choice. Further, be with yourself and be happy with who you are.

"To be or not to be." That *is* the question, isn't it? Hamlet's famous line, in the eponymously titled Shakespeare play of 1601, opens a soliloquy in which he struggles between living and dying. If that's too ominous and finite of a choice, it could be interpreted more metaphorically as: do you want to "be" in this life, in your life, in charge of your life, or throw in the towel and let fate rule it? Do you want to just cash out? This is the essential inquiry of the human condition. Do I exist? If I do, then it's my choice as to how I exist, where I take action, where I passively accept the dictates of some other entity. This, at least, is my assessment.

One more important notion about "be" in this context. As the first word in this phrase, which is actually a full sentence, "be" is in the imperative form of grammar. We use imperative clauses when we want to tell someone to do something. It's a command, literally. Thou shalt be. It has power and it's empowering. Nike coined "Just do it"—Gandhi would say, "Just be it."

That was a lot to take in for only the first word.

Onward to "change." First, I wonder what the fine-line differentiation is between "Be the change" and "Be Change." One could speculate. I contemplated it but have no interpretation that satisfies me. I want to take it this way: Be awake, aware, present and ready. For what? Change. Don't just be change. Be *the* change. In other words, work toward changing. Be the process of change. Then, ipso facto, you will have changed.

To change is part of the human condition, the inevitable

march of time, taking its toll on body and mind but also hopefully enhancing and enriching our understanding of life and ourselves. From birth onward, even from the point of conception, we develop, thanks to the growth hormone produced by the pituitary gland. You don't have to lift a finger to grow and change. This could not be what Gandhi meant by change.

To interpret what Gandhi meant by change, what anyone means when they talk about change, is much more complicated. What do I want to change? What do I need to change? What will I never change even at the risk of health and sanity? This is summed up in the so-called Serenity Prayer, most famously repeated at Alcoholics Anonymous meetings and other 12-step programs:

"Universe (God), grant me the serenity to accept the things I cannot change, the courage to change the things I can, and the wisdom to know the difference."

Change requires, first, an attitudinal change. Yes, I can and will change... if I really want to. One needs to make a strategic plan and stick to it. Pick a simple target, the low hanging fruit of change. I'm going to floss for 60 seconds at least twice a week; the reward (Pavlov's dog thrives, and salivates, on a reward, known in psychology circles as classical conditioning or Pavlovian or respondent conditioning) will be cleaner brighter teeth, less halitosis, more confidence when smiling, less insecurity about speaking closer to others, more friends and lovers, greater wealth, millions of followers on my Instagram account, appearances on major media networks, eternal life... OK, maybe I've gone too far.

Gandhi put it this way: "Carefully watch your thoughts, for they become your words. Manage and watch your words, for they will become your actions. Consider and judge your actions, for they have become your habits. Acknowledge and watch your habits, for they shall become your values. Understand and embrace your values, for they become your destiny."

Ahaaa, to change my habits. Not so easy. The American Journal of Psychology defined habit as "a more or less fixed way of thinking, willing, or feeling acquired through previous repetition of a mental experience." A 2002 daily experience study by habit researcher Professor Wendy Wood and colleagues found that 43 per cent of daily behaviors are performed out of habit. New behaviors can become automatic through the process of habit formation. Old habits are hard to break; new habits are hard to form because the behavioral patterns which humans repeat become imprinted in neural pathways, but it is possible to form new habits through repetition.

In his bestselling and so very instructive book, *The Power of Habit*, *New York Times* and Pulitzer-winning reporter Charles Duhigg gets into the science of habit. The most interesting to me was his look at research published in the February 2018 issue of Current Biology. Albeit with rats, not humans, neuroscientists at MIT found that the more the rodents repeated moving through a maze, the more it became automatic—less thinking, more doing (more "being"). This automaticity depended on something in the brain called the basal ganglia, central to recalling patterns, storing them, and acting on them. It's the same, they concluded, with the human brain. They named this process "chunking," wherein the brain converts a sequence of actions—like flossing!—into habit. They found that certain neurons in the brain mark the beginning and end of these chunked units of behavior; and that habits emerge because our brains are always on the lookout for efficient ways to save effort.

Neuroscience has also opened the mind to the mind's ability to change itself. Scientists in the field of neuroplasticity, known also as neural plasticity or brain plasticity, have demonstrated that neural networks of the brain can be rewired to function differently than in the past. Research in the latter half of the 20th century showed this phenomenon also applies through adulthood.

The worlds of psychology and science collided with meditation, and reinforced each other, when Richard Davidson, Professor of Psychology and Psychiatry and Founder/Director of the Center for Healthy Minds at the University of Wisconsin-Madison, led studies that showed long-term practitioners of several kinds of meditation had altered the structure and function of their brains.

In short, being the change could be a literal breath away—such as the very simple breath meditation I do called Anapanasati (meaning "mindfulness of breath"), the same the Buddha practiced and spread to followers, entailing simply paying attention to one's inhalation and exhalation as they go in and out of the nostrils.

I think of the brain as a circuit board of some sort, with wires attaching one part to another. The wires have split ends; in my imagination, one side goes to the happy place, the other goes to not so happy. One side, which an angel controls, goes to doing something positive for yourself; the other, ruled by the devil, goes to doing self-destructive things. In the end, and ultimately, we (call it our ego, mediating between our id and our superego) control both. Through meditation and other methods, we can facilitate change for the good, and not encourage self-sabotaging agents that block positive change. Aside from meditation, this may also be achieved through a quality I have not yet invoked since it's one I have much trouble with embodying myself, and which may affect my own ability to change: discipline.

Now comes the rest of Gandhi's much-repeated line: "... you want to see in the world."

Thinking optimistically that you have the discipline and desire to change, and have even achieved some degree of success in doing so, you may still ask: so how does this change the world?

I come from the era that introduced and then popularized the phrase: "The personal is political." It first was used by the feminist movement in the late 1960s but was soon adapted by groups that believed personal agendas had political implications and vice versa. In my interpretation, that means when we do the inner work, it's reflected in the outer world. What we bring to each other, to every socio-political situation, therefore depends on who we are ourselves. One event (our change) causes another event (changes in the world around us). In science, metaphysics and engineering, this is called causality; in Hinduism and Buddhism, karma. In Newtonian physics, it's the third law: "For every action, there is an equal and opposite reaction."

All refer to the notion that one event, process, state or object contributes to the production of another event, process, state, or object, wherein the cause is partly responsible for the effect, and the effect is partly dependent on the cause.

The great Vietnamese monk Thich Nhat Hanh put it much more simply: "When we change our daily lives—the way we think, speak and act—we change the world."

Gandhi would have agreed, as do I after dissecting "Be the change."

Easier said than done. Lofty ideals aside, is it possible to live a moral life in these immoral times?

Personally, I've been struggling with this question. When I look around, I see others in an equal quandary. We've lost our moral compass as a society.

Where are the mentors and role models representing a dedication to higher standards of integrity? Who wrote the reliable road map? Where is the *trust*worthy GPS? Is there a paint-by-numbers workbook? A "Moral Compass for Dummies" bestseller? Who models the behaviors we would like to believe we want to follow? In other words, who walks the moral talk? We no longer look to political leaders. Captains of industry also now have tainted backgrounds. Some gurus who have displayed less-than-moral behavior have made us suspicious; so have Catholic priests and other spiritual leaders. Our heroes are often fictional characters, from TV, films and novels, and even they fall victim to immoral acts. I suspect this is why films based on comic book superheroes have become so popular these days. That's how starved we are for real men and women from whom we can glean wisdom applicable in today's real world, as opposed to the blue-screen world of some mythic, fictional past or future.

On a personal level, I have been sinking into a moral morass as well. I'd like to attribute it to all the above, a depressed and depressive reaction to the direction I see too many people moving toward. It's overwhelming for a person with a conscience to witness the decline and fall of Western Civilization in fast-mo.

I admit I am a bit lost—spiritually, physically, mentally and morally speaking. I have demons. I lie, I harbor anger, I covet women and wealth, I want more. I commit selfish acts of gluttony, excessiveness, overconsumption.

At this point, I am having more and more trouble choosing between right and wrong. The line between moral integrity and self-preservation has blurred. The so-called righteous life—right livelihood, as the Buddhists call it—seems like a remote-to-impossible dream, like swimming upstream against a powerful cultural current. I will never get there. The majority of us will never get there. And what worries me, aside from my own struggles to attain the equivalent of moral enlightenment, is that fewer and fewer people care. I face a diminishing number of moral muses to follow, and while I sincerely want to change—or as one of my spiritual teachers puts it, I want to want to change—who will show me how?

Looking around, and without going back to the Great Ones of Yore—Abraham, Moses, Jesus, Muhammad, Joan of Arc, Mother Teresa, the Buddha and the prophets of those times—I see very few in recent history whose moral compass I care to follow. Yet, one stood out in the 20th century: Mohandas Karamchand Gandhi, known as Mahatma Gandhi, or "Bapu" (father in Hindi). He wrote: "You must not lose faith in humanity. Humanity is an ocean; if a few drops of the ocean are dirty, the ocean does not become dirty."

While his life was shrouded in controversy, divisiveness and hypocrisy, some would argue, there is no disagreement that he set among the highest goals for living.

In India he remains an icon, even if some Indians have lost sight of what he stood for. His face is on every rupee. His statue stands in almost every village, town and city center throughout India. Monuments in his honor have been raised around the world, including one installed in 1986 in the center of Manhattan's Union Square, a park historically known for being the site of many protests. The United Nations General Assembly has declared Gandhi's birthday (October 2) as International Day of Non-Violence. The period from January 30 (Gandhi's assassination) to April 4 (Martin Luther King's assassination) has been declared "the Season of Nonviolence" by the Association for Global New Thought, a group based in Santa Barbara, California. Indian-American members of the United States House of Representatives, Raja Krishnamoorthi, Ami Bera, Pramila Jayapal, and Ro Khanna, together with India Caucus Chairmen Brad Sherman and George Holding, introduced a bipartisan resolution to honor the life of Mahatma Gandhi and his enduring legacy in the present world.

Though I have a long history with India, I knew very little about Mahatma Gandhi until a few years ago when I began to research this book. I first went to India in 1973 as a young American would-be hippie disenchanted with America and also disconnected from Judaism, the religion of my parents, grandparents and for generations. India was as far away as I could imagine at the time. Hinduism was even more remote to me. I returned to India some 30 years later as a working journalist, and have gone back almost every year since then. At the time, I found Gandhi hard to relate to as a human being. His life seemed too austere to emulate. I first had heard of him during the Civil Rights movement in America in the mid 1960s. Hearing how much he inspired Martin Luther King Jr., who I admired very much, was my first touchpoint to Gandhi.

Decades later, the day before Barack Obama's historic inauguration, I watched the "We Are One" concert event on TV that took place on the steps of the Lincoln Memorial. President-elect Obama and family (along with many thousands of others) sat facing the giant statue of the 16th President of the United States as great performers did their thing. When U2 paid obeisance to the new leader of Western Civilization by singing "Pride in the Name of Love," an homage to the Rev. King, it struck me how Gandhi had changed the course of American history. I saw the direct transmission of wisdom, the direct lineage from Lincoln the great emancipator to Gandhi the great spearhead of independence to Dr. King the great civil rights leader to Obama the great hope of American politics—men who shared the dream of harmony among all mankind, achieved through nonviolent cooperation.

And so, I turned back to Mahatma Gandhi and the great body of writing he left behind, a virtual how-to instructional on living a virtuous life, one man's guide to moral integrity followed by many people around the world—but not enough people. I set out to follow Gandhi's six main principles literally—to live them on a daily basis—while I went on a global expedition to meet people Gandhi inspired and to assess the success of the Gandhi Movement, especially in locations that changed him. I begin with six main pillars most often cited as the keys to Gandhi's philosophy: Truth, Non-Violence, Simplicity, Vegetarianism, Faith and Celibacy. Some people list as many as 11 principles, but I'm trying to give this experiment at least a fighting chance of success.

In the process, I hope there are a few precious jewels to help you also find the change you wish To Be.

HOW TO GANDHI

So how can we both attain Gandhi-hood? The first step is to forget about that as a goal. Let's take it day by day, adding one good thing, eliminating one bad thing. Keep your eye on the moral compass. When you see yourself losing your way, as I have many times, gently steer yourself in a direction that leans toward the winds of change.

Don't try to take on all six of these at once. You will crash and burn out. Committing to them and then avoiding them like the plague will only lay more guilt on your head, as if you didn't feel bad enough about yourself. See this as a process, not a product. Pick a moral a day, or a week, or a month to spend time in your day contemplating what you can do to address it—and then act on it. Enjoy the ride, or at least endure the ride at first.

It's never too late to start, never too early to take steps to change.

Use these six principles, and Gandhi himself, as a prism through which you can examine all the dimensions and implications of living a moral life, personally and globally.

This is an experiment so there will be many fails. But as the old Zen counsel goes, fall off the cushion seven times, get back up on it ten.

INDIA

Where It Began, Where It Ended

"An India awakened and free has a message of peace and goodwill to a groaning world."

—Mahatma Gandhi, in *Young India*, 1921

"If India becomes the slave of the machine, then, I say, heaven save the world."

—Mahatma Gandhi, in *Harijan*, 1946

"India's destiny lies not along the bloody way of the West, of which she shows signs of tiredness, but along the bloodless way of peace that comes from a simple and godly life. India is in danger of losing her soul. She cannot lose it and live. She must not therefore lazily and helplessly say, 'I cannot escape the onrush from the West.' She must be strong enough to resist it for her own sake and that of the world."

—Mahatma Gandhi, in *Young India*, 1926

"India lives in several centuries at the same time."

—Arundhati Roy, Indian novelist and columnist

"To other countries, I may go as a tourist, but to India, I come as a pilgrim."

—Martin Luther King, Jr.

On the day I arrived in New Delhi in mid-December 2019 for the India leg of my journey in Gandhi's footsteps, this time literally, most Indian newspapers were blasting the alarming headline that the World Air Quality Report named the country's capital the most polluted city in the world. By the end of 2022, as I write this, it had retained that dubious distinction for the fourth consecutive year.

Gandhi could have predicted this predicament, not just in India but on a global level. In fact, he did. He was prescient in sounding the alarm. As far back as 1906, writing from South Africa in his *Indian Opinion*, he expressed his concerns: "Nowadays, there is an increasing appreciation among enlightened men of the need for open air." Even earlier, while he lived in England as a law student, he observed the impact of the growing number of factories sprouting up since the Industrial Revolution that began in the mid 18th century. He wrote:

"A man can do without food for several days and live a day altogether without waters, but it is impossible to carry on without air even for a minute. If a thing that is so very vital to life is not pure, the result cannot but be deleterious...This matter deserves consideration by Indian leaders. We suffer much because we do not realize the value of pure air, and this again is a strong reason why diseases like plague spread among us."

A comprehensive 2019 paper I read in the Indian Journal of Medical Research, entitled "Gandhi as an Environmentalist," attempted to conclude optimistically. Wrote Dr. Rajnarayan Tiwari, director of Indian Council of Medical Research at the National Institute for Research in Environmental Health in Bhopal, Madhya Pradesh: "As a matter of historical record, Gandhi was acutely aware of environmental pollution and of its consequences to human health. He was especially concerned about the appalling working conditions in industry, with workers forced to inhale contaminated, toxic air...The world and in particular India is today facing the harmful effects of urbanization that Gandhi envisioned decades back. The application of Gandhian principles can stall the further progress of these effects."

But very few listened, in Gandhi's time or after, as my first day in India showed. I would see more examples of how Indians use their corner of the planet as a literal dumping ground.

Friends in India had advised me to buy a bunch of N95 masks, which filter out at least 95 per cent of airborne particles. But in the San Francisco Bay area none were to be found because we were suffering our own air quality calamity. Wildfires 60 miles north of us, at the time the worst in the state's history, were leaving the skies an apocalyptic shade of orange, thick smoke clouds full of bad stuff to breathe that blocked the sun entirely. We woke up one morning to a scene from some End of Days sci-fi flick. We were warned to stay inside as much as possible or suffer the consequences of inhaling tiny toxic particles like PM2.5—consequences such as asthma and increased risk of cancer. Health officials said breathing that air was the equivalent of smoking seven cigarettes in a day. The worst of this was that California wildfires were becoming a seasonal thing, as predictable as fall harvest, the result of droughts that left forest floors carpeted with dry tinder by late summer, waiting for an errant flickering cigarette butt or felled live telephone wire.

You can imagine why my fellow San Francisco Bay area residents, prissy and precious Californians who believe it is their God-given right to live in an environmental nirvana, ran for the cover of N95 masks. Walgreens, CVS, Rite Aid—none of the leading drugstore chains in my area had them. So I came to India virtually unmasked, but for a flimsy blue surgical mask (aka medical procedure masks), which, I later learned, are not recommended by health pros since they are not tight fitting and therefore not highly effective at blocking out tiny particles in the air.

Within hours after my arrival in New Delhi, I realized the pollution I had experienced in San Francisco prepped me for this trip... and that my mask would be of little help against the thick air full of who knows what! Still jetlagged, the next morning I walked to meet my editors at Simon & Schuster India. I crossed a crowded pedestrian bridge and looked down at street vendors grilling chapati and stirring pots of uncovered chai.

My plan in New Delhi was to undertake a whirlwind tour, visiting a few of the museums and monuments dedicated to the man considered India's founding father.

First stop was the Gandhi Smriti (translation: Gandhi Memorial/Remembrance). This is the National Gandhi Museum, formerly known as Birla House or Birla Bhavan, formerly the house of noted and ungodly wealthy industrialist Ghanshyam Das (GD) Birla, where Gandhi spent his last 144 days and was assassinated in 1948. Birla was a close associate and a steady supporter of Gandhi, whom he met for the first time in 1916. Birla had launched several companies and his sons and future generations carried on with their own business successes. At his death in 1983, GD had an estimated net worth of about $9 million, a paltry sum compared to the Aditya Birla Group, chaired by GD's great grandson, Kumar Birla. The commodities empire, with interests in cement, aluminum, telecom and financial services, claims $41 billion in revenues. According to Forbes,

Kumar has an estimated net worth of $14 billion, as of 2022. (These financials will all become relevant shortly).

The memorial is located on Tees January Marg, which translates to 30th January Road—the date of Gandhi's assassination.

I walked the grounds, absorbing every vintage photograph, paintings, sculptures, frescos and inscriptions on rocks and extended captions explaining the historical significance.

There was a lot of history and a lot of significance. At the main entrance, some 3,000-plus daily visitors are greeted by a large statue of the Indian sculptor Sri Ram Sutar of the Mahatma, his arms resting on the shoulders of a girl and a boy holding a dove in their hands on either side. At its base, the famous Gandhi line: "My life is my message."

The first wing of the house is where Gandhi lived. The two simple rooms have been preserved. One can see Gandhi's bed, his office and in a glass case on the wall, there are some of his personal belongings, including his round spectacles, walking stick, some cutlery, the stone that he used instead of soap, his wooden desk with the Bhagavad Gita on it, and a white mattress on the floor. It looked as though he could have just stepped out of the room and would be back in a moment.

I watched kids, mostly bored, led either by their parents or on school field trips. I saw couples holding hands as they toured the property, awash in somber obeisance. I walked through the Eternal Gandhi Interactive Multimedia Museum at the Smriti with all kinds of hands-on computer-generated ways to launch more information. Though some of the displays struck me as a bit tacky, and technologically dated, I could see they engaged kids more—and that is always a good thing, countering the refrain that the next gen does not fully understand or care about what and how and who got them to now.

The eeriest interactivity I experienced, unrelated to the bells and whistles of multimedia, was walking literally in Gandhi's footsteps, etched in concrete, bigger than life size, on the winding path that leads from his room to the Martyr's Column that commemorates the exact spot of his death. These would have been the last steps he took. I slowed down to take each step with great reverence and attention, in the tradition of walking meditation I learned as a student of the Vietnamese monk Thich Nhat Hanh. Then, as tradition holds it, I circumambulated the pavement encircling the Martyr's Monument. In Hindi this sort of walk is called a parikrama, a clockwise meditative stroll around sacred objects, such as stupas and statues. In Buddhism it's called a *pradakshina*, often three trips around a devotional object or sacred mountain.

I left that afternoon feeling spiritually high, like after darshan with one's spiritual teacher.

I then went to the National Charkha Museum, located in the heart of Connaught Place, built on the Palika Bazaar garden. Inaugurated in 2017, the museum features what is claimed to be the world's largest chromium stainless steel spinning wheel (charkha) weighing 5 tons and measuring 26 feet in length and 13 feet high. The museum houses 14 vintage models of charkhas and showcases its journey from kapas to the final khadi product. There is also another multimedia presentation of Gandhi's life. The museum honors the rise of the simple tool to a symbol of Indian nationalism, thanks to Gandhi.

For me, this was the first time I'd been to Connaught Place since I'd first come to India in 1973 with my then-wife Iris. I was blown away by its own evolution. When Iris and I first arrived in India, we stayed at a funky hotel a block from the circle and near the American Express office where we could cash our AmEx checks. In the center of the circle was a large lawn, no concrete anywhere, as it is today. There were—as clichéd and dated as this sounds—snake charmers in dull-colored plaid lungees, coaxing cobras out of straw baskets with their flutes (pungis) made of hollowed gourds. Men in dirty white pajama pants offered us head massages. A man, himself charmed by my wife, the petite blue-eyed blonde, wanted to offer more than a head massage, as well as proffer local ganja "at special discount." We refused all gestures of hospitality.

Looking at Connaught Place now, I was blown away in a different manner, both impressed with the change but also melancholy for the simplicity we saw some 50 years earlier. Gone is the expansive open lawn. Now I saw young middle class Indian couples surreptitiously stealing quiet moments together on the steps that ring the circle. They wore nice sports jackets and appropriately modern attire for women. Yet, I still had to fend off vendors and hawkers; that has not changed in India. I looked for the United Coffee House, a popular chain back then, where Iris and I had our first taste of the heat of Indian food. I remember that, after one bite, I stuffed white rice into my mouth and drank sweet lassi to put out the fire.

I felt Gandhi-fied and ready to make the journey to the epicenter of Gandhiland.

In the many years I'd been coming to India, I'd been to several of the 28 states—including UP, MP, HP, Bihar, Goa, Kerala, Rajasthan, Karnataka, Telangana and Maharashtra—but never to Gujarat. You can call me a Gujarat virgin. All I knew about Gujaratis was based on hearsay, literally. Several years earlier, I was at lunch with colleagues at the Taj Palace Hotel's Sea Lounge, the virtual dining room for well-to-do Indians and foreigners, when our conversation got drowned out by a boisterous group of six seated at a corner table as though they owned the place. "Oh they are Gujaratis," someone at my table apologized. How did she know, I asked. "Gujaratis are always the loudest people in any room."

It sounded like a grossly stereotyped generalization. But I had no experience to judge it; at the time I did not even know it was the state where Gandhi was born. The only other thing about Gujarat I knew—actually a very big thing—was that in 2002 the state was the scene of violent riots between Hindus and Muslim that left more than 1,000 dead and 2,500 injured. I learned about the riots after profiling acclaimed Indian actress-turned-director and social activist Nandita Das for the Wall Street Journal with the 2008 debut of her film "Firaaq" ("Separation," in English). The film, which won several international awards, is set one month after the bloody conflict and follows the lives of several Gujarati people and the effect on them. Gujarat is bounded to the northwest primarily by Pakistan, the world's second largest Muslim population which in 1947 attained independence with the Partition of India. It was while researching for the Nandita Das piece I wrote that I discovered the then Governor of Gujarat was Narendra Modi, Prime Minister of India at this time of writing, who was accused of condoning the violence, as were police and government officials who allegedly directed the rioters and gave lists of Muslim-owned properties to them. In 2012, Modi was cleared of complicity in the violence by Special Investigation Team (SIT) appointed by India' Supreme Court.

Otherwise, so naïve was I about Gujarat that I did not know it was a dry state; the sale of alcohol is prohibited, as it is in only three other states in India (Bihar, Mizoram and Nagaland). This meant that I would not be imbibing alcohol, wine and beer for the month. Since it was my plan anyway for the long run of my experiment, I considered it an enforced kickoff to my own dry spell. The only time I even saw alcohol for sale was at a hotel with a restaurant where I learned I could show my American passport. The waiter directed me to a neon sign in a dark corner of the dining room that announced "bar." Curious, I went in the door to the bar. It was not a bar; it was a retail sales shop that sold alcohol by the bottle. I dodged the temptation to buy a bottle as I continued my travels through Gujarat.

The other issue I had not anticipated or been aware of was that the majority of restaurants in Gujarat serve only vegetarian cuisine. This was also good for my new diet, there would be no temptation to resist on that either.

All of this sobriety and abstinence from meat, fish and fowl is directly due to the state's native son. Modi led the move to ban alcohol sales in his home state, though authorities tend to turn a blind eye when it comes to bootleggers.

Since 2014, when I began dipping my toes into what would become this experiment, I became fascinated—and frustrated—with the attempt to designate as a national heritage trail the route Gandhi took from Ahmedabad to Dandi Beach—which came to be known as the Salt March, or Dandi Path. To kickstart my experiment, I thought I could get an assignment from The *New York Times* about its progress, or lack thereof, even possibly undertake the 239-mile (385 kilometers) trek myself, experiential journalist (aka nutcase) that I am. But the project continued to stall due to the type of bureaucratic hiccups familiar in India.

As I waited, on a flight from somewhere to somewhere I must have been bragging about my plans to a couple from Pennsylvania, who generously shared the name of an American gentleman involved with that very project. Within a few days, Thomas Jones enthusiastically emailed me. A historic preservation planner and urban conservator, he's an academic advisor to the Centre for Heritage Management at Ahmedabad University, which has a master's degree program in heritage management, the first of its kind for India. What got me especially interested was his role in developing a "Statement of Intent to Cooperate between the Centre and the United States National Park Service's National Center for Preservation Technology & Training," which agreement enabled him to assist in identifying and conserving Gandhi's march to Dandi.

Over several years we had some long conversations (he is a loquacious gentleman) but we never met, either in the United States or India. Instead, he recommended I work with his Ahmedabad-based colleague, Debashish Nayak, who has been involved in managing urban conservation issues in historic cities both in India and abroad. He was Director at Ahmedabad University's heritage management center. Since 1996 he has been working as advisor to the Heritage Programme of Ahmedabad Municipal Corporation for the revitalization of the Historic Walled City. He cut through a lot of red tape over 20 years to get Ahmedabad designated as India's first UNESCO World Heritage City in 2017. He's been dubbed India's "Heritage Man," not exactly an enviable title in a country that has "at best an ambivalent relationship with its own very long history," as Sabyasachi Mukherjee, a former director of Mumbai's Chhatrapati Shivaji Maharaj Vastu Sangrahalaya (formerly the Prince of Wales Museum) told me in an interview. This was my man.

Debashish Nayak and I began chatting on WhatsApp. He was my only contact in the city, so I was nervously dependent on him to be my advance man, my eyes and ears, my connector and my guide. Through him, I landed a nice deal at the Silver Cloud Hotel & Banquets. I prefer to scout out my own hotel accommodations but from the website it looked OK enough for a 4-star Indian hotel, but its biggest selling point to me was that it was on Ashram Road, diagonally across from Sabarmati Ashram, where I thought I'd spend considerable time. The ashram was home to Gandhi from 1917 until 1930 and served as one of the main centers of the Indian freedom struggle. Now it's a museum dedicated to the life and work of the Mahatma. This would be my base camp for nearly a month.

Debashish came to my hotel the morning after I arrived, just a few days before New Year's Eve. We spread maps and books and brochures on a table and sorted out an itinerary. He was well dressed in a wool vest and kurta. He was soft spoken and also well spoken, with a tight slightly graying mustache. Though friendly, there was a reserve about him, born, I was sure, of working in the bureaucracies of both academia and government—careful to never say anything that might bounce back and bite him. A bit stiff, he would not be the guy to take to a karaoke bar in Ahmedabad. But he was a wealth of knowledge.

He freely admitted Gandhi, the man and his philosophy, were not his area of expertise. But in putting Gandhi in the context of India's heritage, he said: "Honoring our heritage heals the souls of Indians who have been separated from their past or have pushed it away to focus on the urgency of now and a more promising future."

This seems an idea relevant to any country and any man or woman.

The delays of officially making the path of the Salt March a heritage trail drove him nuts, he said. The project has been mired in delays and unkept commitments since about 2006. But now, he promised, "we're at a tipping point," as Gandhi's 150th birth anniversary had just passed (his DOB is October 2, 1869). This milestone motivated the government to release close to $2 million to complete setting up signage and "night halts," simple accommodations and kitchenettes where Gandhi spent each of the 21 nights it took him to reach the Arabian Sea at Dandi, where he famously picked up salt in defiance of the British tax laws in 1930.

Debashish agreed to let me follow him for an 80-mile stretch of the route he had not yet charted so I could witness him collecting stories from descendants who saw Gandhi firsthand, and others who only remembered what their parents and grandparents told them. With a degree in architecture, he had particular interest in finding remains of buildings and schools where Gandhi stopped to give a lecture. In the process, he compares existing documents with new findings, tracking the route on a Google Earth app, "The Salt March to Dandi," created in 2017 on the 70th anniversary of India's independence.

For myself, my motive to trace the route began one way but shifted as I walked it...and continue to shift still. At first, there was the macho motive. If Gandhi could do it, I'd give him a head start of a decade in age difference and prove I still "had it." While Gandhi undertook the march as a demonstration of freedom from the unfair taxes against mining India's own salt, I wanted to declare my freedom from my own body—one that had undergone a pair of hip replacements and had overcome an autoimmune dysfunction called Polymyalgia rheumatica (PMR), an inflammatory disorder that causes widespread aching, stiffness and flu-like symptoms. As well, I wanted to examine the 240-mile corridor that runs southwest from Ahmedabad to Dandi as a barometer to measure how much of Gandhi's hopes for a brighter future in India had been fulfilled, or not. The passage moves through urban congestion, rural poverty, mountains (literally) of garbage, half completed industrial parks and logistics centers, unforgiving traffic and dusty roads blocked by cows, and villages that seemingly have not emerged from the medieval period—a virtual cross section of India today.

I was certainly not the first to retrace the path. It almost seems every time an Indian politician wants to garner favorable publicity and rejuvenate his flagging party he hits the Salt March trail, with reporters in tow. In 1988 Rajiv Gandhi (son of the Prime Minister Indira Gandhi and no relation to the Mahatma), Prime Minister from 1984 to 1989, started the march—but stopped after 7 miles. Of no small note: both Indira and Rajiv were assassinated. Tushar Gandhi, the Mahatma's great grandson who ran for office and lost, tried it twice, both times halted.

The next day I walked across the street to visit the Sabarmati Ashram. It's nothing like I thought it would be. I imagined a group of devoted Gandhians living simply, communally, as in ashrams I've been to in such places as Bodh Gaya, or Thich Nhat Hanh's Plum Village in the South of France, or Hill House, a commune in Western Massachusetts where I had friends in the 1970s. Instead, it's a museum, and a lovely one at that. Half a dozen buildings, mostly upgraded versions of the originals, are spread across the grounds just off the banks of the Sabarmati River. Wide cement steps lead down overseeing the river, where people sit and gaze, absorbing the aura of the space. One building houses wall hangings with historical notes on the life of Gandhi. There's an open airy feel to the hallways. In one corner is a series of offices where the IT staff updates the Gandhi portals and other details.

This was not Gandhi's original ashram. That one was established in Kochrab, on the outskirts of Ahmedabad, in May of 1915. It was small and Gandhi wanted more area for farming, animal husbandry and other uses. So two years later he relocated to the 36 acres that became Sabarmati Ashram. Now about 700,000 visit it every year.

I dropped by every day, as though it was a meditation center, strolling the grounds and revisiting the exhibitions, as Gandhi might have intended. I spent a lot of time in the bookstore. If I weren't going to be traveling so much after Ahmedabad, I would have bought shelves full of books. The only one I allowed myself, though, was a 665-page opus, *On the Salt March*, by Thomas Weber, an Australian academic who teaches in the Politics department at La Trobe University in Melbourne and co-ordinates its Peace Studies Area. He has a special interest in Gandhi and has published several other books on Gandhian conflict resolution and ethics.

On the Salt March was originally published by HarperCollins New Delhi in 1997. I have an edition published in 2009 by the Indian publishing house Rupa. It is an unbelievable book, detailing nearly every inch of the march, which he undertook in 1983. It includes 120 pages of the route, lists of the 81 marchers or "The First Batch," postscripts, notes, bibliography, glossary. To confess, I skimmed it looking for small points; it would have been too exhausting to read the whole thing page by page. If I did, I might still be sitting in a room at the Silver Cloud.

I wrote to Dr. Weber with a few questions, mainly why he decided to do the research, march the march and write the book. He replied by email:

"There is a great deal of history written about the Indian political events of 1930 that encompassed the Salt March. But...there was very little written about the march itself. For corroboration see the Indian history books available at the time. Some published Gandhi's speeches along the way. Little else."

Wearing two hats, one of the meticulous academician, the other of the memoirist, he tried to merge academic rigor with sentimental first-person narrative prose.

My own daily self inquiry: Did I really want to do this thing? I asked that for months back in Berkeley before I went to India. I had gone into training mode. Having read that Gandhi walked 10 miles a day, I ramped up my walking regiment. I'd begun tracking my daily walks back in Berkeley, my Samsung pedometer becoming my bestie. I built up from 2 or 3 miles a day to at least 6 or 7. In Ahmedabad, the days before I was to start the actual event, I used the walking path along the Sabarmati as my track.

They were glorious walks too. It was hot during the day and cold at night in late December but I never tired of the river view. My walking companions were several species of birds, flapping their wings and chirping as they literally sky dived into tiny holes set into the walls. There are nearly 120 species—native and migratory—spotted along the riverfront, an increase of population attributed to a cleanup of the river once considered to be one of the most polluted rivers in India (along with the Ganga and Yamuna). On Sundays the birds and I had lots of company: cute couples shyly cooing and cuddling along the few miles of riverside benches and grassy areas.

When the day had come to begin the march, I had dropped so much weight that I needed to tighten my belt to the tightest notch. I was the thinnest I'd been in the last 30 years.

Waiting to take off, Debashish took me to Gujarat Vidyapith, the university Gandhi had founded in 1920. His intention was to further separate Indians from the grasp of British indoctrination; this would be a school of students form the villages and based on Gandhian philosophy, all classes in the Gujarati dialect. This was all part of Gandhi's goal to encourage and reinforce Indians' self-esteem and identity. Although considerably modernized in its structure and curriculum, the university maintains its commitment to Gandhian ideals, human studies, social service and development work.

The school's foundations were eventually emulated in Benares, Bombay, Calcutta, Nagpur, Madras and many other cities across India. Thousands of students and teachers left British colleges to join the Vidyapith.

The day I dropped in with Debashish, I witnessed a special morning ceremony. It opened with prayer and songs, followed by lengthy speeches. I was so tempted to step out but I held on. The music was mesmerizing. Later in the morning I attended a typical session—equivalent, I assumed, to what we used to call "homeroom." The difference was that while teachers from various departments made announcements, the close to 100 students sat on the floor spinning their own small book-size portable charkhas. This was mandatory and happened every morning. The only comparison I could make to American schools was... nothing! There are no schools outside of Gujarat Vidyapith whose curricula is based on Gandhian ideals that are woven into each subject area.

Quite to my surprise, the principal asked me to say a few words that he would translate to Gujarati because they would not necessarily easily understand English, especially with my New York-ish accent. I don't recall exactly what I said, nor did I think they listened, so focused were they on spinning, except that I was so impressed by their diligence and commitment to this style of education.

A forward journalism teacher seized the opportunity and invited me to his class immediately afterward. The students were so eager to hear an American journalist's perspective on how we research, how we come up with ideas and how we write. I may have gone too far to critique Indian newspaper writing, but I actually saw nodding heads, wide eyes and many hands going up. They were eager to learn beyond their usual horizon. Geez, I thought, how cool it would be to spend a semester teaching there.

My next mission was to visit the city of Gandhi's birth, Porbandar. Debashish had connected me with a tour guide who would take me to Porbandar. Girish Gupta was more than a tour guide. He had all the credentials of a Ministry of Tourism regional tour guide, and is a founding secretary of the National Heritage Volunteer (NHV) based in Gujarat, a not-for-profit organization that creates training and awareness programs for cultural heritage, walking tours, historical monuments and the Salt March. He was erudite, entertaining and had the perfect deep voice for radio—and got some of my wry New York humor. All in all, a good travel companion.

Girish, I and the driver he had hired for the trek, Pandey

Vijay, left early the next day for Porbandar, approximately 390 kilometers from Ahmedabad. Midway we stopped in Rajkot, some 133 miles from where we set out, for a few reasons. On the drive there Girish told me that Rajkot is an important manufacturing center and famous for the invention and manufacture of the 3-wheeled diesel-driven vehicle called the chhakda. At one point Vijay noticed one and we pulled over so I could examine it. Rajkot's green chutney is said to be legendary. I would not taste it, or my stomach would revolt. To avoid mid-day heat, locals have developed the term siesta into their businesses; most shops close from 1 pm to 4 pm and reopen after for the night.

To the two main reasons:

At the age of 9, Gandhi moved to Rajkot with his family when his father became counselor to the ruler there and later the Diwan (finance minister). Mohandas learned the basics of arithmetic, history, and geography at a local school. When he was 11, he attended Alfred High School in Rajkot. He was not an outstanding student; records show he was good at English, fair in arithmetic, weak in geography, good in conduct, and bad in handwriting. The school was shut down in May 2017 after 164 years to make way for the Mahatma Gandhi Museum, which I visited. The 39 classrooms are now exhibition halls lined with photographs, memorabilia, sayings from the Mahatma. There's a 3D projection-mapping show, with sound and light effects. By now I was recognizing many of the images I'd seen before—and would continue to see in Porbandar, and then would see again in South Africa and London.

According to the Rajkot Municipal Corporation (RMC), there were 1.14 lakh (114,000) visitors in the first year of its opening. There were not many people there the day I went, other than groups of students that teachers were having trouble keeping calm.

The other reason I wanted to stop in Rajkot—a city with a population of 2 million in 2021, named the 7th fastest growing city in the world—was that Girish had arranged for me to interview one of Gujarat's largest publishers, and the publisher of many books about Gandhi. We met with Gopal Mohan Makadia, director of Pravin Prakashan PVT LTD, the brother of the founder. His English was not good so Girish served as translator. He did not hesitate to laud some of his controversial authors writing about Gandhi. He cited the most successful title as a biography of Gandhi's oldest son Harilal, an alcoholic gambler trading in imported British clothes even as his father was urging a boycott of foreign goods. Harilal even converted to Islam and changed his name to Abdullah before his death in 1948, only months after his father was assassinated.

Mr. Makadia went on for a while in a very professional manner, extolling the virtues of his line of books. Then I asked one of the questions I asked everyone, the one that revealed to me the human impact of Gandhi:

"How much has Gandhi and the Gandhi philosophy influenced you personally? Do you follow any of the 6 principles that I am trying to follow?" I listed them for him.

This set him off. His face changed; a dark cloud came over him, not the reaction I thought I'd get at all. He adamantly rejected Gandhi the man, a flawed and hypocritical human in his opinion, and therefore he could not bring himself to honor or live by any of Gandhi's prescribed principles.

"While Gandhi was a mahatma," he said, "he was simultaneously a human being. As a human being, he was a common person. He made mistakes. You cannot separate his six principles from the actions of the man, with his human flaws. The image of Gandhi is dented."

He said, "India is suffering due to Gandhi's principles and thought processes. To practice Gandhism today is not possible. Laws cannot be enforced now. Look, he was shot dead before we celebrated even one year of independence. If some new Gandhi came along now, he will be shot in 24 hours."

Things ended slightly awkwardly.

Was this book publisher not hypocritical himself? He was making money publishing and selling books revolving around Gandhi, a man he fundamentally did not believe in. There was something two-faced about the basis of his business model, which itself was a lie.

After chai with him (of course), we moved on to Porbandar, another 180 km (111 miles) away to see the house where Gandhi was born, now, again, a museum.

Porbandar State was a princely state during the British Raj, one of the few princely states with a coastline. Before Gandhi, the city was best known as the birthplace of Sudama, friend of Lord Krishna. Most recently and most unfortunately, it made headlines around the world as the city from which Pakistani terrorists with a group called Lashkar-e-Taiba stole a fishing boat in November of 2008, landed it in Mumbai and launched an attack that came to be called 26/11, killing 166 people.

Gandhi's family home is now part of the Kirti Mandir museum complex, surrounding a center courtyard. There are, predictably, rooms with images and descriptions of Gandhi's life and works. The national museum part was built and opened in 1950, just two years after the Mahatma's death. Since then it has been visited by dignitaries from around the world; 1,500 visit it daily. It's Porbandar's main—its only—tourist attraction.

In the house where he was born, the actual spot of his birth is marked with a swastika on the floor (long before Hitler co-opted the symbol, it represented divinity and spirituality in Hinduism, Buddhism and Jainism, coming from the Sanskrit, meaning "conducive to well-being"). The three-storey house has narrow hallways and steep steps up to each floor. The day I was there it was crowded. Older people struggled to make their way up the steps, but nonetheless made their way, some with the help of someone behind them pushing them up.

I'd read that the house was in a state of neglect, that the walls were moldy, that garbage was here and there, that there was little access for disabled people. I'm sorry to report I did find some of this to be true. Nonetheless, there's always something to be garnered from seeing the place where people who made a difference in the world got their own start. Gandhi did not have humble beginnings. Some would say he had a running start, with a father in a high position. So it's all the more remarkable that he chose to live humbly, eschewing the trappings of wealth—going from riches to rags, one could say.

Porbandar was an affluent port city even during the Mughal rule, dating back to the 16th century. "Bandar" means port or harbor. The backbone of the city's economy is the fishing industry.

Therefore, protecting the quality of the water is imperative, one would think. So it was with true dismay that I learned of blatant pollution when I met Narottam Palan of Gandhi Prakriti Pariwar, a group of citizens working for environmental protection. A retired professor of Gujarati literature at Saurashtra University in Rajkot, he is the author of some 50 books. I'd gone to meet him about another environmental issue I'll get to in a minute, but first he dropped this story on me:

A cement factory was blatantly pumping effluence into the bay. The pipeline was visible running down the beach into the water. After being severely scolded, in response the company simply ran the pipe under the sand and into the bay. No way, I said. Way, he replied.

"Look for yourself," he said, pointing out a few hundred yards out to the top of the water. "See that dark area?"

I did not see it at first. I squinted, put on my baseball cap to block the glare of the sun and looked closer. Then I saw what looked like a huge black slick on the surface of the water, floating there like an ominous blob from a doomsday sci-fi flick. I pictured fish and fowl covered with gunk. But here's the kicker, the irony of ironies to my mind: The factory is owned by the Birla family, descendants of the same G.D. Birla who hosted Gandhi in his last 144 days. If I was an investigative reporter, I would track down a spokesperson or a Birla himself for comment, raise bloody hell with the media and force justice. But this was not my karma. All I can do is write about it here and hope it opens eyes—and minds.

I saw a ray of hope on India's otherwise polluted landscape in impassioned individuals who have started NGOs because they see the GOs moving too slowly. Prarthi Shah, my researcher, is one of them. It was how we connected in the first place. She was among the team from Gujarat Vidyapith, the university Gandhi founded in 1920 in Ahmedabad, who I accompanied as they traced the trail Gandhi followed through villages just near the city. Grandparents on both sides of her family were Gandhi followers who fought for India's freedom. She seemed shy and mousy at first but as the group walked, she and I ended up side by side. I made a passing remark of sadness that at almost every step trash and various other forms of garbage were strewn along the way, in gutters, piled in front of shops, paving the streets as well. She sprang into a verbal tirage of rage, disappointment, and frustration. Over a period of time, I found she was anything but shy. She is a passionate environmentalist. She founded Baroda Strickers, a youth group aimed at involving and encouraging young people to come work for the cause of environmental awareness, education, and action. She explains the name of the group on its website: the role of a cricket striker is to hit the ball. "We want to hit people's mind about the environmental issues." The added 'C' stands for Change. Baroda is the other name for Vadodara, Prarthi's hometown. The group has led clean-up drives, tree-planting projects and other activities. It was partly her progressive work that convinced me to retain her to work with me. Her group's efforts and those of other small initiatives in India and elsewhere are living examples of American cultural anthropologist Margaret Mead's most frequently quoted and hopeful thought: "Never doubt that a small group of thoughtful, committed citizens can change the world. Indeed, it is the only thing that ever has."

The months, even years that I built up in my mind had finally arrived: to begin the Salt March. I was both excited and anxiety-stricken. It turned out to be more and less than my expectations.

Debashish had made it clear to me that not only was it fairly impossible to follow Gandhi's exact route due to the buildup of infrastructure—buildings that blocked the original path, highways that paved over his path, the crazy traffic that made it unsafe—but also that, due to all that, I would not be able to replicate Gandhi's march with any kind of verisimilitude. Further, he convinced me it was unsafe for me to walk alone in these times. And who would want to do the walk with me anyway? Some friends had made sounds like they would but logistically that was impossible too. Even Gandhi did not walk alone. I had miscalculated how long it would take me and still keep to my schedule of next adventures and flights. So I made a compromise. Day One I would go by car with Debashish and two of his team from Sabarmati Ashram past the first place Gandhi stopped and continue to the second night stop where we would meet a group of Gujarat Vidyapith heritage management students studying the Salt March. That seemed interesting. As soon as we were on the road for 15 minutes I saw what he meant: among foot traffic, motor rickshaws, vehicles, buses, trucks, wooden carts, bicycles, cows—just a normal array of street life in Indian cities—I would have been at risk with each step. It would have been nothing like what Gandhi experienced either. From there I would still go with

Debashish and team by car, but they would let me out of the car to walk alone for miles on end, and meet them again at the other end. In villages where Team Debashish was conducting research, we'd disembark, walk by foot and then jump in the car to the next village. Then repeat the drill. This way I could cover the whole Salt March and see what there was to see. I did feel a bit guilty after building other people's expectation—and my own—when I said I was "doing the Salt March." But I quickly overcame my famously Jewish guilt.

Along the way, I marveled at how Debashish worked. He was part detective, sociologist, gum shoe reporter and community builder; part anthropologist, archeologist, and architect; part historian, psychologist and city planner. It reminded me of the many hats we have to wear as journalists.

But he was not a walker. He joined me for one stretch and I could see we did not match: he preferred to stroll while I walked at Gandhi's pace—in other words, fast. Strolling through villages was fine, as there was much to stop and study in minutia that I would never have picked up—rooftops, archways, doorknobs, window frames. He'd stop in a tiny plaza and paint a picture of Gandhi standing on a balcony and speaking to a small or large gathering.

After three days it became hard to keep track of which village had what and when.

There are a few moments that I know will stay with me a long time:

I was left off on a small road in the countryside to walk alone. In India it's nearly impossible to stand anywhere and be in complete silence. Yet there I was, and so stunned by the sound of nothing that I stopped and started recording me talking to me, holding my phone mic in the air, whispering, "Can you hear that? Me neither. That is the sound of silence... in India! I can only imagine that Gandhi might, just might have had some similar moment in 1930. I hope so!"

The funny part was those moments of silence were often interrupted by a motorcycle speeding by, or the white noise of high tension wires. So I'd interrupt myself taping me until another one minute of silence came around again.

Another realization came to me personally at another juncture when I was walking alone. I am, by nature, a loner. I feel entirely comfortable being just me with me. Indians are very rarely alone. Family and friends and others seem to be always around. They seem to enjoy the tumult and chaos. If not enjoy, at least one can say that is the condition they are accustomed to. "Joint family" means parents live with their kids, their own siblings, their kids' wives and kids, sometimes 12 to 15 bodies under one roof. I once told an Indian friend if Americans generally lived like that, they'd have to have a separate room for the family therapist. Gandhi never walked alone on the Salt March. He traveled with about 80 constant followers. When he left one village, the villagers followed him halfway to the next village where the group was joined by the next village while the previous villagers peeled off and went back home.

It was another stark moment for me to realize while I could try to become Gandhi, I would never "be" Gandhi nor would I want to be.

The night stops had been organized by a company that specializes in events. The accommodations were, to be kind, rustic. A step up from country cabins, they didn't have great bedding. The meals were prepared in someone's home kitchen and brought to the guests in a common dining room. I worried about sanitation. Maybe it was just me. But I could not envision Westerners feeling comfortable in this setting.

The last 13 miles of the march were most memorable for me. I'd broken off from Debashish to travel at my own pace to the "finish line" at Dandi Beach. Even then, my very protective driver, Vijay, insisted on traveling behind me in a car. There's a memorial statue dedicated to Gandhi and his followers a few kilometers before the beach. I whizzed past it, so intent on getting to the sea. The great relief and release of walking the long beach to the water, stiff and tired as I was, as burning as my feet were, was one of the most fulfilling moments I've ever experienced.

Personally, I had reached this destination I had thought of for almost three years. That alone was rewarding. The beach was quiet; couples by the two intermingled with families of parents and children playing as if on any beach. How many came to pay homage to what happened here, I can only speculate. Over this sweet scene, I superimposed the beach crowded with hundreds and hundreds of followers when Gandhi had arrived there to commit that act of disobedience. Curious onlookers and swarms of media would also have been there. My imagination was filled in with old sepia-toned photographs and the scene from the film "Gandhi." These helped me sense what it must have been like for Gandhi himself, though still I did not and never will fully know.

The five-hour drive back to Ahmedabad seemed endless but the pull to a bed with a real mattress and a long hot shower made me feel like a horse that smelled the barn. Om sweet om, where it was.

Before returning to Mumbai, from Ahmedabad I went to Udaipur, Rajasthan, to see the Maharana Mewar family, with whom I had worked 15 years earlier. I luxuriated in their Shiv Niwas Palace in a grand suite for three days, then I took a side trip to one of the Mewar HRH hotels, the Aodhi, a rustic boutique hotel 100 yards from Kumbhalgarh Fort, whose 15th century 36 kilometer-wall (22.3 mile) is the second longest in the world (far short of China's Great Wall at 21,196 kilometers, 13,171 miles). I enjoyed the hike up to the top and scrambling along the wall. Gandhi was far from my thoughts... until I began to leave the fort area. I saw a crowd of people surrounding the police, full of curiosity as the authorities interrogated standers-by. It turned out a murder had been committed right there on the grounds. Was there nowhere I could go where the realities of violence did not leave a dark shadow?

Returning to Mumbai, and before heading west and then south and then north and then further west, I had two missions. One was to complete a series of interviews and dining experiences for the book I was ghost writing for acclaimed ground-breaking chef, Rahul Akerkar. This would be a test of my vegetarianism. I failed miserably. Chef's menu at his Qualia Restaurant included a number of meat and fowl dishes. It was my professional obligation to eat my way through the tasting menu, wasn't it? There were plenty of veg options, especially since Rahul's wife, Malini, is a vegetarian. But hey! There was one dish shouting for me to try it: braised buffalo brisket. Frankly, he had me at brisket. You see, my mother—shall I say my Jewish mother—was famous among family for her brisket, hers not buffalo but good old beef, preferably the flat, or first, cut of beef. This dish is a staple of the European Jewish holiday table because it was an affordable cut of beef. Rahul, whose mother is a German Jew, easily matched Mom's brisket and I felt zero remorse or guilt for trying it because I felt it was to honor the late great Chef Lillie Garfinkel.

My other mission was to visit Mani Bhavan, the home where Gandhi lived between 1917 and 1934, pivotal years in his evolution as a leader. It was from Mani Bhavan that Gandhi initiated the satyagraha movement. He began to use the charkha regularly here. Here he also decided to abstain from drinking cow's milk in order to protest the cruel and inhuman treatment of them. In 1955, the building was turned into a memorial to Gandhi.

There is a library with a statue of the Mahatma where people offer tributes. A staircase dotted with Gandhi's pictures depicting his life leads visitors to the first floor which has a photo gallery with photographs from his childhood until his assassination, along with press clippings.

The room that Gandhi used during his stay is on the second floor, where through a glass partition people can see two of his spinning wheels, a book and his bed on the floor. Right opposite that room is a hall where photographs and paintings of his lifetime are on display.

I also planned to meet and interview Gandhi's great grandson there, the first of several Gandhi descendants I would have the pleasure to meet.

Note to self: Next time I write a book about a famous person, do not under any circumstance conduct an interview with a descendant in a library where some 40,000 volumes about or by said famous person line the shelves of two rooms.

Now a museum and one of the most important pilgrimage stops for Gandhi aficionados, Mani Bhavan was where I met

Tushar Arun Gandhi, one of Gandhi-ji's great-grandchildren, who was 57 years old at the time of our first sit-down. Literally surrounded by books, pamphlets, papers, documents and other written materials either by or about Mahatma Gandhi, I was so intimidated I almost walked out on the interview. This voluminous collection—many millions of words—made me think several times about whether I had even a syllable to add to these earnest works. Who was I to think I could write anything that would bring new insights to the legacy of India's Great Emancipator? I could only aspire to become some forgettable unnamed meteor in the Gandhi-sphere. Then I thought of Gandhi's own words, not exactly of encouragement but at least they gave me some perspective and a reason to get over myself:

"Whatever you do will be insignificant, but it is very important that you do it."

So I set up my recorder while Tushar settled into a seat across from me at a table in the reading area of the library. I chose to interview Tushar first, among many other living descendants of Mohandas Karamchand Gandhi, specifically because he is a Gandhian paradox.

Firebrand, ingrate, controversial, ne'er-do-well, opportunist. These are only a few of the epithets hurled at Tushar—author, speaker and self-declared "confrontationist Gandhian." He clearly rubs some people the wrong way. When I proposed to profile him for the *New York Times*, the India bureau chief wrote back: "Asked a couple of others well versed in India for their thoughts. He seems more like a crank than anything else."

As Tushar put it when we met: "When someone challenges me, it gets me going. That is the story of my life."

It's a story with quite a few ups and downs.

In many ways, he is as un-Gandhi-like as one could imagine. In other ways he is following in the footsteps of his *bapu* (father, as in Father of the Nation of India): rebellious, outspoken, stubborn, advocate of social justice, defender of the underdog. Just add about 150 pounds (Tushar weighed 240 at the time, the Mahatma weighed 110), a scruffy beard, a full-bellied laugh, a meat eater (the Mahatma was famously vegetarian) and an imbiber of spirits every now and then.

It seems every time he makes a public statement, there is conjecture about his purpose. Does he want to ramp up his political aspirations? Is it all about his ego? Or, alternately, is he so insecure that, failing real accomplishments of his own, he needs to fluff himself up in newspaper column inches and TV airtime?

"Every time I go public with something, people guess what my agenda is," he said. "My agenda is to keep the message of Gandhi-ji alive today because we are drifting away from his ideals. We are becoming radicalized, unsustainably materialistic, divisive. That was even so at his time. He fought against it. But those areas he focused on are actually much more rabid now. Think about the Trump era and Satyagraha—insistence on the truth; the man has real issues with The Truth. And I see that ethos permeating societies East and West. Then think about India and the rest of the world. Think about the global rise of terrorism and the Gandhian principle of Ahimsa—Nonviolence. And it goes on to all the other principles."

Many disagree with Tushar's tactics in drawing attention to causes he feels the Mahatma would also have supported...and a few he likely would not have backed. His confrontations have gotten him in hot water numerous times and continue today. Just a few:

- In 1995, upon hearing someone slander his great-grandfather on a low-brow Fox India TV talk show, Tushar's outraged public reaction led Parliament to denounce the show and issue an arrest warrant against Rupert Murdoch and four other Fox employees, accused of defaming the Mahatma.
- In 2001, he almost sold the rights to reproduce Mahatma Gandhi's image to CMG Worldwide, the company that markets and manages intellectual property rights, eventually pulling out of the deal but not before alienating much of his family.
- His 2007 book, *Let's Kill Gandhi: A Chronicle of His Last Days*—purposely entitled, he told me, as an incendiary marketing ploy—was largely panned but Tushar was quick to tell me it went into a fifth print run.
- In 2015, Punjabi police attempted to book Tushar on charges of making "derogatory" comments against the late revolutionary martyr Bhagat Singh, who advocated violence during India's fight for independence.
- Just a few months after our meeting and probably continuing for many months, Tushar jumped into another controversial fray. When the government ban on the sale of slaughtered cows led to lynchings by so-called "cow vigilantes" (Hindu extremists mostly targeting the country's beef-eating Muslim minority), Tushar privately petitioned the Supreme Court to intervene. After several hearings, though, the lynchings continued and as of this writing, Tushar continued to push against them.

Those are the reported facts but I wanted to get behind the headlines to understand what motivates this man as a descendant who bears the Mahatma's name and lineage, a weighty mantle and an almost impossible moral bar to rise to.

Tushar Arun Gandhi, born January 17, 1960, is the son of journalist Arun Manilal Gandhi, an Indian-American socio-political activist now living in Rochester, New York, where the M.K. Gandhi Institute for Nonviolence is located and which he founded. Tushar's grandfather was Manilal Mohandas Gandhi, the second son of Mahatma Gandhi and Kasturba Gandhi and who spent most of his life in South Africa serving as editor of the *Indian Opinion*, a Gujarati weekly in English.

Tushar is a heavy-set man who nearly bursts out of the thin cotton collarless short-sleeved shirt he wore that day. He's often been seen in a thick gray beard with very long hair either flowing down to his shoulders or tightened into a ponytail, though today his hair is short and his beard is neatly cropped. He moves slowly and he speaks even more slowly, deliberately. He measures his words, as though someone will throw them back at him if they diverge from his great-grandfather's credo, an experience Tushar has come to expect. But every now and then he utters things that make it clear he could not give a hoot what people say about him.

To connect the dots from Bapu to Tushar, I asked him to take me to the spot in the museum that speaks most to him, where he feels closest to his great-grandfather, where he receives direct transmission and inspiration from him. Without hesitation he rose and I followed. As we walked up two narrow flights, we passed a large room where I stopped, momentarily transfixed. I watched young school children one by one stand in front of a group of other students, a long table of teachers behind each speaker. In their tiny high-pitched voices, each kid recited passages from Mahatma Gandhi's writings they had memorized.

With cute hand gestures, and in sing-songy rote style, they delivered their recitations with as much comprehension as one could hope. Tushar explained this was an annual competition sponsored by Mumbai's Gandhi Smarak Nidhi, in association with Mani Bhavan Gandhi Sangrahalaya, two organizations engaged in the propagation of Gandhian teachings. Did they—winners or not—truly understand what they were parroting? And more to the point, from an educator's perspective, would what they did understand stick into adulthood? Would they "be the change?" Would they move forward living according to Gandhi's ideals, realizing his vision of a utopian society, even by the next generation? So far I did not see it...yet.

As I pondered this, we reached the top floor and came to a stop in front of a room with one wall replaced by a thick glass. This was where Mahatma Gandhi lived for 17 years, learning to use the charkha spinning wheel while also spinning his thoughts into what would become India's independence movement. It's almost scary how basic the room is, as it has been preserved the way the Mahatma lived there: a thin cotton mattress on the floor, a low writing desk beside it, his beloved charkha against the wall, a small balcony from which he could look through the trees and down to the tree-lined residential street.

I'd seen these types of museum-quality rooms before. In my own hometown of West Orange, New Jersey, we took school field trips to the original labs of Thomas Edison, the late 19th century American who invented power lights, phonographs and motion pictures, now the Thomas Edison National Historic Park. At that time, I pressed my face up against the room, intact as it was when Edison was fiddling with his wires and gadgetry. It was inspiring to imagine the man, a mere mortal of flesh and blood, right there in my hometown, albeit 70 years earlier, almost convincing me I could do anything I set my mind to.

For Tushar, the room at Mani Bhavan had a different meaning.

"This may be the most iconic room in India," he said. "In 1959 the US civil rights leader Martin Luther King Junior was a guest of the Indian government and the first place he wanted to visit was right here. I mean he came directly from the airport to this spot. At the time the room had walls on all sides. So when he went in alone, no one knew exactly what he did but he said he meditated." He was in there alone for hours, perhaps meditating on how he would leverage the wisdom he gained from Gandhi to lead thousands of nonviolent civil rights demonstrators on a five-day march from Selma to Montgomery, Alabama, campaigning for African Americans' voter rights.

Tushar continued: "Finally the director came and said he must leave because they were closing. But Dr. King asked if he could stay there only, in that room: 'I want to live in Gandhi's house? Can you make some arrangements for me to stay here?' Of course this sent everyone into a panic. As a distinguished state guest, arrangements had been made for him to stay at the best suite at the nearby Taj Mahal Palace Hotel. On his insistence, though, they put a cot and a few other things in a room across from this room. When he left after three days, King wrote in the visitor's book: 'I stayed here and have been in communion with Gandhi. I feel his energy emanating from here. I am charged to go back and fight for the rights of my people.'"

There was another famous American visitor five decades later, Tushar went on, for whom this room had very special significance. In 2010, then United States President Barack Obama paid a visit, with his wife Michelle, to the home of the man Obama credits with being his inspiration—not, as one might suspect, Dr. King, but the little man in spectacles from India. Obama had kept a portrait of Gandhi behind his desk while a young senator from Illinois. "I might not be standing before you today as President of the United States had it not been for Gandhi and the message he shared with America and the world," he had told a group. Once asked who he would most like to have dinner with, Obama picked Mahatma Gandhi. Obama's inscription in the Mani Bhavan visitor book reads: "I am filled with hope and inspiration as I have the privilege to view this testament to Gandhi's life. He is a hero not just to India but to the world."

Now standing there with Tushar, I asked him a few questions.

"What is your earliest memory of coming here?"

"I must have been very young. With any guest from other parts of India or with foreign visitors, my parents would bring them here and I tagged along."

"What are your feelings when you come here?"

"In truth, while I honor this as a historic space, I do not commune best with my great-grandfather here, probably because I have never been able to go into the room. Where my emotions run high, though, is at Birla House in Delhi, where he lived the last 144 days of his life and where he was murdered. The latent anger and desire to violently retaliate raise their ugly heads. I feel closer to him there. In my head I can hear him saying to me: 'Tushar, resist the violence. Remember that's part of our message and our legacy.' But there it remains. Ironically that anger brings me closer to a live dialogue with him. Luckily, he always wins out. He's like the angel sitting on my shoulder, while the devil in me on the other shoulder tries to fight back and always loses."

I spent my last few days in India in Mumbai: to see Chef Rahul for the book I was ghostwriting for him, eat at his restaurant Qualia, and do some more Gandhi research.

It was February 3, 2020. At one point driving around the city, the couple were sitting in the front of their SUV, I in the back. Rahul and Malini are brilliant at the sciences, she holds a Bachelors in Microbiology from Imperial College in London, and he a masters in biochemical engineering from New York City's Columbia University. They were bandying back and forth about early reports of a certain virus wending its way from China to India and the rest of Asia, heading west from there. It all went over my head; it sounded like science geeks obsessing over a rare strain of some irrelevant microbiological bug. I heard the word "novel" and thought it meant it was something new and would just as quickly become not novel, and therefore unimportant. I didn't pay attention or care that much. I had "bigger things" on my mind, like making sure I got to the airport at some ridiculous hour the next morning.

Unconcerned, I went on to South Africa via an overnight stopover in Istanbul, where I met Elizabet Kurumlu, a Turkish tour guide who had taken me around Istanbul on an earlier trip. She wears another hat as a documentary film producer. When she saw some of the videos I'd shot in India to possibly use in a video essay about my journey, she offered (or did I cajole her?) to join me on the South African leg and document my interviews and travels in video format. When we met that day of February 4, we went to grab a taxi but when she saw four or five people from China getting out of the car, she steered me away. She had been following the news about the same bug Rahul and Malini had been discussing; Elizabet had read the origin of the novel virus was Wuhan, the capital of Hubei Province in the People's Republic of China, the most populous city in Central China with 11 million people. Liz was just being extremely cautious, more so than I would have been. Little did I know, nor did the world. But after I left South Africa and landed back in San Francisco, on March 11, 2020, after more than 118,000 cases in 114 countries and 4,291 deaths, the World Health Organization declared what was called SARS-CoV-2 virus (commonly known as COVID-19) a pandemic. That was the "novel Coronavirus" I'd heard about five weeks earlier. The world went into "lockdown," masks became required or at least highly recommended. Businesses went broke. Everyone knew someone who died from the deadly virus. Yet, it divided people—those who denied it was serious and didn't wear masks from those who did and took extreme caution.

People wanted to know what to do but when they heard the bad news from experts, like the American immunologist Anthony Fauci, director of the National Institute of Allergy and Infectious Diseases (NIAID) and chief medical advisor to then President Donald Trump, many were still confused and fought the protocols that could save lives. In the end, as if there is ever an end to such diseases, some 6.63 million people died of Covid by November 2022.

Since I was writing about Gandhi, it was logical to see if he had sound advice even if hypothetical or a theory on how to cope in a pandemic.

I had heard or read that he had nearly succumbed to the deadly 1918 influenza pandemic, commonly known as the Spanish Flu, which killed 50 million people in the world. In India, where it was dubbed the Bombay Influenza or Bombay Fever, up to 18 million died, more than in any other country. Many experts analyzing the Covid pandemic looked to how the world handled that early 20th century flu. I wondered how Gandhi was able to survive it, figuring his approach would be how I could cope.

But whatever I read or heard was inaccurate, according to one of his grandsons, Gopalkrishna Gandhi, and others. The younger Gandhi was a diplomat who served as the 23rd Governor of West Bengal; he's also founding Director of the Nehru Centre of the High Commission of India, in London. Writing in April 2020 for *The Telegraph*, the Indian English daily newspaper, Gopalkrishna corrected the record: "...[Gandhiji] was, it is true, ill, grievously ill, within a faltering heartbeat of death, when the pandemic was sweeping across the world. But he was not down with that deadly flu... but a vicious abdominal infection," which turned out to be dysentery.

Gopalkrishna offered his own "suppositions" on how his grandfather would have responded to Covid: "Gandhi was at his intense best when dealing with illness and epidemics, finding some quirky but very specific, practical and demanding 'solutions', in which the enforcing of hygiene regimes was central. Though actuated by his own sharply developed sense of the physical body's working, he was very consultative—seeking and considering the advice of medical practitioners, both 'Western' and 'Traditional'," but keeping well away from superstitious, ritualistic or irrational nostrums."

Repeating that he was only speculating, he continued: These may yield the following pointers not as his, but as those of a vigilant and humble common sense:

1. Recognizing the legitimate authority and inherent conscientiousness of governments, we the governed should treat expert and official advice, especially about

hygiene and disinfection, with respect and observe it scrupulously.

2. Similarly and simultaneously, recognizing the integrated experience and inherent good sense of us, the governed, the government should keep a helpline open—not from but to us—to seek public counsel on the measures particularly as related to restrictions. These must see who and how and where the restrictions hurt the people they are intended to help. Rules are best observed when they have *louvres* for genuine exceptions and exemptions such as for the space-less, job-less, family-less, the elderly, the physically and mentally challenged. If Chelmsford could hearken to the Kheda *satyagraha* in the midst of World War I, this is not asking too much of our administrations.
3. We should replace utterly useless commercial, political, sectarian icons with the real heroines and heroes of this human crisis—doctors and medical workers like nurses and lab technicians who are the brave and endangered Fire Brigade for this conflagration. And those providers of essential services who are working with unflagging and hazardous zeal.

Gandhi walked. He walked a lot.

By many accounts Mahatma Gandhi walked on an average around 18 km (11 miles) every day for nearly 40 years.

A typical person can cover approximately one mile on a brisk 20-minute walk. Gandhi was not your typical person...in this case in physical stature. He was 5 feet 5 inches tall (165 cm) so his strides would have been shorter than mine, at 5 feet 10. But he made up for time by walking faster than the typical homo sapiens. He walked at a race-walking pace in all the old sepia-tone clips I watched from the Mahatma Gandhi Footage Collection, which houses 152 videos from 1922 to 1948.

If you're the type who tracks your steps with your pedometer, he would have walked 22,000 steps a day. For Gandhiji, this means he spent close to 3 hours walking. Who in current times has that much time for that? Gandhi would have made you make time. He once ticked off the venerable Gopal Krishna Gokhale, a senior leader of the Indian National Congress, who was like a mentor for him, for not walking: "You do not even go out for walks. Is it surprising that you should always be ailing? Should public work leave no time for physical exercise?" he asked. Needless to say, Gokhale's reply, that he didn't have the time, left Gandhi unconvinced. That was because no matter where he was, or how busy he was, Gandhi never skipped his walks.

He realized the importance of walking early on in his life. While studying law in England from 1888 to 1891, he initially stayed as a tenant with an English family. Finding himself short of money, however, he decided to cut his expenses by half. He took independent rooms of his own, selected so that he could walk to his workplace in half an hour. That way he saved on public transport fares and it gave him walks of 8 or 10 miles a day. He wrote, "It was mainly this habit of long walks that kept me practically free from illness throughout my stay in England and gave me a fairly strong body."

When he came to Bombay after his stint in London, he lived in Girgaum, but hardly ever took a carriage or tramcar. He would walk to the High Court, which took him 45 minutes, and return on foot as well. This saved him money since he didn't have too much work. In England, he enjoyed walking in the crisp, cool weather; in Bombay he inured himself to the heat. Even when he began to earn money, he kept up the practice of walking.

In South Africa, he went for regular walks with his friend Hermann Kallenbach. During the satyagraha there, he led striking workers on a 35-mile walk to escape the white owners of mines and plantations.

Even when he was recovering from an appendicitis operation in 1924 in Bombay, he walked for 40 minutes on the Juhu seashore every day. In London in 1931 for the Round Table Conference, he continued to wake up at 4 am, pray for an hour, then go for a walk through the deserted streets of the city.

Of course, the walk Gandhi is best known for is the great Salt March, undertaken when the Mahatma was 60-plus. He walked a total of 386 km (250 miles) for 24 days from Sabarmati Ashram to Dandi Beach on the coast to break the salt law. This was the walk that shook the foundation of the British empire in India.

Some ardent Gandhi followers give his walking great significance.

"Walking for miles each day was an integral part of his ethos and his graceful gait was part of his charisma," wrote Madhav Nayar, a writer who teaches History in a Cambridge Curriculum school named Beyond8, in *The Hindu*. "Walking reflected some deeply held Gandhian beliefs and philosophies. At one level, it was an attempt to disrupt, if not deconstruct, the mechanical rhythms of industrial time and reconnect with natural time. It represented forward movement, progress and the onward march of the satyagrahi."

I used to hate to walk, as in walk for exercise. Even more I hated to hike, as in a long trek in heat and being followed by hungry mosquitos. At a summer camp when I was about 10, we had to hike with backpacks. I nearly revolted and bolted.

Then, my walking epiphany struck me in my mid 40s while working as a senior writer for Rodale Press, famous for its health and fitness magazines and accompanying books. There, I had to dive deep into the company's extensive library of science-based facts and studies to corroborate any claims doctors we interviewed made. For one book chapter I was assigned to write, I came upon several studies showing even just 20 minutes of brisk walking (not strolling) does a body/mind good. I found this quite useful because at the time I had very little time or interest to do a full workout. Walking was great because all I needed was good sneakers, a sidewalk or path in the woods and the desire to do so. Getting over the lack of desire would be the hard aspect.

So I started to take afternoon walk breaks while at work. Until then I didn't know Rodale, based in bucolic Eastern Pennsylvania, had a series of trails throughout the company grounds designed for just that purpose. I was reborn as a neophyte walker. I didn't need the science to substantiate the benefits: it cleared my head and pumped me up—I mean it literally pumped up my heart rate. I felt like I was doing something for myself that did not require a Stairmaster, treadmill, weights, rackets, balls or any other sports equipment. Plus if I chose wisely, the views, smells and sounds would stimulate my dopamine, the happy hormone.

Inspired by my own commitment to undertake some of Gandhi's ritual, and my desire to find an exercise I can take around the world with me, I began to walk regularly. At first I became obsessed with fastidiously keeping a diary of how many miles and steps I took every day. I built up my endurance and stamina. Within a few months I was up to 10,000 steps, equivalent to 5 miles and still only half of Gandhi's daily regimen, which I'd read was the health sweet spot. Scientists from the University of Sydney and the University of Southern Denmark found that walking 10,000 steps a day lowers the risk of dementia by about 50 per cent, the risk of cancer by about 30 per cent and the risk of cardiovascular disease by about 75 per cent.

I gave up the idea that I was in competition with The Man. It was not a foot race. There were no medals or winner's circles. It was just me and me, and my mind/body. Soon I began to look forward to my walks, peeking only every now and then at my pedometer. Then they became a must to my daily life. Now they are my sadhana, the Sanskrit term used for daily spiritual practice, a disciplined surrendering of the ego, practiced with awareness and the intention of spiritual growth, practiced alone and for the sake of the individual. I walk and think, I breathe deeply, I intake all that nature and man have on offer when I am simply in the moment.

I had learned "mindful walking" on retreats I'd taken in the mindfulness meditation tradition—stepping carefully and silently in slow motion maintaining awareness of feet touching the ground, from the heel up through the toes. One of my most memorable mindful walks was under the tutelage of the now late but always great Vietnamese monk Thich Nhat Hanh, at his retreat center, Plum Village in the South of France. How blissful walking the grounds wandering with others around lotus ponds and fruits trees. "Walking meditation is first and foremost a practice to bring body and mind together peacefully," he instructed later in his talk.

I bring that feeling with me even walking the gritty streets of my city, or any other; and despite the sirens of fire trucks and police cars, I find that "peace is every step," as one of his book titles suggests.

2

TRUTH

The Answer to Every Question

> "Many people, especially ignorant people, want to punish you for speaking the truth, for being correct, for being you. Never apologize for being correct, or for being years ahead of your time. If you're right and you know it, speak your mind. Speak your mind. Even if you are a minority of one, the truth is still the truth."
>
> —Gandhi

In truth—a very good way to begin—I've had a lot of trouble starting to write this book because I knew I must address Truth very early on, given how Gandhi put it first among the principles he prescribed for himself and others. But truth...and Truth...are elusive and mercurial matters, dependent on circumstance and definition and time. Writing about truth, which changes from moment to moment, from this sentence to the next, is a slippery slope because that last sentence I just wrote has to stand the test of time until you read it, and hopefully beyond. But since truth changes with time, I may just have lied.

To bolster my confidence and kickstart this whole experiment,

I defer to advice from one of my first writing gurus, the 20th century American author Ernest Hemingway. In his 1964 memoir, *A Moveable Feast,* he wrote: "I would stand and look out over the roofs of Paris and think, 'Do not worry. You have always written before and you will write now. All you have to do is write one true sentence. Write the truest sentence you know."

So this is mine:

I lie. You lie.

We lie to protect the feelings of others; for self-protection to avoid punishment; to hurt others. And we lie to ourselves—called self-deception. That last may be the most harmful and not just to ourselves.

Not telling the truth, the whole truth and nothing but the truth is a given among human beings.

Also given is that there is something immoral about lying. Why else would it appear in the Ten Commandments, more or less the moral and ethical compass of Judeo-Christians? *The Quran*, the central religious text in Islam, in many verses also mentions truthfulness as more than speaking with honesty; to Muslims, truthfulness is the conformity of the outer with the inner and is the cornerstone of a person's character. To Buddhists who abide by the Eightfold Path, Right Speech and Right Thought cover truth too.

Some of us speak the truth and seek The Truth. Others not so much.

Gandhi hoped we would value both—but he did not specifically or necessarily mean truth in the literal manner of telling the truth, as opposed to lying one's butt off.

He built his moral philosophy around the concept of Truth. His flip from his original statement that "God is Truth" to

"Truth is God" should suffice to demonstrate how increasingly important it became to him. He used the Hindi term *satya*, derived from the Sanskrit *sat*, which translates variously to absolute truth, the true essence, reality, unchangeable, that which has no distortion, that which is beyond distinctions of time, space, person and pervades the universe in all its constancy. *Sat* is a common prefix in ancient Indian literature and often implies good, true, virtuous, being, existing, lasting, essential. In the Vedas and later sutras, the meaning of the word satya (सत्य) evolves into an ethical concept about truthfulness and is considered an important virtue. Grammatically, which often reveals more than anything, *sat* is the present participle of the root as "to be." To be or not to be in truth, that is not the question because we all be—that is, we all exist. By these definitions and parameters, regardless of whether we tell the truth or believe in a higher Truth, we *are* The Truth simply by virtue of being alive.

Gandhi lived truth by his actions, thoughts and words, written and spoken. In his relationships with people, in his relationship to the environment, to pets, to his spiritual practice, to everything that touched his life. Adhering to truth in all these actions and interactions inevitably and irrevocably led him to lead a moral life. In "Making Sense of Gandhi's Idea of Truth," Philosophy Professor R.C. Pradhan wrote in the New Delhi-based journal *Social Scientist*: "Truth is a moral link between one action and another in so far as it bestows on them the virtues of honesty, sincerity of purpose, and rootedness in the basic moral principles. An action is based on truth provided it follows from the moral principles and is performed in the spirit of truth, i.e. the holding unto truth (satyagraha). All truth-based actions constitute, according to Gandhi, the moral life, which is itself integrated into the spiritual life of man."

Gandhi himself wrote:

"Truth is by nature self-evident. As soon as you remove the cobwebs of ignorance that surround it, it shines clear."

Yet, he also wrote he is nowhere near Truth: "I am but a seeker of Truth. I claim to have found a way to it. I claim to be making a ceaseless effort to find it. But I admit that I have not yet found it. To find Truth completely is to realize oneself and one's destiny i.e. to become perfect."

He did slip and tell a lie, at least once, according to an account in the collective website archives of Bombay Sarvodaya Mandal/ Gandhi Book Centre, a Gandhian Charitable Trust. As a young boy, he stole money from one of his brothers and gave it to his other brother to help him get out of a debt. So guilt-ridden by his action, Mohandas wrote his father a letter, confessing the theft. When his father cried rather than punish him, "Mohandas's heart sank with shame and remorse. His father's tears affected him very deeply, and this time he took a silent vow never to do an unrighteous deed again. This incident marked a turning point in his life and he strove ever after to be ever good and truthful."

Before undertaking an attempt to follow Gandhi's moral guidelines, beginning with this most important of his pillars, I had to slice and dice my way through the very many varieties, variations and variables of being truthful and being Truth and then decide which to follow...or not. There are many. Absolute Truth. Ultimate Truth. Relative Truth. Contingent Truth. Objective, Normative, Subjective and Complex Truths. Sages since ancient times, possibly since the Beginning of Time, have tried to define it but wherever they land on that mercurial effort, they agree that Truth is the central pillar of any belief system, of any social organization with a moral conscience—in other words, of what many people call religion.

Gandhi didn't think we mortals had any chance of attaining Absolute Truth. He wrote: "God alone knows absolute truth... man, a finite being, cannot know absolute truth. Relative truth is all we know; we can only follow the truth as we see it. Such pursuit of truth cannot lead anyone astray."

He cut a lot of slack for us flawed human beings in our slippery journey trying to stay on the path of truth:

"I believe that, if in spite of the best of intentions, one is led into committing mistakes, they do not really result in harm to the world or, for the matter of that, any individual. God always saves the world from the consequences of unintended errors or men who live in fear of Him... Those who are likely to be misled by my example would have gone that way all the same even if they had not known of my action. For, in the final analysis, a man is guided in his conduct by his own inner promptings, though the example of others might sometimes seem to guide him. ...It is my firm belief that not one of my known errors was willful. Indeed, what may appear to be an obvious error to one may appear to another as pure wisdom. He cannot help himself even if he is under a hallucination. Even so must it be with men like me who, it may be, are labouring under a great hallucination. Surely God will pardon them and the world should bear with them. Truth will assert itself in the end. Truth never damages a cause that is just. Life is an aspiration. Its mission is to strive after perfection, which is self-realization. The ideal must not be lowered because of our weaknesses or imperfections. I am painfully conscious of both in me. The silent cry daily goes out to Truth to help me to remove these weaknesses and imperfections of mine..."

This all left me feeling greatly relieved. I am indeed painfully imperfect. If anyone in the room will mistakenly break something, spill something, burn something, trip over something, say something that comes off as "off," do something socially awkward, it will be me. My nearest and dearest know this and accept me for it nonetheless. "Perry's quirky," they say politely. Klutzy, I would say. An accident about to happen, I would say. So the odds that I could achieve the enlightened state of Absolute Truth were decidedly slim. But in this case, I'd decided nonetheless that I was going for it.

Then again, Gandhi made the search for truth sound simple but difficult, as simple and as difficult as trying to pick up a puddle of mercury from the floor: "The instruments for the quest of Truth are as simple as they are difficult. They may appear quite impossible to an arrogant person, and quite possible to an innocent child. The seeker after Truth should be humbler than the dust. The world crushes the dust under its feet, but the seeker after Truth should so humble himself that even the dust could crush him. Only then, and not till then, will he have a glimpse of Truth."

"The very concept of objective truth is fading out of the world. Lies will pass into history." ~ George Orwell, in *Nineteen Eighty-Four* (1949)

In the briefest, these working definitions spun around my head, keeping in mind that speaking and thinking the truth is the first step toward being in Truth.

- Relative Truth: truth in reference to something else. Example: The house is on the left side of the street, depending on where you stand in relation to the house and the street.
- Contingent Truth: truth that depends on something else. The house may be on the left side of the street, depending

on which side you are standing on. It may be true that it may be a house; it may not be. Any sentence that includes "may" or "if" is probably a contingent truth.

- Objective Truth: According to the Stanford Encyclopedia, scientific truth is objective, confirmed by proof, that ideally is universally accepted. An objective statement is factual; it has a definite correspondence to reality, independent of anyone's feelings or biases. It's "evidence-based," meaning rigorously evaluated in experimental evaluations, randomized controlled trials and the like, and hopefully published in professional journals.
- Subjective Truth: Subjective truth, on the other hand, is dependent upon opinion and perspective. Sentences that include the telltale phrases "I think" or "I feel" probably are subjective. Good examples of subjective truth are available every night on the evening TV news talk shows on all sides of the political spectrum, best represented by Fox News on the right and CNN on the left.
- Ultimate Truth and Absolute Truth: These two are not simple to explain or distinguish. It may even be true, depending on what tradition you seek, that they are interchangeable. But considering Gandhi said at least one of them is unattainable, I don't feel so bad I'm not able to break them down. Put another way, if relative truth is how we usually see the world, a place full of diverse and distinctive things and beings, then we arrive at ultimate truth when we see that there are no distinctive things or beings. To say there are no distinctive things or beings is not to say that nothing exists; it is saying that there are no distinctions. The absolute is the unity of all things and beings, unmanifested.

In another world view, all knowledge is comprised of two truths—the Two Truths. In the 6th century BCE, according to one Buddhist sutra, Siddhartha Gautama became "The Awakened One" once he fully understood the meaning of the two truths—conventional (relative) truth and ultimate (absolute) truth. Knowledge of the conventional truth informs us how things are conventionally, and thus grounds our epistemic practice in its proper linguistic and conceptual framework. Knowledge of the ultimate truth informs us of how things really are, ultimately, taking our minds beyond the bounds of conceptual and linguistic conventions.

I garnered a speck of insight watching, of all things, the George Lucas film "Star Wars, Episode III: Revenge of the Sith" (2005). Anakin Skywalker is having a Dark Side meltdown in a final showdown with his mentor, Obi-Wan Kenobi.

Anakin: "If you're not with me, then you're my enemy."

Obi-Wan: "Only a Sith deals in absolutes."

In other words, Sith see life as an either-or situation, as black or white, no in-betweens.

To remind those unfamiliar with "Star Wars" (I can't imagine who that could be), the Sith is the arch enemy of the Jedi, the quintessential bad guy versus the good guy. The Jedi believe themselves to be peacekeepers. They act based on a code of selflessness, intentionally giving their lives to the protection of the freedom of others. Their philosophy leaves no room for the self. Your identity as a Jedi is significantly less important than your responsibility as a Jedi. Very much like how Mahatma Gandhi saw and lived his life, and what he recommended for all. On the other hand, for the Sith, their emotions are the direct source of their power, which they use for personal gain. Fear, anger, and passion guide them to manipulate the world into the shape that they desire. They believe that their power is the only one that matters, and they will do anything, even bend the Force to *their* will, to take that power for themselves. The antithesis of a Gandhian way of living.

What does any of this have to do with Gandhi and truth? The answer lies in the just mentioned Force. Its description reminds me of what I believe Gandhi meant when he said, "Truth is God." Just replace Force with Truth or God in the following explanation from a Star Wars blogger:

"The Force is an energy that exists in all things. It *is* all things. Everything living within the universe came from the Force, and everything living shall return to it. And though the Force contains all things, it is more than just a cosmic construct, it has a will of its own. It wills, almost purely, for balance."

Sounds like God/Truth to me. It also sounds like Buddhism: "Nothing ever exists entirely alone; everything is in relation to everything else," the Buddha told his disciples. This is not surprising, as filmmaker George Lucas is said to have dabbled in Eastern thought and been informed by it in writing the script, and as mentioned in a paper entitled "Space Buddhism: The Adoption of Buddhist Motifs in Star Wars." This was not written by a blogging fan but by Christian Feichtinger, executive director of the International Astronautical Federation and senior advisor on exploration at the European Space Agency, and published in Contemporary Buddhism.

In short, I think Gandhi would have given a thumb's up review to "Star Wars." He might even have been cast as Yoda in the Bollywood adaptation.

Let's look at this from the perspective of another American film.

I am a big fan of the 1999 cult classic film "Galaxy Quest," a parody of and homage to science-fiction films and TV series, especially TV's "Star Trek." Little did I (or, very likely, you) think that this film would show up in a book examining Gandhi's principles. Yet, here it is—and with good reason...

One night, watching it for the approximately 23rd time, it hit me like a meteor shower from far outer space: this is a film about Truth. In it, the cast of a long cancelled but once very popular television series called "Galaxy Quest," with a cult-like following, is taken to outer space by friendly aliens who have gotten hold of the series. Thinking the TV show, which the aliens call "historical documents," is actual fact, they've built a spaceship based entirely on the one on the TV series set. Even more significantly, they have taken the values, virtues, credos and oft-repeated slogan from the show.

These aliens are a peaceful species from the planet Thermia invested in the search for knowledge, averse to violence though capable of defending themselves if necessary. They also believe the actors are real space heroes. The Thermians are completely unfamiliar with the concept of lying.

The computer officer (played by Sigourney Weaver) is incredulous.

"Does no one on your planet behave in a way that is contrary to reality?" she asks.

The human commander (played by Tim Allen) tries to explain to the aliens in the simplest terms.

"We pretend... we lie... On our planet we pretend in order to entertain."

Yes, it's science fiction...and a parody at that. It would have to be: who could imagine a society where lying does not exist?

What if we lived on a planet where the entire concept of lying was alien to our species? Would we even have needed a man named Mohandas Gandhi to remind us to follow "the way of Truth?"

What if we didn't have to conceal anything—our motives, our failures and flaws, our weaknesses, our own tendencies to manipulate evidence-based and observable actions or statements to our Machiavellian advantage? What if we actually believed each other—and could believe in each other? In ourselves? In a Higher Being, whatever you call it/her/him? What freedom! But what burden! To be true to your values at all times, to not just parrot Hallmark Card quotes about morals, but to act them, believe them, speak them, do them—this would be an achievement unparalleled in human existence.

Who would even suggest we could live with such a righteous way to organize any society? Well, actually some others have already offered society a proposal that asks humans to do just that. Buddhists call it the Eightfold Noble Path of the "right" things to do in most every situation: right views, right thought, right speech, right action, right livelihood, right effort, right mindfulness, and right contemplation. Siddhartha Gautama, the Buddha (literal translation: the "awakened one"), suggested this so-called "Middle Way" approximately 600 years before the birth of Jesus. Jesus later also tried to codify basically the same principles in his Sermon on the Mount. Six hundred years later, the Prophet Muhammad, in the Quran, orders the Muslim to tell the truth even if it is against one's own interest, to not cheat or betray other people. Allah ordered Muslims to be truthful in word and deed, privately and publicly alike.

Did any of that sway enough Earthlings to become like the

Thermians? Not enough to close secret Swiss bank accounts, nor end cheating on spouses, keep politicians from lying or any other deception humans enact on a daily basis. Unlike in "Galaxy Quest," humans continued to go deeper into the rabbit hole of lies and deceptions, taking along with them any semblance of a civilization built on believable truth. It's unbelievable to me that I have to even include the adjective "believable" before "truth" but that is the depth to which our belief in truth has fallen.

Earthlings have been lying since the beginning of Earth. We find the world's first liar in the original Origin Story in the Garden of Eden, where and when a certain snake (aka serpent, aka possibly the devil) and a certain woman named Eve colluded on a lie to a certain man named Adam about fruit from the Tree of Knowledge of Good and Evil. Upon eating "of the fruit" and convincing Adam to eat it as well, they both gain knowledge that makes them "like god," which God dislikes, to put it mildly.

As it's told in the Book of Genesis, the first book of the Hebrew Bible and the Christian Old Testament, God throws them out of the paradisial Garden and curses both of them—Adam with getting what he needs only by sweat and work, and Eve with giving birth in pain. All this because the snake tricked and deceived the young couple. The snake paid too: God punished it, and all its descendants, to crawl on its belly and eat dust. It's all downhill from there, a sin—not just a sin but the Original Sin, according to those of Christian faith—that all humans carry forward from birth. There's no way that even compensatory "good works" can erase the sin of our lie.

Even if we accept the story of Adam and Eve as only a metaphor, it speaks volumes regarding how we regard lies and deception—as no-no's from the get-go of humankind.

> "Researchers speculate that lying as a behavior arose not long after the emergence of language. The ability to manipulate others without using physical force likely conferred an advantage in the competition for resources and mates, akin to the evolution of deceptive strategies in the animal kingdom, such as camouflage."
>
> —*Why We Lie* by Yudhijit Bhattacharjee, *National Geographic* (June 2017)

Lying can begin as early as our toddler years and today's psychologists consider it to be a normal behavior on the path of cognitive development. Studies have revealed a wide range of reasons we lie, mostly with the goal of self-preservation or self-promotion, though occasionally the impetus is altruism or politeness. The primary goals include: covering up a mistake or transgression, avoiding unwanted situations or people, financial or personal benefits, presenting a positive self-image, or for humor. Interestingly, a study at University of College London showed through scans of the amygdala that a person's negative emotional response while lying can decrease with each additional lie. In other words, the brain gets used to the stress of telling a lie, which then enables the liar to continue their deception without added discomfort, even if the lies become more significant. We all do it sometimes, but the danger is that lying can become habit-forming.

> "...A disregard for facts, the displacement of reason by emotion, and the corrosion of language are diminishing the very value of truth."
>
> —Michiko Kakutani, in *The Death of Truth: Notes on Falsehood in the Age of Trump (2018)*

Donald J. Trump, the 45th president of the United States, did not invent the phrase "fake news," though he claimed to be "the one that came up with the term...and very proud of it." Though he certainly popularized it to the point that it became part of our lexicon, he lied about that factoid, of course. BuzzFeed News media editor Craig Silverman was in fact the person who popularized the term "fake news" before Trump got his greasy paws on it. Silverman first started using it in 2014 while he was running a research project at Columbia University's Tow Center for Digital Journalism.

Further back, the term actually dates from the late 19th century, when it was used by newspapers and magazines to boast about their own journalistic standards and attack those of their rivals. In 1895, for example, *Electricity: A Popular Electrical Journal* bragged that "we never copy fake news," while in 1896 a writer at one San Jose, California, paper excoriated the publisher of another: "It is his habit to indulge in fake news. ... [H]e will make up news when he fails to find it."

Going even further back, the ubiquity of fake news and scientific misinformation was already a serious problem for leading thinkers of the Renaissance. In his *Novum Organum* (1620), the philosopher Francis Bacon describes for the first time the psychological phenomenon that underlies so much of our modern worries about trust and truth—what would only much later be christened "confirmation bias," a nifty term only philosophers and linguists could have coined. Our minds, he notes, tend to lend more weight to "affirmative" (or positive) than to negative results, so a person is likely to "seize eagerly on any fact, however slender, that supports his theory; but will question, or conveniently ignore, the far stronger facts that overthrow it." In the book, Bacon considers the factors that lead people's thinking astray, which include wrong-headed notions accepted from bad philosophy and science, various "systems now in vogue"—and inaccurate language: "The ill and unfit choice of words wonderfully obstructs the understanding."

But back to Trump and why this matters in a Gandhian sense. At first the media had trouble calling his lies lies. They used more delicate words like "false" or "misleading" or "disinformation" or "erroneous" or "mistruth" or this convoluted end-around: "inconsistent with facts." Why the hesitancy? A debate within newsrooms went something like this: Could a presidential statement, no matter how blatantly false, be deemed a "lie" since, by definition, the word implies awareness of falsity and intent to deceive? In the strictest sense, how can journalists know what's in Trump's mind, even when he repeatedly says transparently untrue things? Plus, to call a president on a lie, though it may be, would be almost treason in some worlds, certainly in very bad form, even sacrosanct. That is how precious truth is...or should be.

"Alternative facts" entered into our collective conversation thanks (or no thanks) to Kellyanne Conway, United States Counselor to the President, during a TV interview in which she defended White House Press Secretary Sean Spicer's false statement about the attendance numbers of Donald Trump's inauguration as President of the United States. As she told Chuck Todd on NBC's Meet The Press: "You're saying it's a falsehood and Sean Spicer, our press secretary, gave alternative facts to that."

And it's not just fake news either: it's also fake science (manufactured by climate change deniers and anti-vaxxers, who oppose vaccination), fake history (promoted by Holocaust revisionists and white supremacists), fake Americans on Facebook (created by Russian trolls), and fake followers and "likes" on social media (generated by bots).

Lying became so rampant in his administration that the *Washington Post* tracked his lies on a daily basis and published them. By the end of his 4-year term, Trump had accumulated 30,573 untruths during his presidency, averaging about 21 erroneous claims a day. As a result of what some called Trump's pathological lying nature, a ripple effect coursed through society that let people feel that, "Well, ok, if the President of the United Sates can lie... and get away with it... so can I."

In her 2018 book, *The Death of Truth: Notes on Falsehood in the Age of Trump*, the former *New York Times* chief book reviewer, Michiko Kakutani, primarily targets Donald Trump but makes sure one understands Trump did not invent lying. She instead blames everyone, writing: "Trump is emblematic of dynamics that have been churning beneath the surface of daily life for years, creating the perfect ecosystem in which Veritas, the goddess of truth... could fall mortally ill."

CNN's media commentator, Brian Stelter, warned that fact-based journalism will become an "endangered species." CNN went so far as to run a series of promo commercials for the cable network in the Fall of 2017, mainly because of so much distrust in simple news reportage. With a stark white background to an undeniably red apple, the narrator says: "This is an apple. Some people might try to tell you that it's a banana. They might scream, 'Banana, banana, banana,' over and over and over again. They might put banana in all caps. You might even start to believe it's a banana, but it's not. This is an apple."

This lying syndrome, in turn, has led to possible ill health and shorter lives among people who lie. Research has linked telling lies to an increased risk of cancer, increased risk of obesity, anxiety, depression, addiction, gambling, poor work satisfaction and poor relationships, according to Deirdre Lee Fitzgerald, PhD, assistant professor of psychology at Eastern Connecticut State University in Willimantic. Lying is stressful; it is taxing both physically and emotionally, with one lie leading to another and a nerve-wracking cycle of lies that becomes harder and harder to keep track of.

Covering up past deception can be traumatic for entire nations of people as well. The concern about telling the truth prompted more than 40 countries over the past three decades to establish truth and reconciliation commissions. Gandhian thought has been credited with contributing to the truth commission in South Africa after Apartheid, as a powerful influence for both Nelson Mandela and Desmond Tutu. Unfortunately, or predictably, these processes have been used cynically as tools for governments to legitimize themselves by pretending they have dealt with painful history when they have only kicked the can down the road.

> "The people have a right to the truth as they have a right to life, liberty and the pursuit of happiness."
>
> —Epictetus, 1st century Greek philosopher

Pondering the preponderance of evidence that truth is losing the battle for truth, justice and something concrete we can confidently lean on, something close to a reality we can all agree on, and also realizing Mankind has lied since the beginning of "creation," I wondered what hope there was for true Truth. What do the two truths have to do with each other? Because, I believe, the simple act of telling the truth is the first step toward Being in Truth. It is especially critical to be true about and to ourselves as we look for the Truth Gandhi hoped we strive for. A big fan of Shakespeare, the Mahatma would have read and been influenced by this from *Hamlet*:

> "This above all: to thine own self be true,
> And it must follow, as the night the day,
> Thou canst not then be false to any man."
>
> —Polonius to his son Laertes, in Act 1 Scene 3

Gandhi himself did not put all of his stock in Shakespeare, though. He once said, "All of your scholarship, all your study of Shakespeare and Wordsworth would be vain if at the same time you did not build your character and attain mastery over your thoughts and your actions."

Aha, mastery over my thoughts and actions. There's the rub.

My ambivalent relationship with truth and The Truth goes back to about the time I began to breathe. I lied to my parents when I wet my bed at a very early age. "I didn't do it," I claimed, even in the face of verifiable evidence to the contrary. I lied the time I made a tiny log cabin out of wooden matches in my bedroom, the bedroom with the wood floor, then lit a match in the middle of the cabin simply to savor the flame, which left a burn mark on the floor. I tried to literally cover the lie by moving a throw rug to conceal the mishap. I thought I got away with it until one day, while I was in the den, I heard a shout from my bedroom: "PERRY, come up here this instant." I think I still tried to lie my way out of it but there was no way out. Again, visual evidence.

Then, always the quick study, I learned to lie about things that could not be detected or visually contradicted. When my parents asked me how I was doing in school, I said, "Good," when the truth was "Not so good." My lie was safe...until my report card came and outed me. Nevertheless, I continued that until the day I graduated from college, with barely passable grades.

Other lies followed. Big lies. Little lies. Inconsequential lies: "I lost 10 pounds" (when I lost only three). Consequential lies: "Yes, I sent the check" (when I had not even written it). And the one I became quite adept at: "Yes, my piece is coming along nicely" (when in fact I was struggling with the first paragraph). I lied about when—and to whom—I lost my virginity. I told my made-up version so many times about what really happened, with whom and when, that I began to buy my own lie. The lie became the truth, and no one was the wiser.

I lied about my height all the time; I've said I was 5 feet 10 inches tall when actually I was 5 feet 9 and a half inches. That half inch may seem a petty and pitiable fine line but that's what men do. A study of online dating profiles, published in *Personality and Social Psychology Bulletin*, found that their height is one of the most frequent lies men tell. In my first book, *In a Man's World*, I reported on studies that showed men have some financial incentive to lie: one study concluded than men 6 feet or taller made 8 per cent more than men 5 foot 6 inches and shorter. Now, given the physiological reality that as cartilage between our joints causes the spinal column to become shorter, I am lucky if I am 5 feet 9—but I'm disinclined to check.

I lied about my age on dating websites. I got away with it because my father, boyish looking into his 70s, left me good genes. My justification for not sharing my actual age: "Well I've seen guys my age who look much older and have less energy than me." This too eventually and inevitably blew up in my face when anyone smart enough to deftly google me could ascertain my true age.

I lie to the IRS. Not entirely lie, but let's say fudge. Pad? Underestimate (income), overestimate (expenses)? Embellish? I pay what my accountant, a dear friend who knows my financials inside and out, can justify at the very edge of but more or less inside the bounds of truth.

I lie to people who ask, "How are you?" I respond, "Good." The true answer is much too subtle, and most people don't really want a true report on my condition.

These are all superficial lies that pale in comparison to the lies I tell myself. That I'm doing fine. That my finances are not too bad. That I am OK without a significant other in my life. That I am fulfilled professionally and accept the realization I may remain only a B-list writer. That I am quite fine about my male-pattern balding, inherited honestly from my father. I used to say I was very happy with my body, even though I wished I was at least 6 feet tall and 7 pounds lighter, with a stronger jaw and more bushy eyebrows. I am, however, blessed with having what all agree are sparkling baby blue eyes, a genetically recessive trait that only 8 per cent of the world's population possess.

I lie about my self-confidence. I walk into a social situation with bravado, belying the truth that I lack belief in myself. Secret: when I am stuck mid-writing, I pull out my old clips and links of my previously published work, often good work, to convince myself that since I did it once, it's in me to do again.

I lie to myself about how much I am doing for humankind by virtue of my writing, thus alleviating my need to volunteer for the Boys Club, and justifying that outlandish claim because so much of my writing, in my opinion, helps people where it matters: in gaining knowledge and insight into their nature and how to achieve that. *But Perry, don't you know of writers who find time to do volunteer work as well as write?*

But I reserve my Biggest Lie, which happens every single day when I wake up. You probably do this too.... We open our eyes and invent ourselves anew with each day, pushing the lie that we—this amalgam of flesh and bones, organs and veins, this thinking brain and this subtle thing we call our soul—are somebody. Specifically, A Somebody. We put on our armament—jeans and t-shirts, suits, skirts and other dress—and we present a personality which is a composite of how we perceive ourselves, how we want to perceive ourselves and how others perceive us, or how we think people think of us. It's all a fabrication, a projection of an insecure ego, not our true selves. I would imagine this kind of thinking would never occur to Gandhi. He woke up Gandhi; he went to bed Gandhi.

Are there times when telling the truth backfired on me? For sure. There's that old saw about the dilemma someone faces when their loved one asks if their outfit makes them look fat. The correct answer, even if it is a lie, should always be, "You look great. How do *you* like it? How does it make *you* feel? From here you look fabulous." I figure that out after a few fails.

When I have told the truth, that did not always work out so well in some circumstances. Somewhere in my DNA I believed it was my duty, almost my moral obligation, to say what was on my mind about someone. My thinking was, "This may hurt them at first, but it will be good for them in the long run." This did not work out well, either for me or them. Once, when my new girlfriend and her friend were out and about, I asked her friend what she did for the slight hair I saw growing above her upper lip. Before I could go on to explain that my sister had had electrolysis for her own undesired facial hair, my girlfriend rolled her eyes and cringed in embarrassment for her friend and in anger at me. Later she scolded me. I began to temper my so-called obligation to say unfiltered critical judgments that come into my head that should not come from my mouth. More lately, I have learned to catch those things even before they come into my head.

> "The man who lies to himself and listens to his own lie comes to a point that he cannot distinguish the truth within him, or around him, and so loses all respect for himself and for others. And having no respect he ceases to love."
>
> —Fyodor Dostoevsky, in *The Brothers Karamazov* (1880)

How was I going to turn this around, to go cold turkey from habitual liar to squeaky clean truthsayer? Soothsayers were betting against me.

The first steps would be easy. Yes, I corrected my age on dating sites. I would be honest about my weight, to others and myself. Add my height to that list.

From there, it got harder. I told people how I feel, not how I think they want to hear me say I feel. My honesty made people feel uncomfortable, I quickly found. *"Now what do I say?"* I could almost hear them thinking. *"Do I confess and complain and kvetch like Perry just did?"*

I would try to tame my passive aggressive nature (see next chapter on Violence for more on that attempt). When struggling with an assignment, if an editor asked, "How's it going?" I would not say "Going well," as has been my M.O. for the last forever years.

Then I turned the lens onto myself, and my Self. I began to take the time to look in the mirror and assess my health, my emotions, my mind, and my soul without the rose-colored glasses—*and* without the shit-covered glasses either. Too often I have lied to myself about where I am at. I romanticize my situation to help me either love myself or hate myself, as my moods and circumstances shift. Why can't I just look—without judgment—at my long nose, and my nonexistent chin, at the inevitable balding spot few but me see (or that's what I lie to myself about)? Why can't I appreciate my body without chastising myself over the five pounds that I eternally tell myself I will lose? Why can't I see my bright baby blues? The hard-earned wisdom reflected in the wrinkles around those eyes? My warm smile? Why do I sometimes look in the mirror and swear I could be mistaken for my film idol, Paul Newman? Why can't I savor the fact I can stand, breathe, think relatively cogent thoughts? And this big one: why can't I look at the body of my writing work and accept that I'm not an A-List writer, rather than accept and embrace that I've made a living all these years at the thing I never would have had the gumption to dream I could do?

For the answers to all these questions, I turned to Gandhi's Truth. Luckily, he gives us latitude:

"But how is one to realize this Truth, which may be likened to the philosopher's stone or the cow of plenty? By single-minded devotion and indifference to all other interests in life, replies the Bhagavad Gita. In spite, however, of such devotion, what may appear as Truth to one person will often appear as untruth to another person. But that need not worry the seeker. Where there is honest effort, it will be realized that what appear to be different truths are like the countless and apparently different leaves of the same tree. Does not God himself appear to different individuals in different aspects? Yet we know that He is one. But Truth is the right designation of God. Hence there is nothing wrong in every man following Truth according to his lights. Indeed it is his duty to do so. Then if there is a mistake on the part of any one so following Truth it will be automatically set right. For the quest of Truth involves *tapas*—self suffering, sometimes even unto death. There can be no place in it, even a trace of self-interest. In such selfless search for Truth nobody can lose his bearings for long. Directly he takes to the wrong path, he stumbles, and is thus redirected to the right path. Therefore, the pursuit of Truth is true *bhakti* (devotion). It is the path that leads to God. There is no place in it for cowardice, no place for defeat. It is the talisman by which death itself becomes the portal to life eternal."

OK, attainment of Truth will not be easy, but not for the reasons I imagined. I had thought my spiritual background would already make this complicated for me: raised Jewish, the religion of one God; explored Hinduism, the religion of, some say, millions of gods and goddesses; and now a practitioner of Buddhism, actually not a religion, as the Buddha had explained, but a psychology of happiness in which the Judeo-Christian belief in God is nonexistent. Gandhi gives a lot of room for the many different varieties of belief. But no, my issues will be about faith itself—not just faith in God of any persuasion, but in my own willingness to leave no stone unturned in my quest for Truth.

Later, in Chapter Seven on Faith, I will dive deeper into how, or if, I can find my way there.

For now, and maybe for always, I need to trust my Truth. What I thought I had learned from my study of Buddhism is that truth is ever-evolving. What is true in this moment may not be true in the next. Studying Gandhi taught me a deeper level of truth. It brought me back to a line I remembered from my Rutgers College yearbook, a quote from a 19th century song entitled *In A Quaint Old Jersey Town:* "Ever changing yet eternally the same."

Who am I? Where am I? Why am I here?

These are the start-up questions that any person with a curious brain will ask themselves if they have an iota of desire for self-awareness. It's these same questions that are at the core of the great religions, the compelling scientific inquiries and sincere personal quests. They are also the questions that drive my search for my Truth.

They often come up at critical turning points in life, and at various stages of human development, like as soon as little ones realize they are not a part of or attached to their mother. Psychologists identify the fourth or fifth month of a baby's life as the stage called differentiation, when he or she becomes aware that Mom is a separate being. Swiss psychiatrist Carl Jung called "individuation"—when people become aware of themselves—an important step in the discovery of their purpose and the meaning of life.

My first "I'm me" moment came at an early age. Introspective even as a child, I observed my thoughts and marveled at what strange and seemingly uncontrollable things were going on upstairs between my ears. Were my thoughts unique, I wondered?

At first I decided they were. No one else could be playing these bizarre runaway-train steam-of-consciousness mind games. Then, as time went on, I concluded that yes, people had thoughts that were not mine, but they were remarkably similar. Otherwise, why would they laugh or cry at the same things that moved me as well?

From this, I came to believe that who I am—aside from an amalgam of billions of cells, plus tissue, bones, muscles and organs, the body itself a phenomenal example of "me-ness"—is what I think.

Then one asks, "Where am I?" What is this world I was born into? What holds it all together physically? How are we all related to each other in the complicated and intertwined social web of Mankind? We leave the womb and enter a strange world of air and pain and laughter and others who look like us, more or less. In expanding circles, we move from Mom's nipples, then bravely to Dad's arms, then from crib to room to house to street and city, to state and country. We read how great scientists explain the mystery of it all: Sir Isaac Newton (gravity), Edwin Hubble (the Cosmos), Charles Darwin (natural selection, aka origin of species), Galileo Galilei (the stars and planets), Aristotle (biology).

And then what I, and Gandhi, consider the Big Question: Why am I here? What is my purpose? One measure is by what I do in this world, and for this world.

For the longest time, starting at the age of about 6, my identity—what I thought was my purpose and meaning in life, my USP or Unique Selling Point, as Indians put it—was as a drummer, which I started studying in first grade. My mother says I played drums prenatally, using the inside of her belly as my bass drum. This is not extraordinary in and of itself, as many mothers will attest, but Mom maintains my kicks came in rock-steady 4/4 time—with a syncopated backbeat.

A formative moment of my identity came in fifth grade when the teacher needed someone to stand in front of the class to play a clave to keep good time while the class sang some silly kids song. She and everyone else pointed towards me. I reveled in it; that became my defining moment. I was a somebody, the guy who held it all together, rhythmically speaking but in my mind also metaphorically. I could detect the word "drums" or "drummer" in any running text. I went on to be selected as one of five percussionists to perform with the New Jersey high school all-state orchestra. I captained the Rutgers University marching band drum line, gigged with a jazz trio through college and other bands after graduation (I continue to play with bands to this day as an avocation).

At 22, though, I did not see a viable future as fulltime professional drummer. That was when I began to more seriously consider writing, at which there had been some indication I could put words together coherently and cleverly. Yet, even after eight years as a staffer writing for newspapers and magazines, I did not see it as my much-coveted purpose... until my first book, *In A Man's World* (NAL, 1985), was published. The close to 100 poignant letters I got from men pouring out their own experiences touched me so deeply that I realized if my writing could help others to understand themselves, that would be service to people, a purpose for my existence.

It was only then that I looked back—at the homework assignment in second grade that earned triple-star stickers, at the essay I wrote in high school that won me the opportunity to be an exchange student with another high school in town, at the funny cards I wrote to my parents, at the essay I wrote to get accepted to graduate school, and mostly at the great pride I felt in such accomplishments—and saw the signs everywhere in retrospect, but which I was unaware of since my tunnel vision had remained focused on being "the drummer."

When, where and why did Gandhi find his purpose? If I could figure that out, it might provide a key to how I and others could open the door that goes deeper into their own purpose.

By most accounts, for Gandhi that wake-up call was an event on June 7, 1893, in Pietermaritzburg, South Africa, which woke him up to what would become his life's path and work. The then 24-year-old beginning lawyer, sitting in a whites-only train carriage with a valid ticket, unceremoniously and forcefully was expelled because the train official assumed he was black, thereby breaking segregation laws. Sitting alone in the small dark waiting area where he was sequestered would have humiliated and burned him to the core. This pivotal moment has been so seared into Gandhi's life story that a small museum now stands at the Pietermaritzburg station marking the start of his active nonviolence. Righteous indignation understates how a man of moral principles must have felt.

It probably did light a fire of indignation and protest under him but Gandhi's grandson, Arun Gandhi, has a different take on that incident.

"It was not the moment of revelation for him," he said when I visited him at his home in Rochester, New York, "although a lot of people think that was the moment when it dawned on him to bring in nonviolence and all that. I think it was just the last straw. This was building up, his experiences in India with the prejudices against the untouchables, then his experiences in England, where he suffered some prejudices and he saw all the hate and things going on. And he realized that this went more deeply. All this negativity that we see in our lives today is deeper than it appears, that it's become part of our nature. When this Maritzburg thing happened, then it confirmed his feelings. He had defined this as a culture of violence."

This made me realize purpose does not come in one "aha." It can build over time, as I believe it did for Gandhi. All I need to do is take the blinders off and look for the clues along the way.

The purpose of life, one could say, is to find one's purpose, and in so doing find one's Truth. But there is an added perk to it: an 11-year NIH-funded study proved a high correlation between purpose and longevity. The research shows that people who know their life purpose and why they wake up in the morning, who can express having clear goals, tend to live longer, better lives. This is because individuals who understand what brings them joy and happiness tend to have a "right outlook." They are engulfed in activities and communities that allow them to immerse themselves in a rewarding and gratifying environment.

In another project funded by *National Geographic*, the researcher Dan Buettner identified communities around the world with a high per cent of octogenarians, people living to age 100 and up, which he calls the Blue Zones. The idea of why they wake up in the morning is an integral part of their culture. Okinawans call it "ikigai"; Nicoyans of Costa Rica call it "plan de vida." This strong sense of purpose may reduce their chances of suffering from Alzheimer's disease, arthritis and stroke.

How, then, is finding purpose related to truth and to leading a moral life? If I'm reading Gandhi correctly, your purpose *is* your truth, your true being, why you landed on this Planet, in this uniform, with this personality, wrapped in this ego. Finding purpose will be tested against your own truth; if you proceed in one direction, thinking this is your purpose, but you find that not only is it not coming together as you'd hoped, but also that you find it unfulfilling on the deepest level. Perhaps your reasons were more about the fame, glory, and how it "looks" to others. You may find that path full of barbed wires, obstacles and mishaps. The red flags warning me against the life of a professional drummer came when I did not pass a few auditions. Or when the members of a jazz group I toured with stopped to hear a group at a club and the band leader told me he wished I played like that group's drummer and that I was holding our band back. A harsh slap to my ego, but a necessary step for me to focus instead on what has been my true calling. Playing drums, though, remains a rewarding avocation, absolutely enjoyable and essential to my whole identity—just not my Big Purpose in life. In other words, you have to turn over a lot of rocks to encounter your purpose and at times purpose speaks louder than what your mind wants.

However, if your purpose is to destroy relationships, property, civility, peace and basically be a buzz kill, this would not be in keeping with a Gandhian approach. But are even these unappreciated purposes immoral and reprehensible? In a world of relative realities, no. Who is to say this is good and that is bad? That kind of call belongs only to The Great Judge—not to those of us humans with bias...and we all have some bias.

The business world has picked up on the idea of purpose by emphasizing "moral purpose" as a critical factor in a company's brand identity. One source defined it this way: "a value that, when articulated, appeals to the innate sense held by some individuals of what is right and what is worthwhile." In the workplace, asking yourself these questions may help reveal if your work aligns with a moral purpose:

What is the greater reason for my work? Who or what am I helping by doing my job well? In my role, how am I making a positive impact on the world? What is the meaning of my responsibilities?

A world in which each of us follows her or his Moral Purpose would be a much better place than what we have now. We would trust that any given decision was founded on their own Truth, and not on an ego-driven motive. Without moral principles, we would be reduced to a chaotic culture, like what happened to the British boys left on an island without adult supervision, in William Golding's 1954 novel *Lord of the Flies*, where the kids' behavior degenerated into savagery.

Furthermore, research over the years has demonstrated how central a set of morals is to who we are. One study in the *Journal of Personality and Social Psychology* found that "moral character" is the most important element of "impression formation" when we're getting to know someone new. In another, in the journal *Cognition*, researchers declared that moral traits "are considered the most essential part of identity, the self, and the soul," more than any other mental faculty. In other words, our morals are a fundamental part of who we are and how we interact with others.

Moral principles are the guidelines that help us decide how to handle different situations that may come up in life. They are quite simple common-sense behaviors, actually almost obvious... if we lived in Utopia at least.

Imagine, as John Lennon imagined in his iconic song "Imagine," a world full of people who tell the truth, who live The Truth, who follow the best moral principles. He asks us to imagine people living for today, in peace, sharing as one, a "brotherhood of man." He concludes that some may think he's a dreamer but he's not the only one. I, for one, stand with him. I think Gandhi was that dreamer too. I just wonder how close to that dream the two of them, one born in 1869, the other in 1940, would think we have come in the intervening years when looking at the world today.

HOW TO GANDHI: Truth and Purpose

These are nice aspirations, but how does one uphold them in the face of temptations, deviations, distractions, discipline slips and simple human weakness? How do you hold yourself accountable to the lofty morals you've set? It's not so complicated. If you have trouble figuring out your truth and purpose, don't wait until you are 30, like me and Gandhi. Here's a to-do list to kickstart your attempt.

Set written goals. Research from Dominican University in San Rafael, California, shows that people are 42 per cent more likely to achieve their goals if they write them down. Do an internal inventory. Think about your ideals, principles, standards and morals. Then think of your physical, emotional and mental talents, strengths and abilities. Clear your mind and get to what you really want to contribute to the world. You'll know you're getting close when you have a strong emotional reaction to something you've written. Create your personal Purpose Statement. Follow your nose to incorporate what you like to do and where you can share your talents.

Find a partner. Find someone to whom you can communicate your life purpose, along with a plan for realizing it. It can be a friend, a family member, a spouse, or a colleague. Use their honesty as a sounding board for your plan of action.

Listen to your instincts. Let your gut do the talking, especially when you're about to do something that doesn't fit your personal moral code.

Talk to a pro. Speak with a mental health therapist or psychologist. They can help remind you of your essential beliefs to make moral decisions based on them. They can help you forgive yourself when you fall short of them. They can offer a nonjudgmental, unbiased space to explore all this.

Follow the Golden Rule. Treat others the way you want to be treated, with a heavy dose of empathy.

Speak the truth. Speak up for what you want. Share what others may need to make their own decisions for themselves.

Keep your word. Don't make promises that you can't keep. Do what you say. Follow through.

Put your skills into action. Use your passions as a launchpad for your life. Besides (or perhaps because of) the satisfaction that comes from doing good, people who do so have lower rates of cancer, heart disease and depression, as well as lower health care costs.

Dedicate a place in your house to display your passions, accomplishments and the things of which you are proud. Every time you walk by, you'll be rewarded with a surge of pride and a reminder of how you fit into the world.

3

NONVIOLENCE

How to Make Love, Not War

> "When I despair, I remember that all through history the way of truth and love have always won. There have been tyrants and murderers, and for a time, they can seem invincible, but in the end, they always fall. Think of it—always."
>
> —Mahatma Gandhi

"War," written by Norman Whitfield and Barrett for Motown Record in 1969, was one of the most popular songs ever written, according to many best-of listings, first sung by Edwin Starr, and later covered by The Temptations and again by Bruce Springsteen. The lyrics succinctly sum up the endgame of war: many deaths, and a shift of power or land, or both, until another war breaks out.

Gandhi would have rocked and rolled covering this one himself. His own refrain might have been a line often attributed to him:

"An eye for an eye leaves the whole world blind."

And what did this song, or for that matter Gandhi's efforts (and those of a few hundred studies by organizations and institutions around the world with "peace" or "nonviolence" or "Gandhi" in their title) achieve in ending war?

Absolutely nothing.

Gandhi was overly optimistic to think he could lead a movement that not only advocated peace but also laid down a game plan to achieve it. People listened...for a while. Then someone threw a rock or a slur or accidentally-on-purpose bumped into the "enemy."

The cycle of violence is endless.

Need proof? Look at the headline in any newspaper or any TV or other news outlets any day of any year.

I have empathized with all marginalized and oppressed minorities, victims of extreme violence, even genocide, as a person whose religion had been the target of persecution and antisemitic hate activities since at least the time of the Roman politician and philosopher Cicero (106-43 BCE). In my own experience of protest, the closest I had come to violence was in 1969 in Washington, D.C., when police bombarded several hundred of us with tear gas in Dupont Circle. We were part of the half million who'd participated in what was called the "Moratorium to End the War in Vietnam." When the clouds of smoke came close, my buddies and I and everyone else ran helter skelter in all directions. It felt life-threatening, but my thoughts went to the men and women on the ground in the jungles of Vietnam facing truly life-threatening—and life-ending—circumstances.

The Vietnamese suffered deeply, emotionally, as a society of devout Buddhists (remember the Buddhist monk, Thich Quang Duc, who self-immolated in protest against the war, an act that itself violated Buddhist principles forbidding the killing of living things?), and as a culture.

Not until 1995 did Vietnam release its official estimate of war dead: as many as 2 million civilians on both sides and some 1.1 million North Vietnamese and Viet Cong fighters. The United States military has estimated that between 200,000 and 250,000 South Vietnamese soldiers died in the war. In 1982 the Vietnam Veterans Memorial was dedicated in Washington, D.C., inscribed with the names of 57,939 members of the United States armed forces who had died or were missing as a result of the war. Over the following years, additions to the list have brought the total past 58,200. (At least 100 names on the memorial are those of servicemen who were actually Canadian citizens.) Among other countries that fought for South Vietnam on a smaller scale, South Korea suffered more than 4,000 dead, Thailand about 350, Australia more than 500, and New Zealand some three dozen.

Gandhi often used the word *ahimsa*, a Sanskrit word meaning "non-violence," to inform his policy of non-violent protest. The term is derived from the root word *himsa*, meaning "to cause pain," and the prefix, *a*, that means "not." In a broader sense, ahimsa means "universal love and compassion." Practice of ahimsa involves refraining from causing physical and psychological pain to any living being. Ahimsa is forgiveness, divine love and sacrifice. Ahimsa, in short, is being non-violent in thought and action, in body and soul.

It seems we are further than ever from this ideal.

He coined a word—*satyagraha*—after a relative of his won a naming competition Gandhi sponsored in his *Indian Opinion* newspaper in South Africa in 1906. Gandhi changed the winning word to Satyagraha, a compound of the Sanskrit words *satya* (meaning "truth") and *agraha* ("polite insistence" or "holding firmly to"). *Satya* is derived from the word *sat*, which means "being." For Gandhi, satyagraha went far beyond mere "passive resistance." In his words:

"Truth (satya) implies love, and firmness (agraha) engenders and therefore serves as a synonym for force. I thus began to call the Indian movement Satyagraha, that is to say, the Force which is born of Truth and Love or non-violence, and gave up the use of the phrase 'passive resistance' in connection with it, so much so that even in English writing we often avoided it and used instead the word 'satyagraha' itself or some other equivalent English phrase."

He also called it "love-force" or "soul-force."

In later years he disputed the proposition that his idea of civil disobedience was adapted from the writings of Henry David Thoreau, especially the 1849 essay, "Civil Disobedience":

"The statement that I had derived my idea of civil disobedience from the writings of Thoreau is wrong. The resistance to authority in South Africa was well advanced before I got the essay of Thoreau on civil disobedience. But the movement was then known as passive resistance. As it was incomplete, I had coined the word satyagraha for the Gujarati readers. When I saw the title of Thoreau's great essay, I began the use of his phrase to explain our struggle to the English readers. But I found that even civil disobedience failed to convey the full meaning of the struggle. I therefore adopted the phrase civil resistance. Non-violence was always an integral part of our struggle."

Gandhi distinguished between satyagraha and passive resistance in a 1920 letter:

"... I often used "passive resistance" and "satyagraha" as synonymous terms: but as the doctrine of satyagraha developed, the expression "passive resistance" ceases even to be synonymous, as passive resistance has admitted of violence as in the case of the suffragettes and has been universally acknowledged to be a weapon of the weak. Moreover, passive resistance does not necessarily involve complete adherence to truth under every circumstance. Therefore, it is different from satyagraha in three essentials: Satyagraha is a weapon of the strong; it admits of no violence under any circumstance whatsoever; and it ever insists upon truth."

In my opinion, satyagraha, while foreign to many ears, is better than what most people have landed on in adopting the Gandhian way to peace. The labels "nonviolence" and "nonviolent" (hyphens optional) are a publicist's nightmare for brand identity. One of the rules of PR 101 is never use the words "no," can't," "won't," "isn't," "never," or even prefixes of "non," "un" or "anti"—any negative words. Why? Using such words forces us to first think of what we are turning away from, thereby plant the idea of violence back into our heads. We have to envision what violence feels like, looks like, sounds like, smells like. Some might suggest that's a good thing, like rubbing a dog's nose in his own "business." I disagree, and apparently Gandhi did too. Yet, what is the single word that expresses the opposite of violence? Peace? Harmony? Love? Kumbaya?

Terminological misdirection is no excuse for society's failure to realize Gandhi's vision of a world living in peace. But if I was his publicist, I would begin a rebranding campaign.

On the Gandhi portal there is a story entitled "Gandhi's First Lesson in Non-violence." Remember Gandhi's story of lying that

I wrote about in Chapter Two? It comes from the same story. Continuing, a mother replies to her son in the follow-up:

"But, mother, why did his father cry so bitterly? Why did he not beat Mohandas or punish him in some other way?"

"Because, my son, Mohandas's courage and truthfulness moved him deeply. If he had given the boy a beating, that would not have been so effective as his own gentle suffering. And that suffering and that love left its impression on Mohandas far more deeply than any beating could ever have done."

This is cited as: "Mohan's first lesson in non-violence. And later on it was this very weapon with which he fought the British, and won freedom for his country."

This moment—a first awakening for him in terms of non-violence—became indelibly embedded in his being. Not only did this memory become part of his identity, but it also planted the seed for a strategy that later grew into the basis for non-violent protest against all oppressors. On the important and formative emotional level, it would have left him feeling terribly guilty, embarrassed and ashamed; even more, great remorse that he would have let his father down. This remorse was exacerbated later when Gandhi recounted how he left his dying father's bedside to have sex with his wife Kasturba. Perhaps his commitment to non-violence stemmed from a lifelong attempt to absolve that guilt. I'm not the first to speculate on that. Mark Kurlansky, author of many books, wrote this in an essay published in the Spring 2008 Buddhist journal *Tricycle*:

"Gandhi seems like a Freudian feast, starting with his lifelong guilt over having been engaged in sex with his wife at the moment of his father's death. His life was a constant illustration of Freud's thesis that we cannot be happy because our inherent nature is contrary to the demands of our conscience or, as Freud put it, our ego is at war with our superego."

One could argue that Gandhi's commitment to lead a non-violent life was seamlessly intertwined with his devotion to Hindu faith (especially Jainism), his vegetarian diet, his choice to go silent once a week, his choice of non-attachment to material possessions—all these are often predictive of a live free of violent behavior. Often! Aside from his public efforts, Gandhi lived the life of an ascetic, distant in his personal life from the influences that promote violent thought and action.

I, on the other hand, have not lived the ascetic life and have been exposed to violence simply by living in urban American cities.

My kind of violence is one of the worst kinds of violence, though it did not come from guilt related to my father. It seethes and rumbles beneath the surface, barely suppressed under my deceptively sweet charm, then suddenly lashes out with the sharp knife of sarcasm. This violence inflicts more pain because you never know when to expect it so are unprepared and especially vulnerable.

I'm told I was kinetic from pre-birth, kicking my mother's belly from the inside, as previously mentioned. But what I didn't mention was that I was angrily trying to kick my way out. There just wasn't enough room in there for a kinetic fetus and I could not contain my frustration at the whole stay-in-the-womb experience. Frustration and impatience over unfulfilled desires often lead to violence. *Let me out!* It was my first act of rebellion against The System. I was expressing my rage against the machine of existence, concepts I was not conscious of at the time, nor could have expressed in my prenatal developmental stage other than by kicking. Any minority group that has been oppressed, suppressed, held back, spit on (literally and figuratively), beaten, taunted, hosed, a victim of genocide and other unjust and systemic atrocities can relate.

Moving into my toddler years, I took out my rage on pots and pans on the kitchen floor, annoying my mother while she cooked.

As a 10-year-old, during boring summers in Suburbia USA, I took out my nascent violent nature plucking daddy long legs (also called Harvestmen) from the hot slab of cement between the shingles and the lawn. I'd grab one by the leg, take it to the back patio and pull off one leg at a time from its abdomen, watching with great marvel at their legs continued twitching even once removed from the rest of its body. In my mind I justified it as the curiosity of a future entomologist. But I also felt like a bullying Denise the Menace who could rule over and torment living creatures that did not qualify as sentient beings. This last part saved my conscience. Little did I know they *were* sentient beings in the Buddhist sense. Not once did I think I was committing a violent act. But I was.

I was the kid who knocked all the tiles or pieces off the game board—Scrabble, Monopoly, chess, checkers—when I saw that I was going to lose. I hated my sister and father for outplaying me and the phrase "use your words" had not yet entered parents' lexicon. My anger and embarrassment hijacked my amygdala, as "Emotional Intelligence" author/psychologist Daniel Goleman would put it.

I had an inner hostility that I took out, for instance, on my defenseless sister Sue, three years my senior but petite with no sense of humor at all when I kicked her in the back seat of the car until she screamed, "Mom, Perry's kicking me." Then she would scratch my arm. I often had scabs, but still it did not deter me.

My father bought me a punching bag and gloves, hoping I would take out my violence in some socially acceptable form. This was his version of punching a pillow, a psychological approach to venting anger, called catharsis theory, more colloquially called "letting off steam." Popular in the 1970s, it was widely debunked in the ensuing decades. In fact, in a 2002 study, psychologist Brad Bushman and colleagues at Iowa State University found that venting anger reinforces aggressive urges.

Later, no thanks to Dad, I discovered the art of sarcasm, which psychologists would consider a "sublimation defense mechanism." I rather take it in a different direction, that of a strike-first offense before the other guy is even thinking of witty comebacks. It's a coverup for insecurity and one of the clearest examples of passive aggressive behavior.

Gandhi himself utilized sarcasm to prod and provoke, chastise and embarrass. The best example would be on a trip to London when a western journalist asked him, "What do you think about Western Civilization?" Gandhi replied, "It's a good idea." This was during the time when the British rulers of India treated their colonial subjects in a very uncivilized manner.

In his masterpiece, "Masters of War," from the 1963 album "The Freewheelin," Bob Dylan, the quintessential American folk singer, makes the strongest case for the fruitlessness and futility of wars, sanctioned and funded by politicians and Big Money Interests who "build the death planes," and then "hide behind desks."

War, meaning on the military battleground, is hardly the only perpetrator of violence. Nearly every day since I began to write this, yet another heartbreaking act of gun violence in America has dominated the headlines, leaving a cloud of grief and dread over the heads of everyone. These incidents have created war zones amid the everyday environments of schools, churches, synagogues, supermarkets.

"The world is caught in the culture of violence, a culture that has seeped so deeply in us that everything about us is violent. Our sports, our entertainment, our language, our relationships, our religions—everything is violent."

These were the most chilling words I'd heard in months of globe-trotting in Gandhi's footsteps, and beyond. They were saddening to hear spoken by anyone, the more so when spoken by a man who wrote for the *Times of India* for 30 years and founded an organization dedicated to the study of non-violence. But the most jolting part was those words came from the mouth of Arun Gandhi, one of the five grandsons of Mahatma Gandhi.

A few years earlier, I had come to a similar conclusion as Arun—from a sociocultural anthropology perspective—when I was standing in front of a glass case at the Chhatrapati Shivaji Maharaj Vastu Sangrahalaya in Mumbai (when it was still called the Prince of Wales Museum of Western India). I stared in the encasement at the earliest known weapons of war from the beginning of recorded time. This murder thing has been going on a long time, I thought, for as long as Man could distinguish himself and his tribal gang from the other, any "other." The other was his enemy, his competitor for food or drink or territory or, in the case of males, for the bearer of their offspring. My mind flashed to the opening scene of the Stanley Kubrick film, "2001:

A Space Odyssey," which came out in 1968 when 2001 seemed light years away. The riveting scene shows the moment apes first discovered that dried up bones could be used to kill and scare off an unfamiliar shrewdness, in that case a group trying to drink from the same watering hole. No one misses the metaphoric statement when a bone the ape throws in the air morphs into a ship in outer space 50 million years later.

Violence takes many forms. A brief put out by the Centers for Disease Control and Prevention (CDC in short) includes, among them, intimate partner violence, sexual violence, child maltreatment, bullying, suicidal behavior, elder abuse, and neglect. Unfortunately, most of those have experienced spikes in incidence. Former United States President Donald Trump almost singlehandedly brought bullying to the forefront before, during and after his four years in the White House with his verbal diatribes against his perceived enemies, despite his wife Melania's "Be Best" anti-bullying slogan. Whether his aggressive style led to the real violence perpetrated by his followers on the United States Capitol on January 6, 2020, after Trump lost the Presidential election—you can make your own conclusions. Personally, there is no doubt in my mind that, ipso facto, he was the catalyst. In the wake of that day, five died, 139 police officers were injured and approximately $30 million in damage was done to the building.

Sexual harassment is very high up on that list. And signs indicate it's growing. The United States Equal Employment Opportunity Commission (EEOC) reported significant increase in the number of sexual harassment charges it received in the two years following the popularization of the #MeToo Movement. If that increase was the result of more awareness, and more courage in reporting these attacks, so be it. Can you imagine how much was going on before the Movement?

Sexual harassment and rape are increasing in India, according to a compilation by that country's National Crime Records Bureau (NCRB).

The report showed a 13.2 per cent increase in overall crimes against women in 2021 compared to the year before—crimes that include rape, molestation, acid attack, cruelty by a husband or his relatives and domestic violence, among others.

And here's a contributor to potential violence Gandhi never had to deal with, or even imagine, if aggressive behavior can be counted as a precursor to violence. Playing participatory video games like the violence-infested Doom, Wolfenstein 3D or Mortal Kombat can increase aggressive thoughts, feelings and behavior in lab settings and in life, reported studies in the April 2000 issue of the American Psychological Association's (APA) *Journal of Personality and Social Psychology*. This is especially true in interactive violent games that require the player to identify with the aggressor.

One of the lead researchers, psychologist Craig A. Anderson, wrote: "Violent video games provide a forum for learning and practicing aggressive solutions to conflict situations. In the short run, playing a violent video game appears to affect aggression by priming aggressive thoughts. Longer-term effects are likely to be longer lasting as well, as the player learns and practices new aggression-related scripts that can become more and more accessible for use when real-life conflict situations arise."

In a study published in *JAMA Pediatrics*, the monthly peer-reviewed medical journal of the American Medical Association, psychology professor Douglas Gentile at Iowa State University and an expert on the effects of media on children and adults showed that kids who play violent video games over and over again begin to think in aggressive styles that can influence their actual behavior.

The non-violent principles and techniques made famous by Gandhi's fight for independence in India have obviously been influential in the decades that followed. We know non-violence and civil disobedience were central tenets for Dr. Martin Luther King Jr. and South Africa's Nelson Mandela in their fights for equality and justice. But what about modern attempts at changing the status quo? Have Gandhian concepts proven successful more recently, and if not, what went wrong?

One dramatic movement that took hold of American media and consciousness in September 2011 was Occupy Wall Street, when protesters occupied parks and other locales to protest the influence of corporate money in politics, bank bailouts following a global financial crisis, and the growing economic inequality between the top 1 per cent of earners and the other 99 per cent of America. It was intended to be like the civil rights sit-ins of the 1960s, peaceful demonstrations with no violence intended. By November 2011, the New York City Police Department had forcefully evicted the demonstration.

During the height of the movement in October 2011, a representative of Occupy, Guillaume Marceau, was quoted in *The Economic Times* (an Indian English-language newspaper). "The spirit of Mahatma Gandhi is felt tremendously here. Occupy Wall Street is a non-violent movement," said Marceau. He added that Occupy Wall Street is drawing on the "technical and spiritual leadership of the classic non-violent leaders, such as Gandhi." Marceau also told *Forbes India*, "The community here has gone to great lengths—to great success—to reconfirm every day its commitment to non-violence."

However, with hundreds of protests all over the world and no central leadership, Occupy inevitably had confrontations with police. Even if the aggression originated from law enforcement, some heated responses from protesters made it difficult to uphold the peaceful protest paradigm in the eye of public opinion. Ultimately, the movement which began with such naïve optimism ended abruptly with a middle-of-the night action by NYC police. Mayor Michael Bloomberg ordered the raid in which protesters were arrested and evacuated and their property summarily trashed. Though the messages of economic disparity reached a wide swath of America through Occupy, and which spread around the world, the movement is largely considered a failure since its primary objectives did not progress through their efforts.

Similarly, we witnessed what seemed like unprecedented strength from the Black Lives Matter (BLM) movement following the murder of George Floyd in the summer of 2020. As streets filled with protestors around the world, it appeared that a new page in history was being turned and the next step would be a process of real reparations. Instead, protesters were painted as "rioters" by conservative voices, and a backlash rose up. One of the worst bloody face-offs occurred in Portland, Oregon. The movement also caught on around the world with a variety of different groups. Gandhi's legacy got swept in the movement, as protesters vandalized statues of Gandhi, who they accused of racism.

So why is non-violent protest apparently failing in our day when it was such a powerful tool for Gandhi and his followers?

One of the creators of Occupy Wall Street, Micah White, wrote a 2017 article in *The Guardian* titled, "Occupy and Black Lives Matter failed. We can either win wars or win elections." He writes, "Activists assume that if we get enough citizens into the streets then we, the people, will magically exert a popular authority over elected representatives. It is a beautiful story. But it is no longer true... the people's sovereignty is dead and every protest is a hopeless struggle to revive the corpse. It is time to try a different method."

White's answer is not actually waging war but getting people into positions of power who can implement change. The notion is backed up by the extraordinary wave of women and people of color running for elected office since 2020.

The lesson may be that relying on the tradition of non-violent protest alone is not a cure-all for every societal flaw. As Gandhi hoped, self-rule would be an important component holding us together. He encouraged participation in democracy by all people, including women, rich and poor, all races and castes. Non-violence is not just the absence of something, but we must incorporate efforts for positive action as well.

Whether it's a global protest, or one person's internal transformation, we don't achieve change by merely identifying and removing what is harmful, but we must fill up that empty space with better options. Gandhi has summarized that in a democracy good ends cannot come from questionable means.

While cultures, nations, tribes and other peoples fight it out in endless wars driven by the fear or hatred of that which is perceived to be foreign or strange in a country called Xenophobia, I chose to follow a new path of creating internal peace.

My personal road to peace within began with turning off CNN and other TV news outlets, which broadcast so much violence and vitriol...and that's only on the talk shows. I boycotted the American Presidential debates of 2020 that pitted bulldog Donald Trump against poodle Joe Biden. I knew it would be an ugly, nearly violent blood bath of a dog fight. As days went on, tapering down slowly but surely like from an addiction, at first I missed keeping up with the news, even missed the adrenalin of loving to hate watching bad and disturbing news. Then some kind of peace came over me. I found my life could go on without being able to talk news and politics with friends, conversations that also had riled me. I could go on, even better. Life seemed to continue onward without my involvement. Sadly, though, when I returned to watching, the news had not improved. Inevitably, as is the case of late, it had gotten worse. But now I could witness it from an arm's length, more objectively, less anxiously.

Removing yourself from the conversations and influence of violence is a temporary and possibly necessary fix to give you space to find peace within. Once found, that peace would be your tool to re-enter a brutal world with more clarity and intentionality. There were times, as I've read, that Gandhi did a similar thing by not reading newspapers for brief periods of time. He also took a day of silence every week for this purpose as well.

Next, I stopped watching football games and other body-contact sports. I've been a diehard fan of my San Francisco 49ers for many years, and to any other team where I lived (the New England Patriots, the New York Football Giant) and realized I had become desensitized to the physical violence displayed on the field. My mother turned out to be right; when we watched the sport together, at every badass bone-rattling tackle, she would decry "man's inhumanity to Man."

In fact, American football used to be even more brutal. According to the *Washington Post*, at least 45 football players died between 1900 to 1905, many from internal injuries, broken necks, concussions or broken backs, attributed to "unnecessary roughness." In 1905, following public outcry, President Theodore Roosevelt called for reforms to the game rules, intended to make the sport safer, though helmets were not even made mandatory until decades later, in 1939.

And yet football continued to reached crisis levels of head trauma and concussions among players, causing President Barack Obama to call for change again in 2014 over sports-related head injuries. A *Journal of the American Medical Association* study published in 2017 found that 99 per cent of former National Football League players whose brains were tested through autopsy were diagnosed with chronic traumatic encephalopathy (CTE), a progressive brain condition with symptoms including memory loss, confusion, impaired judgment, impulse control problems, aggression, depression, anxiety, suicidality, parkinsonism, and, eventually, progressive dementia.

As I swore off the NFL these last two years, there have certainly been times I've missed the camaraderie with friends and the community spirit of cheering on local heroes. But do I miss the rush of adrenaline mixed with testosterone, overindulgence in the game-day spread of food and drink, and the righteous rage every time my team suffers a bad call or a missed opportunity? Maybe a little, mostly about how I measure seasonal changes around the sport, sensing the passing of time and sunlight from late summer to fall to the dark days of the SuperBowl.

Violence on the field has also sadly spilled into players' personal lives as CTE has been linked with incidents of assault and domestic violence in professional athletes. Studies have shown that violence in the game also increases the likelihood of violent acts by spectators. It's common for fans to fight in the stands, amongst each other and even directed at officials or athletes. Hundreds of fans have died or been injured during soccer match celebrations.

Football is not the only sport in which we accept overt violence and aggression as part of the game. Hockey is notorious for its heavy "contact" and players have even been prosecuted for assaults on the ice that verged on criminal. Regulating violence during a game has generally been left to the professional sports leagues and officials. To deter violence and serious injuries, the industry relies on penalties, fines, and suspensions as punishment after the fact.

A hockey player, for example, may be penalized for numerous violations, including boarding, butt-ending, charging, clipping, cross-checking, elbowing, fighting, high-sticking, holding, hooking, kneeing, roughing, slashing, spearing, and tripping. In football, penalties can result from roughing the passer and kicker, unnecessary roughness, holding, spearing, tripping. If a baseball pitcher intentionally hits the batter, he may be ejected. In basketball, the Flagrant 1 and Flagrant 2 fouls were introduced during the 1990-91 season to address "unnecessary" or "excessive" contact.

Still, these actions seem to have little overall impact on the next game.

As I am not a fan of winter ice sports, golf or gymnastics, the one sport I landed on where competitors are far away from each other on the field is tennis. It actually has a calming and soothing effect on me, the back and forth of long volleys mesmerizing me like the meditative practice of watching my breath go in and out. In recent years, even tennis has been riddled with its own types of violence, with increased code violations in racket abuse, audible obscenity and unsportsmanlike conduct. So out of hand have things gotten that in April 2022 the Association of Tennis Professionals had directed its officiating team to take a stricter stance in judging violations of the Code of Conduct.

In 2020, India banned the battle game PUBG Mobile as being too violent. The move was prompted in part by stories of suicides and self-harm by users, and parents reporting their children's addictive habits around the game. Luckily, gaming is one vice I never fell into.

I was born in New York, raised in New Jersey, also lived quite a few years in Boston and its environs. For anyone from these locales or who has hung out there, you would know that swearing was a vital part of my conversational vocabulary. A well-placed adjectival exclamation comes naturally and is extremely adaptable to all variety of moments and interactions. Just watch a few episodes of HBO TV series "The Sopranos"—about the fictitious Mafia family who fictionally lived in North Caldwell, New Jersey, which factually is only 6 miles from where I grew up—to confirm that.

Cursing, four-letter words, profanities, foul language, swear words, blue language, expletives, obscenities, offensive words, cussing, maledictions if you want to go highbrow and the good old fallback: dirty words. Whatever you prefer to call the many ways, these expressions contain an aggressive, even violent energy, when you utter them.

Some studies have examined the correlation between the use of obscenities and violence. In one, for example, Brigham Young University researchers found that middle school students who watched TV and played video games with profanity were more likely to use profanity, and in turn, were more inclined to being physically violent and aggressive in how they treat others. The results were published in the American Academy of Pediatrics' peer-reviewed journal *Pediatrics*.

"Profanity is kind of like a steppingstone," said study researcher Sarah Coyne of BYU. "You don't go to a movie, hear a bad word, and then go shoot somebody. But when youth both hear and then try profanity out for themselves it can start a downward slide toward more aggressive behavior."

"The foolish and wicked practice of profane cursing and swearing is a vice so mean and low that every person of sense and character detests and despises it," opined George Washington, the first United States President.

There is scant other research to show a high correlation between the use of swearing and violence. In one dissertation paper, Seth Adam Gitter, PhD candidate at Florida State University, wrote: "The absence of evidence does not prove the fact, however. There is a distinct possibility that profane language, even when fleeting, can influence people's behavior in unsavory ways."

When I do use one of these words, I feel a rush—of adrenaline, of anger, of strength and power and finally of a tendency toward violence, even when it is not acted out. I feel more macho, to put it simply. I have dominated the person I am speaking with, shown my darker side and hopefully intimidated them, or at least demonstrated verbally that I am capable of passionate rage.

Studies have affirmed this impression. Research bears out that using swear words triggers a part of the brain called the amygdala. Studies show swearing frequently precedes or is accompanied by physical aggression in children.

With this in mind, one of the ways I chose to reduce, if not entirely eliminate, violence from my own life was to reduce if not entirely eliminate these words from exiting my mouth. I did not find this really hard. There are plenty of alternatives, such as:

Gosh darn it. Holy moly. Geez Louise. Ohhh fudge. Ohhh man. What theeeeee....

I found this language shift, as linguists call it, made me feel like a kinder, gentler person. In the company of other men using profanities, it made me feel almost saintly, even pious. And, to be honest, a little less manly. It challenged me to draw upon my well documented creative skill with words to find different words to express feelings that many have worn thin with over-usage. There are many. So what would I say instead of "That f***ing sucks." Wait, is sucks a bad word too?

I searched online for advice that could help me stop swearing. One source offered three ways: enlist a friend who may also have a habit of swearing, someone who can hold each other accountable; avoid the triggers that get you cursing (but how can you really do that?); or the oft-used "swear jar," in which you deposit some amount of money for each time you violate, with the booty going to charity or a much needed item you all can share.

Having begun to conquer my use of these words in the company of others, and feel my softer less aggressive side, I then tried to block them from my inner monologue. You know what I mean. When you spill your coffee all over your car seat: "Ohhhhh sh***!" When you forget to pay a bill on time: "Perry, you f***ing a**hole!" When you stub your toe: "Mother f***er!"

This attempt was very difficult for me. Blame it on New Jersey and Boston and MoFo New Yawk.

"Sticks and stones may break my bones, but words will never hurt me."

Surely you have heard and probably used that rhyme, delivered in its traditional sing-songy style, intended to increase one's resilience, avoid physical retaliation and to diffuse impending acts of violence.

But it's not true. Words can and do hurt. Long after the black eye, bruised rib or worse has healed, that curse-filled epithet hurled at you will continue to echo off the walls of your brain, convincing you they were right. Many times these mean assessments of your character are intentional, sometimes underhand (for example, through sarcasm and passive aggressive language, in both of which I have had Olympic gold medals), and often unintentionally, through lazy or ignorant application of the language you speak.

Curse words, as I pointed out, carry their own edge of violence. But all words, ill-advised and sloppily used, spoken in emotionally charged haste or strategically timed to hit you at your lowest moments, can leave wounds and scars as deep as those left by sticks and stone and guns and knives. These wounds can hurt both the sender and the receiver of these kinds of communication.

Guilty of this kind of violence and searching for how to minimize the verbal collateral damage I was causing to others and myself, I was fortunate to stumble onto an assignment as a media consultant to an organization whose mission I knew nothing about. It's called BayNVC, an Oakland, California, group. NVC, which stands for Nonviolent Communication (also known as conscious communication), is an approach based on principles of nonviolence, first introduced in the 1960s by Marshall Rosenberg, an American psychologist whose self-help book, *Nonviolent Communication: A Language of Life*, is considered an authoritative text on the subject. Later he founded the Center for Nonviolent Communication, an international nonprofit. Today there are some 900 NVC trainers around the world.

It evolved from concepts used in person-centered therapy, which is basically talk therapy. It holds that most conflicts between individuals or groups arise from miscommunication about their needs, due to coercive or manipulative language that aims to infuse fear, guilt, shame, and intimidation—linguistic violent modes of communication that divert attention from clarifying needs, feelings and perceptions, thus perpetuating the conflict. So it first attempts to create conversational empathy, establishing an environment for easier talk about solutions which satisfy the needs of all parties. The goal is interpersonal harmony, the endgame being cooperation. It rejects coercive forms of discourse; its goal is to gather facts through observing without evaluating, genuinely and concretely expressing feelings and needs, and formulating effective and empathetic requests. Examining it, one might put it under the umbrella of psycholinguistics or psychology of language, the study of the interrelation between linguistic factors and psychological aspects.

The organization lists three practical applications of this communication style:

"Self empathy," explained as "compassionately connecting with what is going on inside us," noticing our thoughts and judgements...without judgment, and looking at the needs that affect us; "empathic receiving," connecting "with what's alive in the other person and what would make life wonderful for them, an understanding of the heart in which we see the beauty in the other person, the divine energy in the other person, focusing on listening for the underlying observations, feelings, needs and requests; "honest expression," in terms of observation, feeling, need, and request.

Using these components together minimizes the chances of people getting lost in potentially disconnecting speculation about what you want from them and why. Very little of this psychological gobbledygook made much sense to me. There was a new agey vibe to it that often makes my eyes glaze over and muddles my brain, despite the fact that I was part of the new age in my 20s and 30s. But I needed to pay attention if I wanted to change my behavior. There was some evidence it worked: a 2013 professionally published analysis of 13 studies suggested an increase in empathy subsequent to the application of NVC.

I took on the gig and went to meet Miki Kashtan, BayNVC's cofounder and lead trainer. Born and raised in Israel, Miki is an intense woman with a no-hold-barred straightforwardness. In our first conversation, she was quite assertive and brilliant. A prolific writer, she is the author of several books and countless training and development materials and blogs. She thought so fast that she interrupted some of my questions and answered what she already knew I was going to ask. She was curt and abrupt, got right to the point. Yet, I sensed an earnest heart and a sincere commitment to helping others find their way to nonviolent forms of human communication.

As she had written somewhere, "I grew up in Israel, one of the most tortured pieces of land in the world. Now I dedicate my life to making war obsolete. I am the Face of Peace."

I attended a few group sessions and found the experience and the method extremely challenging but beneficial in the long run. It seemed that whatever came out of my mouth broke some basic guidelines of NVC. In the beginning, it made me stop at almost every word or phrase, examining it from all sides for possible meanings and possible effects. I was dismayed at how much I said was offending someone, how much violent behavior inadvertently comes from everyone's mouths. Slowly as I previewed whatever I was going to say before I let the words emerge from my lips, I reshaped my thoughts with much more empathy for others...and after a while, I even felt empathy for myself.

She encounters these problems in relationships and in the workplace, where she has consulted with organizations. In a *New York Times* essay, she wrote: "Collaborating to achieve a common goal requires facing dissent. In most workplaces, however, speaking freely is risky. Power differences and habits of passivity lead many people to stay silent.... Time and again, I have seen collaboration foster an environment where everyone is free to contribute to their full potential. With this freedom, and with a sense of joint purpose, people willingly stretch in new directions... Sometimes, collaboration requires transforming deep habits of mistrust... Although collaboration—or 'laboring together' (*collaborare* in Latin)—isn't easy, it becomes easier the more we welcome differences and even conflict in service of a larger whole. The results are higher trust, increased productivity and rich creativity."

This idea of nonviolent communication is embedded in all of Gandhi's writings, in his speeches and in his philosophy, anticipating and informing the work of Marshall Rosenberg, Miki Kashan and the hundreds of trainers worldwide.

HOW TO GANDHI: A Nonviolent Approach

It is nearly impossible to cut oneself off from the bombardment of violent images and actions society throws at us, in person or on the news, all negatively influencing our ability to remain calm and peaceful. Yet, there are some things you can do, and not do.

For example, don't hit a pillow; sit on it—as in a meditation cushion, aka zafu. This is quite possibly the oldest method known to humans to minimize stress, which creates violence in the mind. As lots of research has shown, the simple act of watching your breath in silence, as the Buddha did with vipassana (the Pali word meaning seeing things as they really are, literally "special seeing," and now also called insight) meditation, reduces heart rate, respiratory rate, blood pressure and increases self-awareness, inner peace and calmness.

The most dramatic example I personally witnessed of the power meditation has with even hardcore criminals was when I visited India's Tihar Jail in Delhi, where inmates who attended 10-day vipassana retreats within prison grounds showed lowered incidences of recidivism. That is, once out in society again, under the calming influence of meditation, they were less inclined to the kind of violent behavior that got them in jail in the first place. They had literally re-formed.

Other than that, just say no as much as possible to violence that creeps into your life—to news of school shootings, to stories about rape, to angry rap music lyrics full of swear words hurled like daggers at people, to sports that are defined by violence such as boxing, wrestling, hockey and football, to people you encounter who rage with borderline violent anger, and to thoughts in your own head that beat you up.

GANDHI IN THE UNITED KINGDOM

Searching for Gandhi in the United Kingdom

On October 2, 2021, the 152nd birth anniversary of Mahatma Gandhi, I was fortunate enough to be in London after a frustrating 18-month wait due to Covid. Why was I in London, or England at all? (Those who know this brief historical catch-up can skip ahead to the next paragraph.) In 1888 at the age of 19, Gandhi had left his hometown, the harbor city of Porbandar (population less than 100,000 at the time), headed by ship to London to spend the next three years studying law at the Inner Temple, formally known as the The Honourable Society of the Inner Temple.

London was the world's largest city then (second only to the place of my birth, known as New York City). In 1851, over 38 per cent of Londoners were born somewhere else. Greater London had a population reaching beyond 3 million in the last decade of the 19th century. It jumped to more than 7 million by the 1910s. During the same period, the flow of immigrants rose from a steady stream to a raging river of human immigration.

The earliest records of Indians arriving in the United Kingdom in significant numbers date back to the 18th and 19th century when the East India Company hired many Indians to serve as crew members. The first large influx of Indian immigrants came at the end of World War II and the dissolution of the British Empire; many came as laborers in the textile and rail industries. The number of Indian-born residents increased by almost 45 per cent during the first 10 years of the 21st century. Today, Indians are the largest ethnic minority in the United Kingdom, with a population of 1.5 million, ranking sixth among the Indian diaspora communities.

For young Mohandas the initial culture shock upon arrival would have been nearly overwhelming. But his tunnel vision helped him get through well enough. His singular mission, aside from passing the bar, was to adapt to and adopt the ways of the West. He would gain that experience through this virtual epicenter of the world, in the country that had colonized India in 1858 and ruled over it for 100 years, often without much regard for the well-being of the inhabitants of the "jewel in the crown."

The relationship between Indians and the English has always puzzled me. Some say Indian people revere all things British because they were systematically brainwashed—one could say bureaucratized into numbness and submission, with the help of its military might. Others say India, with its history of kingly monarchies, could relate to the same tradition in England. Still others may appear to like the Brits, showing the stiff upper lip they learned from their overlords, while in private disdaining them with vengeance in their hearts. Either way, why would a people made to feel so diminutive in comparison come around to hold England in such high regard that a young wanna-be lawyer would travel to London and surely be subjected to humiliation after humiliation?

Was he trying to know his enemy? That well-known phrase comes from the 6th century Chinese general Sun Tzu in his *Art of War*. The full quote, by the way, goes like this: "Know thy enemy and know yourself; in a hundred battles, you will never be defeated. When you are ignorant of the enemy but know yourself, your chances of winning or losing are equal. If ignorant both of your enemy and of yourself, you are sure to be defeated in every battle." Did Gandhi already have a battle for independence in mind?

As he struggled painfully to adapt to Western food, dress and etiquette, he felt awkward. His vegetarianism became a continual source of embarrassment; his friends warned that it would wreck his studies as well as his health. Fortunately, he came across the one vegetarian restaurant in town, as well as a book providing a reasoned defense of vegetarianism. Though he'd grown up in a household that ate according to the strict Hindu tradition of the Vaishnavas, the zeal he developed for vegetarianism helped to draw the shy youth out of his shell and gave him a new poise and purpose. He became a member of the executive committee of the London Vegetarian Society, attending its conferences and contributing articles to its journal.

With my eye-witness reporter's hat on, little spiral notebook that fits into any pocket and my trusty phone to record interviews and shoot still photos and videos, I set out to see where Gandhi went and tried to imagine how he lived, and to compare his then with our now.

Preparing to go to London and travel in Gandhi's footsteps, I had found an article in the *Times of India* hyping a first-ever walking tour called Gandhi Walk, funded by a gentleman named Ajay Goyal, an India-born global entrepreneur, investor, philanthropist and writer who'd settled in London. This was a great find, even auspicious, as it reminded me precisely of how

I found Shantum Seth when I began research for my last book, *Buddha or Bust*. Shantum leads tours "In the Footsteps of the Buddha," and his site came up first when I googled that phrase.

The problem was that the Gandhi Walks article was published in 2007, some 12 years before I undertook the search, and my best googling and that of my India-based ace researcher Prarthi Shah, could not find it or Mr. Goyal. So instead I booked a day with Shaju Nair, a registered London Blue Badge Guide who is from Kerala, a lush green tropical state I love that's on the Malabar Coast of southwest India, famed for its tranquil backwaters with ayurveda retreats all around and year-round weather ranging between 84°F (29°C) and 91°F (33°C). I kept thinking Mr. Nair, a nice and competent man, must really have wanted to live in England enough to leave a country that justifiably calls itself "God's Own Country." Then again, maybe London's infamous rains made him feel at home, given Kerala's twice-yearly heavy monsoon rains.

Mr. Nair took me on a tour of Gandhi's London, including where he slept, where he studied law, where he stayed on visits after his years in South Africa and India. I was especially interested in the first place he stayed upon arrival. No. 20 Baron's Ct Rd in West Kensington is where he stayed as a law student his first months in England. It looks like a simple multi-level row house. We couldn't get in because it's occupied by somebody, and there's nothing there to distinguish that Gandhi lived there. The sole identification is one of the only two Gandhi-related Blue Plaques from the greater London Council (United Kingdom's scheme of historical markers), connoting that "Gandhi lived here as a law student." The other Blue Plaque is outside Kingsley Hall on Powis Road, where Gandhi stayed for several months in 1931. That was when he came to discuss Indian independence at the Second Roundtable Conference held in London. Gandhi had declined to stay in nicer accommodations on that trip, preferring to stay at the Hall, which had been a community center in a less-than-posh neighborhood. He was met by a large crowd (there's some old video footage of him on a balcony greeting well-wishers). He was visited there by such luminaries as Charlie Chaplin and George Bernard Shaw.

It took Mr. Nair a while to find the right person to let us get in and see the interior of the building at Kingsley Hall. The gentleman who finally met us there, David Baker, was the groundskeeper of the building and quite a quirky fellow. Inside, the building was a mess. Mr. Baker took me to the room Gandhi slept in. There was no desk or any other indication that Gandhi had stayed there. It was quite disappointing and reminded me of some of the unkempt places Gandhi had stayed on the Salt March. Then he took me to the outside garden area which I found more interesting. Gandhi had planted a tree in the garden in 1931, though it was destroyed in World War II. In 1983, Richard Attenborough used the garden for a scene in his film *Gandhi*, dressing up the building before he could shoot. Today, Kingsley Hall is a center for youth, women's groups and other community needs. The Gandhi Foundation keeps an office on the top floor, which Mr. Baker showed me. It looked unused.

On Gandhi's birthday, it was a typically overcast morning when I took a taxi to Tavistock Square, in the London borough of Camden. Rain was threatening. A small group of people were there, maybe 30 to 50, including members of the Indian diaspora, Parliamentarians and community leaders. The annual event is organized by the High Commission of India in London and supported by the India League, which traces its roots back to India's freedom struggle. One of the esteemed guests I met was the mayor of Camden, Councillor Sabrina Francis.

Attendees gathered in front of the Gandhi statue in the center of the square, a very austere statue which was unveiled in 1968, marking the centenary of Gandhi's birth in 1969. He has a furrowed brow and it's the only statue I saw of him in the three countries I visited where he is sitting down and looking quite somber. I circumambulated it several times, slowly, studying each angle of the man.

The event included a recitation about who Gandhi was and what he meant to the world, floral tributes, and the singing of Gandhi's favorite bhajan, "Vaishnava Jan" by Indian students in London. The ceremony concluded with a Buddhist prayer for peace conducted by monks.

In other parts of the park, there is a bust of Virginia Woolf, the beloved Bloomsbury writer who lived at 52 Tavistock Square in the 1920s and 30s. There is also a memorial to other Brits of historical note. Stones around the park are adorned with plaques such as the Conscientious Objectors' Commemorative Stone with a message Gandhi himself would have admired: "To all those who have established and are maintaining the right to refuse to kill. Their foresight and courage give us hope." He might not have appreciated the Starbucks across the street and other examples of creeping capitalism.

Reflecting on the differences between Gandhi's experience of London and my present-day observations, I had a fortuitous conversation and impromptu tour with Munsur Ali, a Bangladesh-born, London-raised Muslim filmmaker and local politician. Mr. Ali never meant to enter politics but he found himself compelled to get involved after massive redevelopment plans arose in his community.

Mr. Ali, now in his mid-40s, lived in the same Brick Lane area—actually in the same flat—since the time he was two years old. He described to me the threats that permeated his childhood memories. "I grew up in a very racist era, we grew up being constantly racially abused... I have a scar from when I was 13 and I was cut with a coffee cutter by two grown men." His neighborhood of Brick Lane was the heart of the Bangladeshi community. He said, "Bangladeshis came because they were afraid of the daily racial abuse and attacks, so they only felt comfortable in areas with others from their community."

Sometimes this meant squatting in bombed out and rotting buildings, but Brick Lane also boasted great halal shops, Bengali clothing stores, a strong Jewish area and a growing sense of unity. After Mr. Ali graduated from University and began his career in film, a major housing redevelopment began to take place where he lived. "When I heard about the redevelopments," he told me in his filmmaking studio, "I wanted to make sure my friends and neighbors didn't get the short end of the stick." It began with mobilizing the people and ultimately led to his becoming elected as Council member.

Mr. Ali described his motivation to stand up for his community, many of whom faced language barriers and weren't educated about their rights. "It's easy to get marginalized because you might be offered something a tad bit better than what you have, but really you're entitled to *a lot* better. Unless you know how to compare it, you think that's something, but in reality you're entitled to way more than that, because you've not been told the full story...You make a decision based on the level of information that you have."

We took a quick car ride to Brick Lane where Mr. Ali proudly pointed out a wide variety of businesses, the historic Brick Lane Mosque Jamme Masjid, commemorative artwork and architecture. Amid the sounds of traffic, construction and languages foreign to my ear, the area was clearly alive with growth. In recent years, Brick Lane has become a focal point for protests against gentrification and "hipsterfication." Locals object to trendy bars, boutiques and tourists replacing the businesses and families who established the area, fondly known as "Banglatown."

Mr. Ali said he's happy to see how many more people are getting educated, aspiring to businesses and understanding their rights. There's nothing inherently wrong with economic change, in his view. However, he warned, "Progress is when it involves people. When it excludes people, then it's a takeover."

Walking through this narrow lane, I was awed by my principled young guide who was working to empower his neighbors. I couldn't help but think of the impact of another man who journeyed from South Asia to London on his path to making a difference.

Intrigued to learn about other communities where Indian culture has crossed borders and thrived, I searched online for communities outside of India with the highest densities and per centages of people with Indian/South Asian heritage. I came upon the city of Leicester, England. I knew nothing about this place located about 100 miles (160 kilometers) north of London.

Mahatma Gandhi was never in Leicester; the closest he came was the cotton mill town of Darwen, 130 miles (210 kilometers) further north. He'd visited it in 1931 at the invitation of a mill-owning family that wanted him to see the hardship the East Lancashire textile industry was suffering due to the Gandhi-led boycott of British goods.

So there seemed no reason for me to go to Leicester if I was even now still trying to literally follow in the Mahatma's footstep. What is there, though, is a Gandhi statue, which I'd also read had been the target of protests and vandalism, a theme I'd been following with increasing concern as reports of the incidences also increased, ever since I began my experiment becoming Gandhi. Leicester would be just one of many Gandhi statues assaulted literally around the world, from my state of California to South Africa and Ghana, to India, to too many European countries, to New York City. An online petition was filed in Ottawa, Canada, calling for the removal of a Gandhi statue from the Carleton University campus. In the United Kingdom, over 6,000 people signed an online petition to take down Gandhi's statue in Leicester. These petitions described Gandhi as a racist, who called Africans "savages" and "kaffirs" during his two decades living and working in South Africa.

One other significant factoid compelled me to visit the city and it was not The Foxes, nickname for the Leicester City Football Club, the professional team that overcame the oddsmakers to win the 2015-16 Premier League. Rather, in the 1970s, with the rapid influx of immigrants from South Asia and several African nations, which indigenous British clearly did not appreciate, racial tensions were so high and violent that the city established Britain's first-ever race relations council committee in 1976. An ad the City Council published in 1972 in the *Uganda Argus*, a daily newspaper out of Kampala (now called *The New Vision*), rather exacerbated the tensions. The capitalized headline read:

"AN IMPORTANT ANNOUNCEMENT ON BEHALF OF THE COUNCIL OF THE CITY OF LEICESTER, ENGLAND...

Then the notice stated (its caps intact here): "The City Council of Leicester, England, believe that many families in Uganda are considering moving to Leicester. If YOU are thinking of doing so, it is very important you should know that PRESENT CONDITIONS IN THE CITY ARE VERY DIFFERENT FROM THOSE MET BY EARLIER SETTLERS." The ad cited problems with housing, education, social and health services, all "already stretched to the limit." And then this dire warning:

"IN YOUR OWN INTEREST AND THOSE OF YOUR FAMILY YOU SHOULD ACCEPT THE ADVICE OF THE UGANDA RESETTLEMENT BOARD AND NOT COME TO LEICESTER."

Contextually, in 1972 Ugandan monster Idi Amin had expelled 60,000 of his country's Asian minority, giving them 90 days to leave.

The notice backfired spectacularly, as Leicester restauranteur, Dharmesh Lakhani, told me when I hung out with him at his restaurant, Bobby's. It's a virtual community center for all Indians along what's known as the Golden Mile of Belgrave Road that pierces like a straight arrow through the downtown starting from Belgrave Circle and then veers off to Melton in one direction and Loughborough in another heading north-ish.

"My parents, Ugandan Indians, were among thousands who read the ad and were curious to find out why the council would go to such trouble as to take out an ad in the Ugandan papers—and so they decided to come to Leicester to find out. That's just how Indians are; we want what is forbidden! We came and never left."

The Golden Mile—by the way, the origin of the name is often mistakenly attributed to the plethora of shops selling Indian gold jewelry but in fact comes from the early 1970s when a rapid succession of yellow-amber traffic lights began to appear along Belgrave—is now renowned for its authentic Indian restaurants, sari shops and jewelers, the closest that Britain comes to an Indian bazaar. It's also where the largest Diwali festival outside of India occurs every year.

Eventually the white majority became the minority when non-whites of Indian, African and Caribbean origins (many whose own heritages went back to India) rose to some 70 per cent of the population, giving Leicester another first: the first city in England to achieve such a demographical milestone. Now city officials and business people call it a harmonious and diverse city, thanks in part to efforts along the way to smooth things out.

In my research on the petition to remove the Gandhi statue in Leicester, I read a response by Claudia Webbe, a member of Parliament for Leicester East. A bit from how she was quoted:

"I stand in solidarity with the Black Lives Matter protests here in Leicester and across the United Kingdom. I will continue to support all those across the world who are safely and peacefully protesting systems of racist oppression. I believe that the calls to take down the statue of Mahatma Gandhi in Leicester are a distraction from this crucial movement. I recognize that, like many people of his era, Gandhi said and did some questionable things in his life. Yet Gandhi was part of creating a historical anti-imperialist movement in the same way that Martin Luther

King created a ground-breaking civil rights movement. His form of peaceful protest, like Black Lives Matter today, was a powerful force for change. ...Gandhi... remains a hero to many of Leicester's Asian community and to millions across the world."

Ms. Webbe was born and brought up in Leicester to parents of African descent who migrated from the Caribbean island of Nevis to the United Kingdom; she studied race and ethnic relations at Birkbeck University in London. In the mid-1990s Webbe had also founded and chaired Operation Trident, a community-led initiative to tackle the disproportionate effects of gun violence on black communities. She was the first female Member of Parliament for Leicester East.

When I spoke with Ms. Webbe in person at her political office on Uppingham Road, she clarified the actual threat to the city's Gandhi statue. There never was a protest or vandalism; there was that online petition signed by 6,000. There were rumors that a group, possibly not from Leicester, was going to vandalize the statue or stage some kind of event there. Nonetheless, Leicester leaders and citizens of Indian and non-Indian descent organized their own counter-protest by forming a human chain encircling the statue, linked by a white ribbon, followed by some statements.

The originator of the petition in 2020 was a woman from the city of Derby some 40 miles (50 kms) north, an industrial city where 80 per cent of the 260,000 residents are white. Eventually the Leicester City Council got her to close the petition.

A city council spokeswoman said: "Although this petition has not yet been submitted to us, these representations will be considered as part of a wider conversation about the context, relevance and appropriateness of street names, statues and monuments in the city. In such a culturally-diverse city as Leicester, it's important that we respect the histories of all our communities and understand the context for the historical references that are part of our streetscape and built environment."

It was either a tempest in a teapot or a disaster averted.

Ironically, about a week after I met with Claudia Webbe, a report broke that she had been convicted of harassing another woman and she was later expelled from the Labor Party. I took it as a reminder that we are all human. She defended Gandhi's legacy and work while embroiled in a personal crisis that threatened her own.

Aside from examples like this of people losing their personal moral and ethical compass, which can happen even as they are defending Gandhi, what I'd heard about Leicester now being a harmonious community seemed true to me. As is so often true, and seems to be part of human nature (and birds that flock together), ethnic communities establish their pockets within the context of larger society. We are not a homogenous people, no matter how utopian the idea. I know the city of my birth, New York City, very well. It is commonly referred to as the "Melting Pot" of America, yet in the borough of Queens, where my parents and grandparents were born and lived, it's said that 130 languages are spoken: Spanish, Russian, Korean, Urdu, Farsi, Greek, Chinese, Vietnamese, Tagalog among them. The borough might be the most concentrated ethnic mix in the world. Ride the No. 7 train to the end of the line in Flushing and you might as well have been deposited in any number of Asian capitals. The nerve center of ethnic Queens is Astoria, a collision of Greek, Hispanic, Arab and Eastern European cultures. Almost every four blocks you are bombarded with different smells and sounds and languages. But each community basically stays to itself, marry within their own people, dine at their local ethnic restaurants, and the twain do not meet until they go downtown to work.

I found this also to be true not only in Leicester but also in London as well, and many other urban centers in England.

I'm not sure this was the Utopia Gandhi had in mind, even if his vision was a dream that can never become true.

Gandhi himself is not given his due in the United Kingdom, in my opinion. While there are a few Gandhi statues throughout England—two in London, one in Leicester, one in Manchester—the fact that there are only two Blue Plaques and that the places he lived in are not well kept suggest he was and will remain a marginalized figure there. Could that be because he was an Indian? I'm just asking.

Almost literally, Gandhi did not leave a strong enough mark on the United Kingdom and that left me worried, and sad. This country that left such a strong mark on him now thinks of him as an asterisk, a footnote to its own history.

That said, the election of Britain's first Indian-origin Prime Minister, Rishi Sunak, elected in October 2022, is a sign of a change in attitude. Born in the port city of Southampton to parents of Indian descent—his father born and raised in Kenya, his mother from what is now Tanzania—he's a testament to Gandhi's own "Be the change" mantra.

In 2020, when he was chancellor, he wrote to the Royal Mint Advisory Committee supporting a campaign called We Too Built Britain, which seeks representation of non-white icons on British currency. Gandhi's image, and those of Indian-origin British spy Noor Inayat Khan and Jamaican British nurse Mary Seacole, were on the wish list.

I just wish he'd been elected while I was there so I could hear in person more of his views.

The winds of change are inevitable, and ever shifting.

4

SIMPLICITY

It's Not That Simple in Complicated Times

"You may have occasion to possess or use material things, but the secret of life lies in never missing them."

—Mahatma Gandhi

"I always listen to what I can leave out."

—Miles Davis, jazz trumpeter

"To live a pure unselfish life, one must count nothing as one's own in the midst of abundance."

—The Buddha

George Carlin, the late, great acerbic American comedic commentator who aimed his daggered tongue at the injustices and plain weirdness of human behavior and social (and anti-social) rituals did a schtick on stuff. He ranted on in this manner:

"...All you need in life is a little place for your stuff, ya know? Everybody's got a little place for their stuff. This is my stuff, that's your stuff, that'll be his stuff over there. That's all your house is—a place to keep your stuff. If you didn't have so much stuff, you wouldn't need a house. A house is just a pile of stuff with a cover on it. You can see that when you're taking off in an airplane. You look down; you see everybody's got a little pile of stuff. And when you leave your house, you gotta lock it up. Wouldn't want somebody to come by and take some of your stuff. They always take the good stuff. They never bother with that crap you're saving. All they want is the shiny stuff. That's what your house is, a place to keep your stuff while you go out and get...more stuff! Sometimes you gotta move, gotta get a bigger house. Why? No room for your stuff anymore."

I picture Bapu rolling in the aisles, more precisely from his grave, in recognition of this human need to hold onto things. He himself famously wrote: "We have sufficient for everybody's needs, not for greed."

He went on: "I suggest that we are thieves in a way. If I take anything that I do not need for my own immediate use and keep it, I thieve it from somebody else. I venture to suggest that it is the fundamental law of Nature, without exception, that Nature produces enough for our wants from day to day, and if only everybody took enough for himself and nothing more, there would be no pauperism in this world, there would be no more dying of starvation in this world. But so long as we have got this inequality, so long we are thieving."

He himself lived up to his hope to take "enough for himself and nothing more."

Most people are measured by what—and especially how much—they left behind. Gandhi is often measured by how little he left behind. A memorial stands in the room where he lived his last 144 days and was assassinated on January 30, 1948. Formerly the New Delhi compound of wealthy industrialist

Ghanshyam Das Birla, the museum known as Gandhi Smriti (Gandhi Remembrance) is a remarkable study in declutter and non-possession. Zen design before it was cool. A mounted display showcases Gandhi's worldly remains: his walking staff, spectacles, spectacle case, pocket watch, a spoon, a knife and fork, and oddly enough, a sickle. The room we see is just as he left it: bare but for a mattress on the floor, a bolster, a pillow, a copy of the Bhagavad Gita and a short writing table.

For Gandhi, simplicity was part and parcel of a more spiritual and economically practical philosophy, a way to live with ethical and humanitarian overtones. On the economic and political front, in the Big Picture he intended to help India and Indians sever the chains of dependency England had over this subcontinental country. That was part of his strategy to spur the popularity of spinning with a charkha; as well, the march to Dandi to encourage Indians to rebel against paying taxes to England for their own salt. On the personal side, he was very thrifty out of necessity and tendency—the former especially when he lived in London during his medical school years.

In Gandhi's vision, prescribing to the less-is-more philosophy is a moral decision if you believe, as I do, that we have a moral obligation to protect the Planet, protect the sanctity of our minds and our bodies. Simplification at its extreme requires one to strip down to bare essentials, forcing you to choose what really matters to you. In doing so, Gandhi reasoned, you inevitably come down to the questions at the heart of all the great belief systems: Who am I? Why am I here? What is my purpose? And Gandhi would add one more: what do I need from the material world in that self-exploration? The answers to these questions, in turn, circle back to Gandhi's moral code, which in these times might be summarized as "living lightly on the Earth," a phrase that entered our lexicon in the 1970s, with the first Earth Day and, later, the advent of the Environmental Protection Agency (1970), the Clean Air Act (1970), the Clean Water Act (1972) and the Endangered Species Act (1973), among others.

If Gandhi's influence on us to live more simply will have its greatest impact, it will be in two areas, and they are not your closet or desktop: they are the limited natural resources of the planet and the limitless value to your mind. We don't need Al Gore to tell us that the more we manufacture and produce, the more we farm and eat, the more we buy, acquire, consume and dispose.

Gandhi's ideas about living more simply drew directly from pioneers in the field. Among the most influential was the 18th century French Enlightenment philosopher Jean-Jacques Rousseau, who praised the simple way of life in such works as "Discourse on the Arts and Sciences" (published in 1750) and "Discourse on Inequality" (1754).

There are several components that drive the increasing interest in a movement that encourages less, not more. Just look around. Traffic, crowded cities, shortages of various essential commodities, shrinking available land and space to grow, exorbitant apartment rental fees, air pollution, limited data to add yet another app to your allegedly smart phone, the cost of all this to your wallet and, not so incidentally, the environment. But perhaps especially costly to your wellbeing, to the limited available space in your mind to balance your increasingly complex lives.

The days of Robin Leach's 1980s TV series "Lifestyles of the Rich and Famous," and his tag line "Champagne wishes and caviar dreams," took upwardly mobile to whole new aspirational heights...and then to nightmarish depths as reality set in, mortgage rates went up, credit card debt skyrocketed, inflation went up, the stock market went down, the dot com boom turned into the dot bomb bust, manufacturing and production dwindled and in some cases disappeared thanks to modern technological advances that replaced humans with chips. Consumption became more of a dirty word than a dream.

But economics alone did not fuel the fire of this movement. Dissatisfaction with what all these material things brought, or even the promise of what they would bring, burst the bubble of hope and left us depleted, cheated and depressed—emotionally bankrupt.

The rock singer Bruce Springsteen's 1992 hit "57 Channels (and Nothin' On)" was a reference to how many cable channels were then available—in contrast to the basic seven network "stations" before then—and lamenting that, even with so many viewing options, there was so little worth watching. Now my Xfinity offers some 1,000 different channels—and still very little worthy of my valuable eyeballs. This example stands as another representation of the dilemma of too much that has added wind to the simplicity sail.

The "too much" movement has spawned an overabundance... of clutter. We are awash in clutter. People's garages are so full of "stuff" that outside storage unit rentals have become the norm. There are 48,500 storage units in the United States, more than McDonald's and Starbucks locations combined, by one estimate.

What happens to a lot of that clutter when we realize we didn't want it or we ran out of room? We dump it. The average American consumer produces up to five pounds of trash a day. That's 1,640 pounds a year. These numbers are higher than the averages for residents in other countries. In Europe, the average amount of trash generated by one person in a year is just over 1,000 pounds. Every year, American landfills add another 140 million tons of waste.

What we don't discard, we keep too long. I thought my apartment was cluttered; then I watched an episode of "Hoarders," a reality TV series that ran on A&E and opened my eyes to how seriously bad things have gotten for some people just can't let go. In fact, hoarding is now categorized as "compulsive hoarding disorder," recognized by the International Classification of Diseases and the Diagnostic and Statistical Manual of Mental Disorders (DSM-5), the Bible of the American Psychiatric Association.

Overbuying that led to owning too much has spawned its own growth industry of people who want to help unclutter your home. *Fast Company Magazine* estimated the home organization market was valued at $11.8 billion by 2021. One of its superstars is Marie Kondo, the Japanese organizing consultant, who became popular internationally with her 2011 book *The Life-Changing Magic of Tidying Up* and her 2019 Netflix series "Tidying Up with Marie Kondo." But she claimed that when she shifted her focus from looking for things to throw out to things that made her happy it did in fact make her happier. "Identifying the things that make you happy: that is the work of tidying," she wrote—things that she says "spark joy," the term she repeats like a mantra. In Japanese language it's *tokimeku*, translated in English to "flutter, throb, palpitate." According to Celebrity Net Worth, Kondo's empire was worth $8 million before she slowed down to be a mother.

What some have done in their own homes, many others

have done to Planet Earth: turned it into a dumping ground. In the last 125 years, global carbon emissions from fossil fuels have significantly increased. Since 1970, CO_2 emissions have gone up about 90 per cent; fossil fuel combustion and emissions from factory smokestacks, for example, contributed close to 80 per cent of the total greenhouse gas emissions. The next largest contribution comes from agriculture, deforestation, and other land-use changes. Airplane emissions also play a role, though not as large as one would think.

There are some signs the world slowly began to catch up to Gandhi's ideas about simplicity—signs in the proliferation of what has become known as the voluntary simplicity movement, aka minimalism, aka downshifting, aka simple living (One wonders if it's so simple, why have so many different names for it?). Signs in magazines devoted to helping people figure how to have less and enjoy less more. Such as *Simplify Magazine*, a free monthly digital publication. Also the print magazine called *Real Simple*, founded in 2000 "for today's busy woman, providing inspiring ideas and practical solutions to help her simplify her life." A 2021 *Real Simple* "special issue" was entitled "The Power of Less." Power to "unload, the stress," to "declutter your thoughts," to "waste less every day," as the cover lines inform us of what will be inside this mag. Why does it always have to be about power? But, just to make things more complicated rather than simpler, in 2010 *Real Simple* added a few apps. Do apps really make life simpler? Or do they suck you into rabbit holes you could have easily done without? It's obvious that *Real Simple* also wants to suck you into the rabbit hole of consumption, with its online magazine's menu directing you to a "Shopping" page.

Can you even imagine how powerful Gandhi would have

been in mobilizing his forces if he had had an app? There actually now is an app, a complete interactive biography of Mahatma Gandhi, packed with rare photographs and videos, made just for the iPad and downloadable via the Apple App Store.

O dear Bapu, look what you have spawned. And speaking of O...

O, the Oprah Magazine, joined the party and put out a special issue in August 2020 with the cover line shouting, "Let It Go!" Cover lines also promise "how to de-stress, de-clutter, recharge, find your center, and finally relax." *National Geographic* dedicated a whole magazine in 2021 to "Simple Sustainability," mostly written by Kris Bordessa, founder of a blog called *Attainable Sustainable* and author of a book by the same title.

These publications are largely aimed at women; *Real Simple* claims 90 per cent of its 7.6 million readers are women. Naturally, the editorial content reflects what editors think women want and need to achieve a vaunted state of simplicity. That thinking may be gender stereotyping at its worst.

Unfortunately the overriding movement in society today is all about more, more, more. But more never seems to be enough. A few thousand years ago Buddhists had identified this human trait as what's called the Hungry Ghost. Hungry Ghosts, or *pretas* from Sanskrit, are beings who are tormented by desire that can never be sated. You got the corner office, but now you want the penthouse suite of offices. You got the perfect love of your life, but you see an even more perfect love. You boast about your Beemer, but then the Tesla came along to seduce you.

In the face of that trend, and coinciding with the wanna-be simple trend, some companies try to capitalize on their recognition that consumers themselves are torn between buying stuff and knowing they don't need the stuff. A perfect example is the mixed message the online travel booking website Expedia brought home—if home is every TV screen in the world—in a 2022 TV commercial that had its premier on the self-indulgent American extravaganza piously known as the Super Bowl, a Sunday worship with an international congregation of some 112 million viewers across television and streaming, according to NBCUniversal. This was the best ratings in five years for the game, a boast NBCU said, "spoke to the pent-up desire to buy, consume, eat, drink and merrily forget the last two years" (this referred to Covid).

In the commercial, the Scottish actor Ewan McGregor, who played, among other roles, Obi-Wan Kenobi in several "Star Wars" films, walks through a sound stage where crews shoot glitzy commercials for cars, perfumes, TVs and the like, as he says:

"Stuff! We love stuff and there's some really great stuff out there. But I doubt that any of us will look back in our lives and think, 'I wish I'd gotten a slightly sportier SUV, bought an even thinner TV or found a trendier scent. Or wish I'd discovered a crunchier chip. Found a lighter lite beer. Or had an even smarter smart phone.' Do you think any of us will look back on our lives and regret the things we didn't buy..."

Then he walks through a door onto a glorious and uncrowded beach and continues, "...Or the places we didn't go?"

Yes, it's a rhetorical question because Expedia wants you to answer: "Yeah, maybe I should travel. How do I book?" This feeds right into Expedia's not-so-hidden agenda to encourage you to spend money booking airline tickets, hotel rooms, car rentals and all your other travel needs via Expedia. By no surprise, Expedia makes the majority of its money through booking accommodations in bulk at a cheap price, and then selling them to their users with a markup.

Expedia is not suggesting that you don't buy just any "stuff"—it's suggesting you buy its stuff. In short, travel itself is a product, a product now available to the middle and upwardly mobile class. In the past it was only the dominion of the upper classes who could spend considerable disposable and/or discretionary income on travel "abroad," as it's so quaintly and colonialistically referred to, and often more for the boasting rights than for the actual experience. I once sat alone at a table too close to a well-heeled couple at a small trendy restaurant on the New Jersey shore. They were going over their travel bucket list. She said she hadn't been to India's Taj Mahal and that certainly must be a must-see, right? He said he'd been and it's no big deal. The UNESCO World Heritage site, one of the 7 New Wonders of the World, the 17th century marble mausoleum in devotion to his deceased wife and the cherished testimonial to love—no big deal? As they rattled through their list, I realized the experience of being at these places was much less significant than their ability to tell others at some cocktail party that they'd been there.

This flies in the face of the Expedia commercial and speaks directly to my thoughts in relation to Gandhi's hopes we live life not just more simply but also with our values in the right place: that we do value where we go and what we do once there is more than the accumulation of experiences for the sake of accumulation. While hotels and destinations promote "authentic indigenous experiences" (a string of cliches I read too often in their literature), with research to substantiate travelers' priorities, I still wonder how much of leisure travel has been commodified among the middle class.

The Buddha, Expedia and Gandhi were not the only ones to recognize the human need for greed. It pops up in the strangest of places in popular culture. "Hungry Ghosts" is also the name of a rock duo from Portland, Oregon. And "Hungry Ghosts" is the title of the fourth studio album, released in 2014, from American rock band OK Go. The Cure, a quintessential English post punk (also called gothic rock, new wave and alternative) band, released a song in 2008 entitled "The Hungry Ghost" that points out we'll never satisfy the hungry ghost that lurks around inside us.

I'm speculating that the members of The Cure, all now said to have a net worth in the millions, came to this song honestly: they had all they could ever want materially and yet they found it, and themselves, empty. At least one can hope the experience led to some new understanding that having too much achieves nothing for the soul.

> "It is preoccupation with possession, more than anything else, that prevents men from living freely and nobly."
>
> —Bertrand Russell,
> from *Principles of Social Reconstruction*, 1910s

The Norwegian-American economist and sociologist, Thorstein Veblen, coined the term "conspicuous consumption" in his book *The Theory of the Leisure Class*, first published in 1899. He warned against this trend, accelerated by the Industrial Revolution, of an increasingly materialistic society in which people strive to acquire more goods and to be admired for their personal wealth.

There's no evidence among the some 400 books Gandhi read, which have been listed online and shelved at Mani Bhavan in Mumbai, that he read Veblen's works. Gandhi would have been 30 when that book was published; he certainly would have benefitted from a read and agreed with the theories but he was quite busy at the time, caught up in South Africa with the Natal Indian Ambulance Corps, which he'd created as a team of stretcher bearers during the Second Boer War. Yet, the Mahatma was either a visionary or early on caught the wave beginning to trend pushing back the inevitable impact of industrialization.

The implications are profound and impact almost every facet of our lives. In a paper about the voluntary simplicity movement published in the *Journal of Consumer Culture*, the two co-directors for the Simplicity Institute, an education and research center based in Ohio, write:

"Overconsumption in affluent societies is the root or contributing cause of many of the world's most pressing problems, including environmental degradation, global poverty, peak oil and consumer malaise. This suggests that any transition to a sustainable and just society will require those who are overconsuming to move to far more materially 'simple' lifestyles. The Voluntary Simplicity Movement can be understood broadly as a diverse social movement made up of people who are resisting high consumption lifestyles and who are seeking, in various ways, a lower consumption but higher quality of life alternative."

Richard Gregg, a peace activist and author of *The Power of Non-violence* (1934), was one of the first Americans to live and work with Gandhi in the 1920s. He later coined the term ""voluntary simplicity" in *The Value of Voluntary Simplicity* (1936). Since then, the ideals were taken up by, among other early thought leaders in the field, economists Ralph Borsodi and Scott Nearing, anthropologist and poet Gary Snyder, utopian fiction author Ernest Callenbach and, most notably among my peers, the

British-German economist E.F. Schumacher. His 1973 "Small Is Beautiful," a treatise proposing human-scale, decentralized and appropriate technologies with the significant subtitle "A Study of Economics As If People Mattered," held pride of place on bookshelves beside Frances Moore Lappé's *Diet for a Small Planet*, Robert M. Pirsig's *Zen and the Art of Motorcycle Maintenance*, Stewart Brand's *Whole Earth Catalog* and Edward Espe Brown's *Tassajara Bread Book*.

In the United States, voluntary simplicity started to garner more public exposure through a movement in the late 1990s around a popular simplicity book, *The Simple Living Guide*, by Janet Luhrs. Around the same time minimalism (a similar movement) started to feature in the public eye.

Has this voluntary simplicity movement caught on? Not so much, says my good friend Wes Nisker, Buddhism teacher and author of *Buddha's Nature* and other books. He succinctly assessed its progress: "Not enough people volunteered."

Am I living a life of simplicity, or am I simply living?

I'd describe myself as a simple person thrust into a complex life—that is, the life of a working journalist. Now, I didn't say I'm a simpleton; I'm smart, or smart enough. Lacking a Mensa level IQ, I have had to struggle hard to catch up to the brilliant people I've been lucky enough to interview. Growing up in bourgeois suburban New Jersey, with the simple aspiration to not end up in my father's footsteps as a traveling salesman, throughout my career I stretched myself to fit in and blend with the likes of Rajasthani royals, Michelin-starred chefs, the Dalai Lama, and billionaire entrepreneurs from India, Costa Rica, and New York.

At various times in my life I've lived quite literally from hand to mouth, a few times scrounging for coinage that may have dropped under my car seat to pay a bridge toll. There was a period of time when I stored most of my "stuff" between storage facilities in New Jersey and Massachusetts, without a steady income or a steady roof under my head. For three years, after a potentially lucrative book deal fell through, and then two more failed projects, I lived with whatever I could cram into my green Subaru Forester. Suitcases, cardboard boxes (I think I counted 15 at one point), each marked for different needs: the library of my traveling books, one whole box for footwear, another for toiletries, one for dry foods including spices, sleeping bag and my pillow (my bestest friend). I couch surfed at friends' homes and apartments, including at my daughter and son-in-law's; bounced among AirBnBs, Craigs List findings, funky motels and the occasional lovely hotel at deep discount with the help of hotelier friends. I'd stay three or four nights, then be on my unmerry way, unpacking and repacking at each pit stop. I'm proudly humbled to say I never slept in my car (and not only because there would have been no room for me to stretch out). Pride was involved, even at that level.

When I got commissioned to work as ghostwriter for a wealthy Beverly Hills psychologist who invited me to live at her home while we worked on it, I jumped at the opportunity. A roof in BevHills? The gig would last more than six months. Eventually I had my trusty Forester shipped to me from New Jersey, thinking I'd stay a while on the West Coast and knowing life in LA without a car is like being in a band without instruments.

After that gig ended, I'd met a very nice woman so I stayed

in LA, bouncing from her lovely house to temporary corporate housing in Woodland Hills. I had to move with all my stuff stuffed to the brim in my car. She called it the Green Turtle. I felt like the shell of my ordinarily grounded self.

This nomadic period in my life was my first lesson in minimalism. I didn't mind having few things to move around; it was something of a relief. But I did feel I was on an endless downwardly spiraling cycle of impermanence. (I learned the hard way the Buddha was right—all is impermanent).

When my mother passed away, my sister and I learned quite by surprise that we had inherited a tidy sum in stocks and bonds to split. This was a windfall and at the right time for me, after three years of rough times and backed up bills. Right away I calculated that I could probably live for 20 years on the inheritance money if I also brought in a trickle of income by writing.

Once I settled into my own apartment in Berkeley, itself a big step up from those years I did not live anywhere, I was reunited under one roof with everything I owned for the first time in some 10 years. For a while, I was overwhelmed with my "possessions." It was scary to realize how much "stuff" I actually had, and remarkable that I had lived without so much of it, and had missed very little of it. I bought indoor plants. I watched them grow. I had roots. I lived eight blocks from my daughter, her husband and my granddaughter.

Now, with enough money not to worry about next month's rent and flush with what I'd only heard from afar as disposable discretionary income, I was drunk with the urge to acquire. I thought of all the things that I had deprived myself of and I went on a spending spree. First priority was a new car, my shiny blue Honda Fit. I have a soft spot for Persian rugs and handcrafted

Mexican ceramics; I proceeded to fill my two-bedroom flat with all the beautiful items I wanted to surround me.

Sometimes I made excuses—I needed this thing or that thing for utilitarian reasons. Like shoes. OK, but the shoes I coveted were made by Mephisto. The last ones I bought had traipsed around the world with me for *National Geographic* and they nearly outlasted me. These new Mephistos I wanted, black dress shoes, cost $300. While expensive to me, I amortized the expense over the many years I would use them. Just one problem: after buying them, I wore them two times, then they have sat gathering dust in my closet.

As I began this journey through Gandhi's principles, I looked closely at my acquisitional behavior. First, I called a moratorium on buying anything new that I did not absolutely need in my life. Food and other monthly bills, gas, holiday gifts for my family—these were non-negotiable. But did I need yet another kitchen gadget? More sweatpants?

Then, it was time to clean out my closet.

> "If one has wealth, it does not mean that it should be thrown away and wife and children should be turned out of doors. It simply means that one must give up attachment of these things!"
>
> —Mahatma Gandhi

I set aside a Saturday to go through my entire closet and chest of drawers, take inventory and decide which charitable group to which I would donate what I didn't need or had rarely worn or outgrown over the last 25 years. I had not set aside enough time: there was a lot, an embarrassing abundance of nothing valuable to me. There were a dozen shirts, several pairs of pants that were either so out of style or so tight fitting that I marveled at how thin I used to be, and would never be again. I had kept one favorite pair of black Levis that had become a goal, my weight loss holy grail. Accepting defeat, I tossed them in the growing pile to donate...along with ties that went out of style with Beau Brummel, sandals even my Dad wouldn't wear, three pairs of worn out sneakers, shirts whose buttons screamed to be released from torture. I found a terry cloth bathrobe from the Ritz Carlton Hotel Laguna Beach with my name embossed on it when I was a mucka mucka in the world of travel journalists—a souvenir I wore so few times it still looked new.

This stuff we carry around—each piece of clothing, each book, each tiny little item, each birthday card that reminds us we are loved—all carry memories that define our past, invigorate our present and quite possibly pave a path to our future. How can you throw those things out? One camp says, "Never." These are the people who run into their burning house to retrieve not books or clothes but family photo albums. The other camp: "Who needs them? They are just dead weight, emotional excess baggage, an albatross around their neck. I had thought of myself in the who-needs-it camp. But when it came to relieving myself of much of it, I held onto each for what seemed like endless minutes. Do I need this? Is looking at it right now enough? Will it now remain in my permanent memory bank, where its endless data storage capacity will hold it eternally as long as I breathe?

When it was all over, I stared at the donate pile and felt relief anew, unburdened of pieces of my past, and proud of my largesse. I took the pile around the corner to a second hand thrift store appropriately called Out of the Closet, an American chain founded in 1990 where 96 cents of every dollar goes to AIDS Healthcare Foundation's HIV prevention and treatment services.

It felt good to give to this org, and for good reason: There is some evidence to suggest that when you help others, it can promote physiological changes in the brain linked with happiness.

O happy day of donating.

My friend Jeff Greenwald, the American travel writer (and more), wrote a book during the pandemic titled *108 Beloved Objects*. He decides to relinquish cherished items that encapsulate moments from his life and to make the decluttering a conscious practice itself.

Greenwald writes, "We seem to understand, at a deep level, that to release our possessions is a path to personal freedom. The ironic thing is how difficult it can be. It sometimes seems as if our possessions own us; we have that little agency over them. Collecting is easy; letting go, not so much. I wish to learn what's essential; to leave a record; and to travel forward, from this point on, more lightly."

Enthused after lightening my own load, I looked at what else I could do to simplify my life. It was obvious: sign off social media. I'd joined Facebook very early on, in about 2009; it was founded in 2008. It was fun for a while; we found old friends from elementary school, old girlfriends or boyfriends. We joined groups with similar interests. We could boast or kvetch and we knew there was a core group who cared, or at least "liked" our posts. Then it became too much. It transitioned from "social media" to promoting one's product service. Then it became an obsession and a sponge of our time. There is plenty of research that shows while it has built consensus groups, good and bad, it has also caused a lot of stress, anxiety, bullying. For those who scroll in bed before they sleep, it causes loss of good rest.

By the time I undertook this experiment, I had been hooked. Between writing sentences, I would check FB. When I had a cute idea, I'd post it rather than use it in whatever I was writing.

So I decided to quit it...but I was addicted and could not. I tried to wean myself from it, first deleting the app from my phone, along with Instagram, which I had resisted for quite a while until I heard Facebook was for old fogies. Realizing the folly of my ways, I signed off completely from both and that lasted well over a year. But like any drug, it sucked me back in after someone said I must see so-and-so's latest post.

A few days ago, my page was hacked for the first time in close to 20 years and that did it for me: I signed off again, though by the time you read this, I may have rejoined simply and strictly for PR purposes. I have enough actual (not virtual) friends who I do not spend enough time with.

Simplicity can be as simple as following a ritual every day, day after day. There's a rhythm to repetitiveness; it does make life simple. It's not necessary, for example, to expend time and energy asking yourself upon waking up every day, "What shall I do first thing this morning?" The answer is, "The same thing you did yesterday, dummy!" In my case, it's heat up water. While doing so, I crush a lemon into juice, add two tablespoons of freshly squeezed lemon and sip slowly along with a pill of folic acid (for a "preexisting condition"). As I do so, waiting for a kettle of water to boil for coffee, I make a small bowl of fresh fruit, and eat after I finish the juice. By that time, I've made one cup of drip decaf. That's all a no brainer, requiring zero thinking, leaving my brain free to map out the rest of what usually is a chaotic day.

So far, I had tackled my worldly possessions, social media addiction, and morning routine in my search for simplicity. Still, I gave myself one more Gandhi-inspired challenge, one I knew they never covered in *Real Simple* magazine.

Since I would not wear a dhoti or lungee (I'm not built for them), or grow a moustache (believe me, I did try but I looked more like a droopy Ringo Starr), I decided to try my hand at spinning yarn from cotton, using the same instrument Gandhi had used. My intention from the start was not to master the technique, nor to exactly "be" Gandhi, but rather to see why this exercise is considered an important piece of the Mahatma's overall hope that people live more simply.

A charkha is a spinning wheel that is so much more than a spinning wheel in the story of Gandhi and of India. To embody and embrace the significance of charkha, I learned to spin raw cotton into yarn in a most challenging and, I can say in retrospect, most ridiculous circumstance. It was that much crazier to learn for a guy with two opposable thumbs that often seem opposed to whatever I direct them to do. Craftwork requiring any sort of manual dexterity is not my thing. In my youth, just watching my mother trying to thread a needle made me anxious. When I saw her struggling, I tried to help but gave up in a cold sweat. Training my hands to a new skill is also not one of my known strengths;

I learned how to type as a kid using two fingers and stuck to my hunt-and-peck method throughout my writing career. Learning to spin with a charkha would not be a quick spin around the block.

I had blown the chance to take lessons in person from any number of experts in and around Ahmedabad when I was there. The location would have been perfect but the timing did not work out and the Dandi Path was beckoning. I figured I'd be coming back to India in a few months and could sign up then. The 2020 pandemic changed all that, making it impossible to return soon enough. So, when I got back home to California I began to track down someone who could teach me via Zoom or any other video platform. Cue the ridiculousness.

Spinning cotton into yarn requires developing a deep and meaningful relationship with the fibers, which are less than cooperative at times. It's a tactile experience and from a distance there is little way a teacher can press your hand to assess how much pressure you're putting on the strands of cotton to twist and spin into sturdy yarn, a reality I learned the hard way.

The other ridiculousness was that I was attempting to learn this skill at my advanced age when the brain works more slowly (brain shouting into my ear, "You really can't teach an old dog new tricks"). All this while sitting alone in an apartment some 8,100 miles from Ahmedabad, without benefit of the cultural context of India, where the whir and rhythm of street life syncopates with the mesmerizing sound of the wheel spinning, where the charkha is woven into the fabric of Indian identity and history.

This exercise in probable futility was already reminding me of my attempt to learn tabla, the drums of classical Indian music. In that case, though, I had been in Varanasi when I started taking lessons from the famed tabla guru Panchu Maharaj, then head of the tabla department at Banaras Hindu University. He invited me to stay at his house for several weeks. I did nothing but take daily lessons, practice all day, watch his kids and nieces and nephews also practicing drums, dance, assorted other instruments, and then try to sleep amid the howls of monkeys outside my barred windows. Tabla also requires great attention to the tactile experience; your fingers and the heels of your hand tap and squeeze out sounds directly on vibrating goatskin heads. The rhythms undulate up from your fingers and palms to the core of the chest, resounding to the core of your soul.

One day, enveloped in the tals—hypnotic rhythmic patterns perpetually ringing in my ears, suddenly every bark, honk, shout, clickety clacking wheels on rocky pocked roads—all fell into the beat with the basic 16-beat teental I'd been practicing. That was the moment I got it. Got that the entire universe was driven by rhythm, that I was privy to a timeless pulse and that the pulse was me. If I could truly get with the beat, then I'd be absorbed into the Great Akash—from the Sanskrit root word *kāś* meaning "to be." I would be in lockstep with my own rhythm, as off-beat as it is, and only then could I achieve and receive all for which I was destined.

I felt so alive, so attuned and at one, in sync and in syncopation with everything and everyone. Once I returned to Boston, full of inspiration, I was lucky enough to find a tabla teacher, Pandit Sharda Sahai, an artist in residence at nearby Wesleyan University's renowned World Music Program. However, continuing to practice in sterile American quietude on a hill above Boston proved so much less than my experience in India that I lasted less than a year trying to learn this most fascinating percussion instrument.

With charkha, I had hoped, even assumed, I would have the same kind of cosmological epiphany and penetrate the veneer of Mr. Gandhi's formidable persona to make a stronger personal connection with him. Maybe viscerally I would understand why he thought this wheel would be the sparkplug igniting the revolution against British rule. But I did not have the advantage of having started spinning in India, nor the advantage of having been a student of Western-style drums since I was six years old. Indians clearly had a running start on me, not that I am competitive or anything.

Against these odds, why did I feel learning to spin was that important to my transformation into Gandhi? It's a question I asked myself the whole time I took lessons, and for weeks after they ended. I honestly thought that by going through the act, the repetitions, I would get into the flow of spinning in the same way Gandhi did, and my muscles would memorize and simulate his own love of spinning.

Young Mohandas would have known and seen charkhas while growing up in Porbandar, the city of his birth, simply as something the women did in the home to produce clothing and such. By the time Gandhi returned to India from South Africa in 1915, Gujarat's textile industry, centered in the state's then-capital of Ahmedabad, 240 miles (390 kilometers) from Porbander, had risen quickly; the number of textile factories multiplied at near alarming rates. Industrialization slowly made the hand weaving of cotton obsolete. By 1965, in fact, American historian Howard Spodek, who has extensive knowledge about Ahmedabad, wrote about the 'Manchesterisation' of Ahmedabad in the peer-reviewed Indian academic journal *Economic Weekly* (now *Economic and Political Weekly*). The association with the gritty United Kingdom industrial city was not a compliment.

Today, India is the world's second-largest exporter of textiles and apparel with a massive raw material and manufacturing base. The textile and garment industry in India is a significant contributor to the economy, both in terms of its domestic share and exports. It contributes about 7 per cent to industry output, 2 per cent to the GDP and 15 per cent to the country's total export earnings. The sector is one of the largest job creators in the country, employing about 45 million people directly and 60 million people in allied industries.

Gandhi also would have been aware of the great wealth textile manufacturing was generating for the families of a small handful of entrepreneurs like Ranchhodlal Chhotalal, Mangaldas Girdhardas and Mansukhbhai Bhagubhai. He also would have been aware of the long grueling hours factory workers were putting in under appalling conditions.

If he wasn't so darned annoyingly humble, Gandhi could quite legitimately take some credit for his part in those impressive numbers. He may well have planted the seeds for the modern artisanal crafts movement and set the stage for sustainability-chic companies that trumpet their cotton clothing, such as Cotton Basics.

Gandhi first came up with the idea to turn the humble charkha into something more—an action plan for independence, a symbol of self-reliance and a peaceful weapon against British rule—in South Africa. As he wrote in his weekly newspaper *Harijan*: "In 1908, in South Africa, I conceived the idea that, if poverty-stricken India were to be freed from the alien yoke, India must learn to look upon the spinning-wheel and hand-spun yarn as the symbol, not of slavery, but of freedom." (*Harijan*, 1946, p. 320).

The charkha might have remained a charming throwback, or another relic lost in the name of progress, had it not been for the marketing genius of Gandhi to, in effect, rebrand it as a symbol of revolution, of perseverance and determination.

We could say he merely reinvented the wheel, which in its many circular variants appear very close to the center of virtually every religion and belief system, ancient and modern. Psychologists, sociologists and design gurus, among others, have pontificated on the importance and impact of circles on us. As one pundit put it: "Circles don't have angles; they feel softer and milder than other shapes. They commonly represent both unity and protection. Circular shapes are much friendlier because they tend to invite the viewers into their completeness," as one expert put it.

Gandhi was tapping into Man's subconscious. Who knows how much he thought about or understood how deeply a circular spinning wheel would affect human psychology? I wouldn't put the idea of subliminal messaging past him.

The charkha became so fundamental to his teachings that he made learning to spin with it part of the curricula at Gujarat Vidyapith, the university he founded in Ahmedabad in 1920. I had conducted some interviews on the campus and was invited to attend, and then speak at, a typical morning opening exercise where teachers and administrators fill students in on upcoming events and offer inspirational talks. Some 200 students gathered in the auditorium, all seated next to their charkhas, busy spinning and listening to the talks. The whir of 200 wheels spinning echoed off the walls, turning the room into what sounded like a chamber chanting ommmmmm. It all appeared so natural to them, something they repeat day after day and with a focus I could never replicate. To me it was a revelation; I could not think of any other educational setting in the United States where such a thing takes place.

Over the ensuing years, the Mahatma was steadfast and persistent in promoting his main message about the charkha (note the chronology here):

"I ... claim for the Charkha the honour of being able to solve the problem of economic distress in a most natural, simple, inexpensive and businesslike manner... It is the symbol of the nation's prosperity and, therefore, freedom. It is a symbol not of commercial war but of commercial peace." (*Young India*, 1921, p. 406)

"The message of the spinning-wheel is much wider than its circumference. Its message is one of simplicity, service of mankind, living so as not to hurt others, creating an indissoluble bond between the rich and the poor, capital and labour, the prince and the peasant." (*Young India*, 1925, p. 321)

"The message of the spinning wheel is, really, to replace the spirit of exploitation by the spirit of service. The dominant note in the West is the note of exploitation. I have no desire that our country should copy that spirit or that note." (*Young India*, 1928, p. 34)

"I have not the slightest doubt that the saving of India and of the world lies in the wheel. If India becomes the slave of the machine, then, I say, heaven save the world?" (*Harijan*, 1946, p. 404)

"If I preach against the modern artificial life of sensual

enjoyment and ask men and women to go back to the simple life epitomized in the Charkha, I do so because I know that, without an intelligent return to simplicity, there is no escape from our descent to a state lower than brutality." (*Young India*, 1921, pp. 228-9)

Not everyone had the same Utopian vision of how the humble charkha could bring Indians closer to self-rule, most notably prominent among them Rabindranath Tagore. The Bengali polymath and Gandhi had great admiration for each other (it was Tagore who, presumably without tongue in cheek, was the first to give his counterpart the moniker of Mahatma) but differed on many points. In a 1925 essay entitled "The Cult of the Charkha," for the *Modern Review*, Tagore argues that this repetitive act of spinning is exactly what Indians do not need, in fact is what reduced them to a colony, effectively enslaved of England. Hand spinning with charkhas he wrote, "...imparts skill to the limbs of the man who is a bondsman, whose labor is drudgery; but it kills the mind of a man who is a doer, whose work is creation. So in India, during long ages past, we have the spectacle of only a repetition of that which has gone before... By doing the same thing day after day mechanical skill may be acquired; but the mind like a mill-turning bullock will be kept going round and round a narrow range of habit. That is why, in every country man has looked down on work which involves this kind of mechanical repetition."

Tagore notwithstanding, I remained committed to finding my Inner Spinner and continued searching for my charkha guru. I thought if only I could find someone in India or anywhere who could teach me, even if only via distance learning. My black belt in Googling led me first to Joan Ruane. An American based in Arizona, she has a long background in teaching classes in person and via video, specifically working with cotton. I was somewhat disappointed when I saw she worked mostly with traditional spinning wheels, also known as the great wheel. But then I saw some of her videos online in which she introduced the charkha, so I gave her a call. After talking a while, she sent me a takli, a small support spindle, sort of like training wheels before graduating to bigger wheels. This little metal spindle was first designed by Gandhi so that everyone in India could be spinning. Every kid in school got a takli and was taught to spin.

"If the spinning wheel is king," Gandhi had written, "the takli is a queen in her own right. If the wheel can be plied by thousands, cores can use the takli that the finest yarn used to be spun in former times."

Despite the Mahatma's praise of it, the device looked so simple that I decided to pass by the takli and go right to the book charkha. I paid heavily for my arrogance once I started spinning.

The next person I uncovered was not a teacher but she was much closer to my home and quite a formidable person in the hand spinning world and the regenerative agriculture community. California-based farmer-scientist Sally Fox is considered a pioneer in developing organic, naturally-colored cotton, as well as raising heritage Merino sheep and a variety of crops, including Sonora wheat. In her bio, she writes, "I am trying to figure out how to farm sustainably and humanely and profitably."

Good luck with that, but Mr. Gandhi would have loved her for her initiatives. I became aware that there is a growing community of organic cotton farmers and spinners at the esoteric end where taking care of the planet matters.

I'd given up on finding a teacher until I got back to India. But with Covid-related hospitalizations and deaths rising at alarming rates that winter, my windows to travel were closed for the foreseeable future. Almost ready to ditch this whole episode, I turned to my ace Gujarati researcher Prarthi Shah, who resides in Vadodara (aka Baroda). She quickly recommended Avani Varia, who lives in Ahmedabad, 100 kilometers north of Vadodara. In India that made them practically neighbors. Prarthi knew Avani from her own studies for her MBA in heritage management.

Avani had very impressive credentials and commendable intentions. With a master's degree in the arts and heritage management, she has taught charkha and other crafts for more than 20 years, has curated a number of museum exhibitions, including at Ahmedabad's Khoj Museum, India's first children's museum, which alone made me like her. But my esteem for her grew when I learned about her initiatives in support of India's indigenous arts and crafts tradition. She wrote a book, *Chalo Charkho Ramiye* (translation: "Let's play with the charkha"), which is also what she calls her charkha movement, again to promote interest in using the charka. On her Twitter feed, she wrote about her highest hopes for spinning: "If everyone in the world spun an hour a day, there would be no more war. Peace means not about 'no war.' It is to have peace in every person's mind. Peace is a by-product of constructive work done by everyone with positive attitude and calm mind."

Lofty ambition, yes. Achievable? Let's see...

I signed up for a month of daily lessons via Zoom. All I needed now was a charkha. If I wanted one just like Gandhi used,

I'd thought I'd have to order one delivered from India, which did not bode well for timely delivery based on my experiences with India's postal service (which in my opinion is a misnomer: postal disservice would more accurately describe its efficiency).

But a company called The Woolery, based in Frankfurt, Kentucky, came to my rescue. The website said "imported from India," which was a good sign of its authenticity; I just hoped they had plenty in stock in Kentucky. I ordered a book-size charkha, billed as "the authentic 'Gandhi' Charkha Wheel." With my authentic Gandhi walking stick from Gujarat, I would have a matched set.

Within a few days it arrived. Unpacking it, I was already intimidated. I could tell it was an Indian invention because it looked at once deceptively simple but actually complicated...or was it deceptively complicated but actually simple? Hand-crafted in teak wood (except for three spindles, a couple of screws, latches and the bases of the wooden wheels), it was in dimensions precisely what the name suggests: the size of a book. It had two sides, each side hinged together to fold and unfold, each side two inches deep, 9.75 inches in length and 6.75 inches wide.

There were lots of parts cleverly tucked into place, the economy of available space a reflection of how well Indians squeeze the most out of limited resources. So daunting was the prospect of properly assembling them into operational position that even after watching a few how-to videos, I still was unsure. I waited to go online with Avani for further instruction.

From the first call I could tell this would not go so well. There were tech issues; poor connectivity from Gujarat shredded or delayed or froze her words and images. There were issues with finding the best camera angle and how to set up my good old

Samsung Galaxy G8, without it tumbling off a stack of books or toppling my tripod. I had to either get up early to meet her schedule in her evening, when I am not at my best, or my evenings for her mornings, when I am also not at my best. We settled on my evenings, so as not to disrupt my writing schedule.

Then there was the problem of where I would set up the charkha. Since my knees would not allow me to work from the floor with legs crossed, I chose my living room coffee table with a low stool beside it. Avani impressed on me that my positioning was crucial; my right knee had to be parallel to the large wheel. My left arm needed room to stretch. But the coffee table is slippery, so the charkha kept sliding. I had to put a placemat under the wheel, then tape it to the table, then tape the underside of the charkha to the mat. This all took up the first session.

Her actual first homework assignment was to simply twist the edge of the cotton puni (in English it's sliver, with a hard i), which looked to me like a tampon, and pull it at the same time until it stretched into a long thin thread. Oh, I can do this, I thought, and I did a few times until I felt comfortable with it. I was beginning to get a feel for the materials, and what the cotton could do. Or so I thought.

Before each class, she asked me to relax my mind and body. In a state of panic, as when you arrive to class without having done your homework and fearful the teacher will call on you, relaxation was the last thing on my mind/body. The next step I had to tie thread to the spindle. My two left thumbs struggled for 5 minutes with that alone. Once that was accomplished, I slowly turned the wheel, at the same pulled the rest of the puni away from the wheel toward the side of my body while lifting my left arm to make an angle with the spindle. What's supposed to happen is the cotton begins to wind around the spindle, on the way to making yarn. But it did not happen that way to me. The thread broke, time after time after time. I could not get the feel of it, no matter how much Avani described the motion.

A painful week of daily classes later, she confided that I was the worst student she ever had and doubted she could teach me. But then, she almost reluctantly admitted, I was beginning to get the hang of it. I did not agree.

All the while, I videotaped in every session for posterity, thinking the world would want evidence I had gone from her worst to most improved student. She kept imploring me to not press too hard, not to pull too fast. Intellectually, I understood but physically it was impossible, and all the more frustrating because I knew if she could put her hands on mine to show me what it should feel like, I'd have a better chance.

By the last week of our month-long sessions, I all but gave up. Mentally I let go. I stopped trying so hard. And that was when it happened. When I stopped stressing about succeeding at it, I began to see some improvement.

Yet by that time, my focus had shifted, not from anything related to the technique of charkha, but to the mirror it had become to me. Stop pressing so hard. Stop pulling so hard. Let the cotton do the work; let it tell you when and how much pressure to exert. She was not talking about my spinning; she was talking about my life, how I approach problems and challenges that arise. I often have trouble letting things unfold as they are meant to unfold, on their own, without my effort but with slight prods and encouragements every now and then. This holds true in my work life, in my relationships with family and friends and in my love life.

If that was the subliminal message Gandhi meant to convey with charkha, then I mastered the wheel.

HOW TO GANDHI: A Simpler Life

Marie Kondo had it right: Spark your own joy by systematically reducing the material things in your life that do not add significantly to your happiness. But keep in mind even she slacked off a bit on the tidying thing after she had her third child, and reprioritized where her joy truly lay.

It's not necessary to spin with a charkha, though I do recommend trying it just to humble yourself. There are other ways to do it yourself without relying on outside manufacturers. Baking is one. We set up Zoom baking sessions with my granddaughter Kasey and her friend Yenna during Covid. We three loved getting hands and kitchens covered with flour—cleaning up afterward not so much—but we did learn so much about how other people spend their days in professional bakeries.

To unclutter the mind is the "tidying" chore that could easily take the rest of your life. But just in the same way you clean out your closet, take one distraction at a time. Do you really need 18 chat apps on your phone that ping you every 10 seconds? Those pings trigger stress hormones that you do not need to bring joy. Do you need those clinging and needy friends who bring only toxic energy in your mindspace? Find a diplomatic manner to put them at a distance.

5

SEX AND THE SADHU

Is Celibacy Your Path?

We live in oversexualized times. Even if you believe in a healthy sex life, too much is too much—and not in a good way. We don't need proof but just in case, the American Psychological Association (APA) Task Force on the Sexualization of Girls found evidence that the proliferation of sexualized images of girls and young women in advertising, merchandising and media is harmful to girls' self-image and healthy development.

The world is so rife with examples from the media that it would be moot to offer any. Just turn on the TV, flip through any publication, look in almost any store window, scroll through your phone, examine highway billboards.

Different cultures and in different periods of time have different mores with regard to sexual activity, no matter whether you call it coitus, copulation, intercourse, fornication, the expletive "F word" in its gerundial form, or the one word that best defines it for me: lovemaking.

I grew up at the dawn of the so-called sexual revolution of the 1960s and 70s in the Western World. Gandhi did not grow up in anything like the environment of that movement.

"That India has been a sexual wasteland for the last two centuries is... due to a combination of British prudery, adopted by the upper classes in what may be called an 'identification with the aggressor' and our own deep seated strain of Brahaminical asceticism," Sudhir Kakar, psychoanalyst, scholar of cultural psychology and the psychology of religion, and the author of 27 books including a translation of the Kamasutra and *The Ascetic of Desire*, told *Scroll*, an Indian digital publication.

Coming from a most devoutly conservative branch of Hinduism, Gandhi would have been prudish in behavior on the outside. On the inside, would he have been a typical young male with desire for physical contact with a woman? Would these two opposing attitudes have caused him personal conflict? We don't know but there are indications he would have had mixed emotions.

For myself, a red-blooded American male exposed to all that "free love" and "make love, not war" ethos, the idea of celibacy was anathema. Yet, for the purposes of my experiment, it was not hard to abstain from sexual relations for the duration. I had not been involved romantically or sexually with anyone for six years, despite my best efforts otherwise. Abstaining from physical sexual activity was not the problem; the problem was and remains the sexual fantasies of the mind, bombarded as we are by sexually seductive and suggestive images and innuendos.

The difficulty in writing about this revolves around Gandhi's own relationship with sex, and the controversy that has followed him since his days in South Africa. Yes, I will go there. First things first:

In Hindi the word brahmacharya often translates to celibacy in English. But that is not quite accurate. Etymologically, the

Hindi word stems from two Sanskrit roots: *Brahma*, which means one's own higher self, ultimate reality, absolute consciousness, and the name of the Vedic god of creation, ergo Divine Creator; and *charya*, which means to follow, engaging with proceeding. Together, it means behavior that leads to Brahma, to stay true to one's Self, or on the path of Brahma.

Celibacy, on the other hand, at its simplest means non-indulgence in sexual activity. The root comes from the Latin word, *caelibatus*, a grammatical form of *caelebs* ("unmarried"). It usually refers to a state of voluntarily being unmarried and sexually abstinent for religious reasons—within acts of renunciation. Throughout history in virtually all the major religions of the world, celibacy has been a part of their practices in one form or another. In other religions and cultures, celibacy is opposed, such as in the Shinto tradition. So too with most African and Native American traditions. The Romans considered it an aberration; they created laws levying monetary penalties against it. Jews and Muslims embrace marriage and family, so they denounce celibacy. In classical Hinduism, asceticism and celibacy in the later stages of life, after one has met one's societal obligations (meaning marriage and kids), are encouraged. And Jains, more austere than Hindus and the religion Gandhi's pious mother leaned toward (though both his parents were Vaishnavas), preach complete celibacy as the path to attain *moksha*, the release from the endless cycle of birth, death and rebirth, according to its doctrine.

There's also some confusion about the difference between abstinence and celibacy which even above I use interchangeably, but they are not the same. Sexual abstinence, also called continence, is abstaining from some or all aspects of sexual activity, often for some limited period of time. Celibacy may be defined as a voluntary religious vow not to marry or engage in sexual activity. And one more working definition, critical to my assessment: asexuality. This is the lack of sexual attraction to others, low or absent interest in the desire for sexual activity, which some consider a sexual orientation.

Of these, and after reading about Gandhi's activities and thoughts about all these, I believe Gandhi had moved through several of those categories but after declaring himself brahmacharya, he shifted his energies to asexuality. As his austerities increased, moving him higher and higher into realms approaching monkhood, it's my sense that his sacral chakra, the one located just above the pubic bone and responsible for passion, sexuality, intimacy and money, closed and his desire for sex with anyone went on complete lockdown.

His history of sexual intimacy gives more insight into how this happened, and how and why he tested his own sexual desires; and, further, how his opinions and actions on this subject affected mine.

In 1883, the 13-year-old Mohandas Karamchand married 14-year-old Kasturbai Makhanji Kapadia in Porbander, the city where their parents lived. It was a traditional arranged marriage and their youthful ages to wed were not uncommon then. He once wrote of that wedding, "As we didn't know much about marriage, for us it meant only wearing new clothes, eating sweets and playing with relatives." His wife stayed with her parents for some time, according to custom. Her husband, being a teenager full of male testosterone, had written that he regretted his natural lustful feelings: "Even at school I used to think of her, and the thought of nightfall and our subsequent meeting was ever haunting me."

The sex drive is a potent potion, very difficult to ignore without a foundation of austere self-discipline. It can distract even men and women trained to a celibate life. To wit: in 2019 the United States Roman Catholic Church reported that allegations of child sex abuse by clerics had more than doubled in a 12-month period. Countries around the world see similar trends.

In 1888, at the age of 18 and a month after his first son Harilal was born, Gandhi left his wife and newborn to attend law school in London. He did not see her again for three years. Gandhi returned from England after finishing his education, but soon went to South Africa on a work assignment as a lawyer. After this, Mohandas came to India in 1896 and then took Kasturba with him. From then on, Ba, as she was known, stayed with her husband.

Gandhi carried great remorse that with his father Karamchand Uttamchand Gandhi close to death, young Gandhi, then 16 years old and his high voltage sex drive probably peaking, chose to go to his wife's bed. As he wrote in his autobiography, "...Every night whilst my hands were busy massaging my father's legs, my mind was hovering about the bedroom and that too at a time when religion, medical science and commonsense alike forbade sexual intercourse. I was always glad to be relieved from my duty and went straight to the bedroom after doing obeisance to my father."

Of the night his father died, he wrote, "No one had dreamt that this was to be the fateful night. The danger of course, was there. It was 10:30 or 11 pm. I was giving the massage. My uncle offered to relieve me. I was glad and went straight to the bedroom. My wife, poor thing was fast asleep. But how could she sleep when I was there? I woke her up. In five or six minutes, however, the servant knocked at the door. I started with alarm. 'Get up', he said, 'Father is very ill'... and so I guessed what 'very ill' meant at that moment. I sprang out of bed... So all was over! I had but to wring my hands... I saw that if animal passion had not blinded me, I should have been spared the torture of separation from my father during his last moments... The shame...of my carnal desire even at the critical hour of my father's death... It was a blot I have never been able to efface or forget, and I have always thought that, although my devotion to my parents knew no bounds and I would have given up anything for it, yet it was weighed and found unpardonable wanting because my mind was at the same moment in the grip of lust. I have therefore, always regarded myself as a lustful, though a faithful, husband. It took me long to get free from the shackles of lust, and I had to pass through many ordeals before I could overcome it."

This is one clue as to why, with this trauma leaving a permanent scar that he associated with his lust, he tried to distance himself from what would ordinarily be a normal desire. Most of his commentary on sexual relations refer to sex as "lust," and as an act reserved solely for the purpose of procreation. "Human society is a ceaseless growth, an unfoldment in terms of spirituality. If so, it must be based on ever-increasing restraint upon the demands of the flesh. Thus, marriage must be considered to be a sacrament imposing discipline upon the partners, restricting them to the physical union only among themselves and for the purpose only of procreation when both the partners desire and prepare for it," he wrote in 1926 in *Young India*, his weekly journal published in Ahmedabad from 1919 to 1931.

Did Gandhi go as far as Epicurus, the Greek philosopher of the third century BCE, who cast sexual passion as a kind of illness that has the power to upset the equilibrium of soul and the state? Not completely but close.

He grew up in a country and at a time when sex was looked upon as taboo. Without recounting the entire history of attitudes toward sex in India, which would take us back to approximately 1500 BCE. In the Indian epics, the *Ramayana* and the *Mahabharata*, sex was considered a reciprocal duty within matrimony, equal satisfaction of both partners being the norm. There are stories about out-of-wedlock sex, sex between siblings, sex between father and daughter. Yet this from the *Mahabharata*: "O sexual desire! I know thy root. Thou art born of thought. I shall not think of thee and thou will cease to exist."

Then there's the Kama Sutra, much ballyhooed as the erotic sex manual in the West written somewhere from 400 BCE–200 CE and attributed to an Indian philosopher Vatsyayana. But it is much more: a guide to the art of living well, the nature of love, finding a life partner and maintaining one's love life that would compete with Hallmark Valentines cards for earnest love vibes.

Another deceptively emboldened Indian gesture of sexuality are the Khajuraho Group of Monuments, built between 885 CE and 1000 CE in the state of Madhya Pradesh. The UNESCO World Heritage site, a popular "must-see" stop on the tourist trail that I visited on my first trip to India, features sculptures in bas relief on the exterior walls, famous for those depicting men and women in various sexual positions that the West had not yet thought of. One can rest assured couples studied them, practiced yoga positions to gain greater flexibility before attempting them.

But, in one of the earliest examples demonstrating that even a little bit of sex sells, only 10 per cent of the images actually portray sex in action.

Then came the Brits in 1608. They—meaning the first representatives of the East India Company—landed in Surat, Gujarat, coincidentally just 600 km from where Gandhi was born. With superior weapons, economic muscle and a European cockiness Indians envied, they quickly took over the subcontinent. By 1858, England had made India a colony of "Empire," and thus began what's politely called the British Raj, officially the Government of India Act. India, it was said, was the jewel in the British crown.

With the Brits came their mores, their cultural customs, their organizational skills and their very puritanical and prudish attitudes toward sex. Layer that over India's already mixed messages. Gandhi grew up in this environment, most likely confused or at least ambivalent and curious. Then, while in law school in London, he must have picked up additional mixed messaging in England, where he was trying to blend.

There is much written, and much more criticized, about his... let's call them for now...extracurricular sexual activities. I have some conclusions and opinions.

In South Africa, long before he was called Mahatma, young barrister Gandhi met a Lithuanian architect and bodybuilder named Hermann Kallenbach. The two became fast friends. Kallenbach soon built Gandhi a house, which they shared. It's clear from letters Mohandas and Hermann had fallen in like, a mutual admiration society, as in platonic love. Why not? Both brilliant men, one with ideas, the other to execute them. They were inspiring to and inspired by each other.

But this became a very public problem for Indians when *New York Times* former executive editor and Pulitzer Prize winner Joseph Lelyveld wrote a biography entitled *Great Soul*, published in 2011 by very prestigious American publisher Knopf.

Lelyveld explores the relationship of the two men. He never flat out writes that Gandhi was gay or bisexual, but his framing, hints and tawdry innuendos that they had something more than a strong friendship lead the state assembly in Gujarat (Gandhi's home state) to unanimously and immediately ban *Great Soul.* The ban was based not on any Indians reading it—the ban came 10 days before the actual pub date of the book—but on media reviews. The state's Chief Minister at the time, Narendra Modi, said that its contents were "perverse and defamed the icon of non-violence." Modi, born in Gujarat as well, later became the country's Prime Minster and often uses Gandhi as a political flag to wave showing his patriotism.

Critics cite a few lines from the Gandhi-Kallenbach correspondence. In one widely quoted sentence, Gandhi wrote, "How completely you have taken possession of my body. This is slavery with a vengeance."

Lelyveld denied the accusations by critics, saying his work had been taken out of context: "I do not allege that Gandhi is a racist or bisexual in *Great Soul*," he told the *Times of India*. "The word 'bisexual' nowhere appears in the book."

This is true but when you open a section with "They were a couple," quoting esteemed Gandhi scholar Tripid Suhrud, it smacks of a savvy author setting up thoughts in the reader's mind by attributing someone beyond reproach.

One wonders if Lelyveld was being manipulative, perhaps even suspecting this will be of enough considerable interest to incite Gandhi-loving people to recoil. That they did.

Only in 2018 did India's Supreme Court rule that gay sex is no longer a criminal offence. The ruling overturned a 2013 judgement that upheld a colonial-era law under which gay sex had been categorized as an "unnatural offense." Before that and in Gandhi's time—and despite the laws even in these times among a large per cent of the population—there was a long-standing stigma against homosexuality, even more so than in many other countries East and West.

Stay with me now as I scrutinize, analyze and try to break down the next aspect of Gandhi's life that so often raises eyebrows. And rightly so.

But let me start not by apologizing for or explaining away his behaviors here by putting it in the context of the man.

Gandhi was an experimenter, as he put it in the subtitle of his autobiography, *The Story of My Experiments with Truth*. He explored, examined and innovated—with education, with diet, with nonviolent forms of protest...and with his own sexuality. Like Thomas Edison, inventor of electricity and much more; like Leonardo da Vinci, inventor of the flying machine and water systems; like ornithologist Salim Ali, known as the "birdman of India"; like Albert Einstein, inventor of nearly everything—men who had more failures we don't read about than their successes. I would count Gandhi among them.

His "experiment" sleeping beside young women was a deeply flawed experiment on several levels. For one thing, for a man who seemed so strategic about garnering publicity to rally people behind his causes, this experiment had the opposite effect. Even his inner circle of confidantes strongly advised him against it.

After Kasturba died in 1944, Gandhi shared his bed with naked young women a number of times, a number of women, including his personal doctor, Sushila Nayar, and his grandnieces Abha and Manu. He was some 50 years older than them. He said, and openly wrote, that he was testing his vow of brahmacharya. We don't know precisely what happened between the sheets, so to speak. The experiment was flawed not for reasons of morals, which surely one could claim to be the case for any person but especially for the man whose whole brand was based on living a moral life. Rather because, to my mind, and looking at his experience with sex, it showed how little he knew about the relationship between love and sexual arousal, between his heart organ and his sex organ. You don't simply lie next to a niece and expect to get an erection, nor would the women try to seduce him. What did he prove to anyone, and mostly to himself? Detractors would say he proved he was a pervert who obsessed about sex but only in the theoretical. Supporters...I don't know. I can't really justify it. Presumably director Richard Attenborough *was* so perplexed and concerned about how Gandhi would come off that this episode is never mentioned in the Academy Award-winning film that left such an indelible mark on so many people.

If he had tried this in the 1960s in California at the Esalen Institute, where public nudity and other social experiments helped inspire what became known as the Human Potential Movement, his activities would have fit right in. But in the India I've described, he was condemned. Perhaps even teachers at Esalen would have frowned on him in this case, failing a detailed rationale for the attempt.

While some writers and advocates say Gandhi had an

enlightened attitude about the role of women in society, I can't say I agree. This comment from him demonstrates how ancient his thinking was:

"I have always held that it is physically impossible to violate a woman against her will. The outrage takes place only when she gives way to fear or does not realize her moral strength. If she cannot meet the assailant's physical might, her purity will give her the strength to die before he succeeds in violating her... It is my firm conviction that a fearless woman, who knows that her purity is her best shield can never be dishonored. However beastly the man, he will bow in shame before the flame of her dazzling purity."

Is this the attitude that Indians picked up that may have led to such sad statistics when it comes to the incidence of rape in India? The country's National Crime Records Bureau reported that the number of reported rape cases rose from 59,945 in 2001 to 1,33,836 in 2018—an increase of 70.7 per cent in that period of time. Equally disturbing are reports of so-called "honor killings" in which family members murder their female relatives for suspected sexual activity, even if the women or girls had been raped. Of course one can't hold Gandhi responsible for any of that but what he said can be seen as absurd at best or misogynistic, in the 21st century.

Since abstaining from the physical act of sex was not the issue for me, what other way could I eliminate sex from my thoughts?

While I had been earnestly looking for love on Internet dating sites, I realized that just skimming through photos and profiles left me with desire: desire to meet someone special, go out on dates, imagine, kiss and...there it was: make love. So I quit Match.com, OKCupid.com, BrazilCupid.com and LavaPlace.com and quickly felt the pull to couple up begin to dissipate. With the release from the pressure of "the search," my energies found balance between me and me. Love myself first, I thought, and love will find me.

Being the male that I am, though, I still had sexual urges and there was no distracting my testosterone but, for better or worse, in my era there are free porn websites. Back in the day almost every teenage young man and his father stashed copies of *Playboy*, *Penthouse* and other so-called "adult" or "nudie" magazines somewhere they thought the women in their lives could not find. But they always found them. We did not read these for the articles. These rags were both a sign of masculinity and embarrassment. Today there are endless free porn websites to satisfy the urge. I'm not embarrassed to say I was a "user." I even got caught watching them when I was involved with a woman. So I "broke up" with my many pixelated girlfriends, Mia, Autumn, Katy, Bella, Reiko...etc. I couldn't believe how much free time I now had. I also began to sense my drive went down, not up. I also carried a lot less guilt and shame. I was onto something.

This gave me another idea in the letting go category. I've carried the sadness of the ones who got away who I still wanted back. These go back to junior high school up to last year—from Susan L. to Laura F. and Adriana P.

I also silently apologized to the ones whose hearts I broke: Elyse R., Margot A., Iris G. and others.

All of this was aimed at cutting ties with women with whom I had had sexual relations. Because I so strongly believe that the heart is or should be connected to the lower body parts, I felt that these were ways to exorcise the sexual dynamic with them that still resided in my head. Did it work? Partly. Yes, it helped further distance me from them emotionally, even though some of these relations went back so many years. Did it erase some memories of our sexual encounters? Not entirely. But the exercise to exorcise cleared the slate of my guilt.

Would I continue to be celibate if I met a woman I loved? Absolutely not. I consider the act of making love with a woman—not just "having sex" with her—is the physical expression, perhaps the highest express, of the deep connection I would feel for her. Plus enough studies have shown that sex is good for you, while abstaining not so much.

Having sex has repeatedly been associated with improved moods and psychological, as well as physiological, relaxation. The reason has to do with the region of the brain called the hypothalamus, which releases the hormone oxytocin. Not only does oxytocin make us calmer, but it also dampens our sense of pain. According to a 2013 study, oxytocin relieves chronic headaches. Another study suggests that the hormone endorphin, often cited for the high one feels from exercise, which is released during sexual intercourse, also relieves headaches.

Would I then argue that perhaps Gandhi, the man so conscious of healthy options we follow today such as vegetarianism, should have had more sex, not less? I won't venture to say. I just know for me, still the red-blooded male, if I fall in love, it will be a grand day in my life.

The question looming over all of this is whether sexual intercourse is moral or immoral? It is neither: it's a normal human function, like breathing and eating. Will abstinence get you closer to God? Gandhi seems to have thought so. Or it was his early guilt that made him think so. But Gandhi seems to have taken everything he did to the extreme. It is clearly not the determinant of whether we will achieve anything close to enlightenment. What is true, from a biological perspective, is that orgasm releases the hormone oxytocin into the bloodstream. Oxytocin, typically known as the "love" or "cuddle" hormone, can decrease stress. The cliche is that men go right to sleep after orgasm, and women want to cuddle. Now science proves the cliché is fact.

Nowadays, with so many ways to openly express our sexuality, alongside society's wider trends toward sex-positivity, polyamory, destigmatizing sex work, and more—who can say what is moral and what is immoral? Those lines feel blurred. In fact, the question itself seems moot. Personal choice and consent are the criteria that matter most.

If Gandhiji lived today, he would either entrench deeper into his belief that celibacy is the better path or throw up his hands and embrace a sexual revolution that leaves everyone ready to cuddle.

HOW TO GANDHI: To Sex or Not to Sex

Sexual abstinence may or may not be your path to attaining some sort of enlightened perspective on what is right and what is wrong, both with yourself and with society at large.

Ask yourself if you personally think sexual activity leads to a value system based on a moral code of ethics. Ask yourself if you feel even thoughts about sex are diverting your attention from things that should matter more to you.

Sex happens as much in the head as in the loins. If you feel you're thinking too much about sex to the detriment of your wellbeing, just as I suggested how to deal with the onslaught of violence in society and from the media, turn your eyes and ears from the barrage of sexually enticing imagery and messaging.

If you think sex enhances your appreciation of life through the tactile connection of skin to skin, go for it. If sex equates to the wholesome expression of love for a mate, go for it.

6

HE WAS WHAT HE ATE

Going Vegetarian...Or Close to It

> "He who is able to control the palate, will easily be able to control the other senses."
>
> —Mahatma Gandhi

I've already covered so many deep and lofty principles at the heart of Gandhi's concept of morality that the question of what we eat might seem a minor consideration. Gandhi, however, considered health—and specifically diet—to be of the highest importance. He devoted decades of study and personal experimentation to questions of food and drink.

> "There is nothing so closely connected with us as our body, but there is also nothing perhaps of which our ignorance is so profound, or our indifference so complete."
>
> — Mahatma Gandhi, "A Guide To Health"

No big surprise that he condemned the use of tobacco, opium, alcohol, and even tea and coffee as poisonous to a healthy body. But his recommended ideal diet for man does raise eyebrows:

Gandhi referenced science and human biology to conclude that man should live on a fruit-based diet, like our closest monkey cousins. He further declared that adopting a raw diet would meet all our nutritional needs and save untold time and resources currently spent on cooking.

The Mahatma described the results of his own attempts at a fruit-only vegan diet (consisting of plantain, groundnut, olive oil, and lime or another citrus fruit). "During this period, I have been able to keep well where others have been attacked by disease, and my physical as well as mental powers are now greater than before."

After a fruit diet, he espoused the vegetable diet as second-best, and wrote at length about the value of different vegetables and grains, recommending against sugar, salt and other condiments. He described the "pure superstition" that values milk as "so deep-rooted that it is futile to think of removing it."

He might never have imagined milk consumption in the United States would decline 42 per cent over the past half century, with similar patterns reported in the United Kingdom, as plant-based milks and other alternatives emerge. When he wrote of substituting the almond for cow's milk in 1921, he unknowingly predicted the billion-dollar sales of almond milk in 2022.

In addition to *what* is eaten, he had strong opinions on *when* and *how much*. He suggested fasting at least once every two weeks. He wrote: "I can also say from my experience that there is absolutely no need to eat more than twice, for a man who has passed the period of youth, and whose body has attained its fullest growth."

Gandhi compared one's body to a king who "may do infinite good to his subjects, or be the source of untold mischief. Indeed, the body may be a good servant, but, when it becomes a master, its powers of evil are unlimited."

He concluded, "All sins like lying, cheating and stealing are ultimately due to our subjection to the palate."

It's clear that, in Gandhi's opinion, food choices have a lot to do with self-control. He challenged himself similarly to his stances on celibacy and simplicity, to re-train the pleasure impulses in which so many others indulge. If an extravagant meal with a variety of rich foods is a luxury for some, Gandhi sought the exact opposite. His pleasure came from renunciation, from eating the bare minimum for survival and limiting his intake with attention some called obsessive.

But there was more to it for him than just compulsive self-control, which modern psychologists recognize as a key aspect of eating disorders like anorexia. His diet and his greater purpose fed into each other.

Nico Slate explains in *Gandhi's Search for the Perfect Diet* (University of Washington Press, 2019): "The pillars of his diet—vegetarianism, limited salt and sweets, rejecting processed food, eating raw food, fasting—were all deeply connected to his politics and, in particular, to his conception of nonviolence... Equality was at the core of his nonviolence—and of what he ate."

Ahimsa dictates considering the lives of all creatures, and Gandhi considered vegetarianism the most ethical choice, so as not to live off the deaths or suffering of other animals. This goes for both the individual and the body politic.

Vegetarian and pet groups often cite Gandhi who wrote: "The greatness of a nation and its moral progress can be judged by the way its animals are treated."

The timeline of the man's lifetime relationship with food is not a straight progression, but a series of experiments, discoveries and reversals. The evolution of his beliefs around diet gives me a bit of hope for my own approach to eating well: it's the journey not the destination.

He equated lust for food with other sensual desires he felt should be denied. Gluttony of the tongue could lead to moral collapse in all areas. "Gandhi rejected any food that might tempt him to put bodily cravings above spiritual and political pursuits. Yet he struggled to distinguish dangerous pleasures from healthy delights," wrote Slate.

Born into a vegetarian family in 1869, a young Mohandas spent a year in his late teens secretly eating meat before swearing off it again and joining the London Vegetarian Society in 1890. He apparently had a love-hate relationship with mangoes, and found them so irresistible that he later declared, "Mango is a cursed fruit." Even his decision to eliminate milk from his life was fraught as he ended up reintroducing goat's milk several years after vowing never to consume dairy products, dramatically referring to his milk consumption as "the tragedy of my life."

A lot of Gandhi's dietary principles are extremely popular today, brought into the mainstream by authors like Michael Pollan, vegan celebrities like Joaquin Phoenix, Benedict Cumberbatch, Natalie Portman and vegetarian icons like Sir Paul McCartney, who took it up under his wife Linda's influence. Vegetarian and health-focused documentary films that might have been seen at food conferences in the past are now reaching millions: "Cowspiracy" (executive produced by Leonardo DiCaprio and streaming globally on Netflix, despite some claims of inaccuracy), "Forks Over Knives" (the hit documentary that sparked a series of best-selling books and a movement of its own), "The Game Changers" (executive produced by Arnold Schwarzenegger and Pamela Anderson), "Fat Sick and Nearly Dead," "What the Health," "Earthlings" (narrated by Joaquin Phoenix), and more.

Just to break out the consistent message from one of these films, consider "The Game Changers," directed by Louie Psihoyos, of the Oscar-winning 2009 dolphin advocacy film "The Cove." His 2018 documentary follows an unlikely proponent of plant-based eating, an English mixed martial artist and UFC (Ultimate Fighting Championship) competitor. Wilks is astounded to learn that ancient Roman gladiators were primarily vegetarian. Raised on eggs and lamb chops, Wilks had been immersed in a macho athlete culture with an unswerving belief that "meat gives you energy." Through speaking with elite vegetarian athletes, nutritionists and scientists, he discovers incredible performance-based results from changing one's diet from meat to plants. Even for those of us without Olympic aspirations, the outcomes are eye-opening. The doc states a plethora of health benefits. Switching to a plant-based diet can reduce measures of inflammation by 29 per cent in just 3 weeks. People who get all of their protein from plants reduce their risk of heart disease by 55 per cent. Studies have shown a plant-based diet can even reverse heart disease.

A study published in 2020 by the American Journal of Clinical Nutrition summarizes that "consumption of animal products increases the risk for cardiovascular disease, cancer, diabetes, obesity and other disorders." Furthermore, it concludes, "When omnivorous individuals change to a plant-based diet... the risk of these health problems diminishes."

Meanwhile, statistics demonstrate the staggering environmental impact of meat-based agriculture. Research at the

University of Oxford found that while meat and dairy provide just 18 per cent of the world's calories and 37 per cent of protein, meat and dairy production use up the vast majority of global farmland, 83 per cent. Simply growing enough animal feed for livestock requires huge amounts of deforested land and water, and contributes to pollution on a massive scale. Meat-based agriculture contributes nearly 15 per cent of total greenhouse gas emissions worldwide, greater than all emissions from transportation combined. Shifting away from livestock farming in the United States could reduce agriculture emissions up to 73 per cent. Paying attention to these measures now could alter the fate of humanity as we try to beat the clock on catastrophic climate change.

It's hard to hear these statistics and deny that the less meat we farm and consume, the better it will be for both individual health outcomes and our planet's environmental crises. So, are we being the change yet?

Choices like eating raw, eating local, whole grains and unprocessed food have reached well beyond their original niche. Gandhi would be thrilled by the food justice movement which works to provide healthy and nutritious foods to people experiencing poverty, and grassroots efforts that support organic and independent farming. As magazines like *Vegan Life* make clear, it's not just a diet, it's a lifestyle and a personal form of activism. From its website: "A truly cruelty-free life is more than just the food you eat, so while you'll find plenty of amazing vegan food here, we also highlight inspirational vegan activists, environmental issues, and vegan lifestyle tips and advice."

Ironically, restricting your food options can represent its own kind of freedom.

Nico Slate summed it up: "Freedom from craving, freedom from desire—that was the independence, the swaraj, Gandhi most prized. Like the British Empire, meat and wine deprived the individual of that most basic right—the freedom to be at peace with oneself."

People in India practiced vegetarianism long before Gandhi was born. Recent statistics indicate that Indians have the lowest rate of meat consumption in the world. The actual numbers are tough to pin down as various studies and surveys have shown per centages of vegetarianism ranging from 20 per cent to 40 per cent of the population. Some theorize the survey responses are skewed by a tendency to underreport meat consumption because of cultural expectations and pressures. It appears meat-eating is slightly on the rise in India. Regardless, even among those who do eat meat, less than 30 per cent of Indians report eating it regularly. Globally, even at the lowest end of the range, the rate of vegetarianism exceeds the next closest nation, Mexico at 19 per cent. Other countries trail further behind.

In his day, Gandhi's precise way of eating was considered strange even in his homeland. He did not convert the masses to his diet. Most felt he was too extreme.

While in England, he found vegetarian restaurants and kindred spirits. The London Vegetarian Society, which Gandhi joined in 1890, still exists today (now goes by the name of The Vegetarian Society) and is the world's oldest vegetarian society celebrating its 175th anniversary. The charity organization encourages plant-based eating through community awareness and actions such as the annual National Vegetarian Week, a vegan food bank donation program and a cookery school with a teaching kitchen on the grounds of its Victorian mansion headquarters in the town of Altrincham, outside of Manchester, England.

I had hoped to spend time there but due to Covid, it was closed. So I spoke by Zoom to the Vegetarian Society's Chief Executive, Richard McIlwain, about the organization during Gandhi's time and today.

Richard explained that shortly before Gandhi's arrival in London in 1888, there had been a kind of ideological split within the Vegetarian Society. A section of members felt the Society should be about more than vegetarianism, and should also require abstinence from alcohol and tobacco. They felt the movement was about clean living in all areas, not just food. These hardcore reformers were some of the folks that Gandhi spent time with during his years at law school in London.

When Gandhi arrived, he already didn't eat meat, based on the strict disciplines of his mother's branch of Hinduism. But, adds Richard, "he also starts to see the wider morality around not eating meat. Rather than it just being a religious thing, it becomes a sort of secular moral thing as well... I think those two have been triggers for a long time. One sort of moral and outward facing and other a bit more inward facing, maybe even a bit selfish." Today, Richard noted in their surveys on why people choose to avoid meat, "It's still very much health and animal welfare, but the environmental angle is starting to creep up. And it's not just climate, it's biodiversity loss as well. I think these are the things that ultimately, actually are going to really affect our lives at the end of the day."

For Gandhi, there was a moral imperative and a health imperative to vegetarianism and both developed over the course of his lifetime through influences like his family of origin, his time with the vegetarians of London, and his own thoughts and experiments. Today, those imperatives still drive diet choices, plus the urgency of environmental catastrophe brings us to a new level of responsibility and guilt. If you can't eat right for yourself or the animals, we are reminded, what about your children and grandchildren's air and water?

McIlwain again: "We've got this fantastic history, but we need to be fighting fit for the 21st century... Clock is ticking, eight years to really do something around climate and some of the other issues... Fundamentally, [diet's] the one thing they can change. Not everyone could afford an electric vehicle or take the bus to work every day and get rid of the car or turn the heating down, but they can actually change their diet tonight."

I was impressed by McIlwain's open-minded approach to new outreach, which frankly sounded like the opposite of many die-hard vegans I've encountered. He was a realist about the movement. He acknowledged that roughly 3 per cent of the United Kingdom population identifies as vegetarian or vegan, admittedly still a niche in terms of people who have completely committed to eliminating meat and/or dairy and eggs. But according to him and others, the classification doesn't need to be so binary.

New labels have come out for people along the spectrum of meat eating:

Reducetarians: Committed to eating less meat and dairy and fewer eggs—following their own heart and individual motivations (which may include improving their health, protecting the environment, and sparing farmed animals from cruelty).

Flexitarian: Follows a semi-vegetarian diet centered on plant foods with the occasional inclusion of meat.

Then we have Mark Bittman's book *VB6: Eat Vegan Before 6:00 to Lose Weight and Restore Your Health...for Good*, in which he followed a healthy vegan diet (no meat, dairy, or processed foods) until 6 p.m. every day; after that, he'd eat however he wanted, though mostly in moderation. Bittman's book debuted at #1 on the *New York Times* bestseller list in its first week on sale and was followed by a *VB6 Cookbook*, naturally.

McIlwain describes the other movements this way: "You're reducing your meat. So you're not going full on as vegan, but you are going some way towards, [and] I've said we need to celebrate that. We need not berate people just because they aren't full on vegetarian or vegan. If somebody does a meat-free Monday or does a couple of days meat-free, that's great. They're on that journey. They're on that treadmill. Actually, the very fact that they've had that initial thought to say, 'Maybe I should reduce meat,' suggests that they're now open to a little bit more, a little bit more...

No one's ever perfect. Vegans often get shot down because some of them try to put themselves on pedestals. Of course, the second you put yourself on a pedestal, all anybody wants to do is throw rocks at you."

Meat in moderation may be a more achievable goal for most of us than total elimination, and even Gandhi was tortured by his own demands for purity and perfection, and sometimes frustrated family members with his rigidity.

McIlwain says, "It's not about do no harm, it's about minimize harm as far as you can."

So I've been on my own journey through vegetarianism over the years with varied success. I grew up with meat at the center of every meal: my Dad was a meat and potatoes man, my Mom pulled out all the stops on holidays and special occasions with her legendary brisket, corned beef and tongue. If we had the occasional frozen TV dinner, it was the Salisbury Steak. This, to me, was living the good life.

Then in my twenties, I found a new way. No more steak and burgers, nothing frozen or packaged, my body is a temple. I learned how to cook magical new ingredients like tofu for dinners with my daughter, who had become a vegetarian herself in 7th grade after reading the savage pig hunt scene in *Lord of the Flies*.

Still, chicken and fish have always been a mainstay of my Jewish culture. Smoked salmon, gefilte fish, and at least 42 chicken recipes straight from my mother's cookbook. I wasn't ready to give them up. Plus, as a travel writer covering the restaurant and hospitality world, I was invited to taste some of the most decadent and revered preparations of animal flesh available. I have experienced firsthand the gluttony that Gandhi decries. If I'm enjoying the taste of something, I can't turn it off. I've paid the price over more nights of indigestion than I care to admit.

So, this would be my chance to make a major change both for my personal health and my quest to be a better person with a smaller carbon footprint. I took myself out for one last meal of meat, appropriately enough, in Jersey City.

I started by tapering off and then went cold turkey (as in *no* turkey, chicken, fish or meat). I didn't go full vegan but I tried to minimize eggs and dairy. I had a head start on cutting down milk and cream as I had learned it triggers the symptoms of joint inflammation from my Polymyalgia Rheumatica (PMR). That was enough incentive for reduction. But how do you motivate for change when it's *not* self-serving?

Over the two years of this project, I've struggled to maintain my vow of vegetarianism. I've gone months in accordance, making holier-than-thou demands of dinner party hosts, and then suddenly fallen off the wagon for a week-long binge of endless meat. When I was carefully watching every meal portion, I did feel lighter as those morning-after regrets were fewer and far between. But I needed something more than grains and vegetables. Lately, I've settled on a pescatarian compromise. Eating fish seems to give me the protein I crave and while it is decidedly not vegetarian, I do feel better physically and morally. Step by step.

"For many vegetarians—and particularly for organization leaders—'being' a vegetarian is not a static state; it is a process of 'becoming' through shifting personal motivations and increasing degrees of commitment."—Donna Maurer, *Vegetarianism: Movement or Moment*

Gandhi was disciplined about *what* he ate, but he is especially known for the periods of time when he ate nothing at all—his famous extended fasts.

Sources report that he fasted 18 significant times throughout his life for various reasons.

The first instances were in 1913, while in South Africa, when he fasted for one week as atonement for a moral failure of two other people at his ashram, and later that year when he ate only one meal a day for a period of time to mourn the police killing striking laborers during the Miners March.

Back in India, he continued to use fasting as a method of atonement, community harmony, and to add pressure to movements and demands in progress (increased wages for mill workers, change in election policy, protesting violence). The fasts ranged in length from days to weeks, lasting as long as 21 days on more than one occasion.

He fasted while in Yerwada jail in 1932 in protest of the treatment of "untouchables" and caste separation. This resulted in the Gandhi-Ambedkar Poona Pact, providing a common electorate for all Hindus and new rights for the untouchables in the legislature. Gandhiji considered fasting a non-violent tool against injustice and also as a route to penance when violence or wrongdoing occurred. He engaged in hunger strikes to highlight the righteousness of his moral principles and change the minds of opponents or obstacles to liberty.

As for me, I looked forward to—yet had anxiety about—fasting a la Gandhi. Unlike his fasts, all as protests against injustices toward mills workers and others, I took them on as protest against my physical body, to prove I was not a prisoner of my own gluttonous desires.

Gandhi was oriented to fasting watching his mother keep long ritual fasts. In one account I read, the Mahatma followed his own ritual routine for long fasts. He would have lemon juice and honey with warm water before he started. He'd drink water, occasionally with salt or lemon juice, through the day. To conserve energy, he would sleep more than usual. And *Time* magazine reported in 1943: "Each morning the Mahatma was wheeled on his bed to a palace bathroom to be shaved and washed. He was massaged twice daily, had mud packs placed on his head. He was given occasional enemas."

In the realm of protests, fasting has another name: hunger strike. Among people who have undertaken hunger strikes are

Mexican labor activist Cesar Chavez, black civil rights activist and comedian Dick Gregory, Hollywood actor Mia Farrow and many others. There have also been protest fasts on behalf of the Tamil diaspora, Palestinians, Irish Republicans, Cuban dissidents and more.

Nowadays many people fast for reasons of personal health: to purify their bodies, clean out their intestinal systems or lose weight quickly. People go on fruit fasts, calorie restriction fasts, micronutrient restriction fasts and the increasingly popular intermittent fast.

I realized I've been doing the last type for many years. The first I took were during the Jewish holiday of Yom Kippur, the holiest day for Jews. The Torah commands all healthy Jewish adults except for new mothers to abstain from eating and drinking between sundown on the evening before Yom Kippur and nightfall the next day. The fast is believed to cleanse the body and spirit, not to serve as a punishment. But for a kid of 13, it was punishment and a test of discipline. I watched my grandfather, a devout Jew who also had heart problems and Type 2 diabetes, struggle to get through to the evening without a midday pick-me-up. The reward of not eating all day would be a big dinner of deli cold cuts, which certainly did not help Grandpa's heart but which I relished.

Now there are whole movements and medical protocols revolving around intermittent fasting. An intermittent fast simply means not eating for periods of time—the time varying from 12 to 18 up to 48 hours. These fast are good for one's health. A 2019 paper in the *New England Journal of Medicine* found that eating within an 8-hour bracket of time and fasting for 18 hours can reduce risk of disease and promote longer life.

My friend Peter Moore and his co-author David Zinczenko, both former editors of *Men's Health* magazine, wrote the bestselling *The 8-Hour Diet* (Rodale Book, 2012) with a subtitle that tells us its motive: "Watch the Pounds Disappear Without Watching What You Eat!"

For myself, over the years, and especially as an editor working in a frantic newsroom with my famously delicate stomach all aflutter, I often skipped lunch altogether. I still do; once my mind gets revving, my tummy does too.

But a longer fast would be another matter.

My longest fast during these last two or so years was only three days. I can see Bapu smirking. I did them about once every few months. But it was enough to reap the benefits of giving my digestive system a break, and to observe what goes on in my mind about food, and my attachment to the eating ritual. One question I had to think about: With all that new free time, what would I do constructively with it?

What I learned was how much time I spend thinking about what I want to eat, how long it takes to buy and prepare a meal, how much it costs to eat and more so how much it costs to go out to eat, how quickly it all goes down, how little I appreciate the taste while I am eating, how much I dread cleaning up afterward. And finally, how much weight I put on if I don't monitor my desire to put another bite in my mouth just because the food is on my plate.

HOW TO GANDHI:
Eating Plant-Based (More or Less)

With a tip of the hat to Michael Pollan—"Eat food. Not too much. Mostly plants." (from his *In Defense of Food*)

Set a goal to eat only vegetarian or vegan for a minimum of 30 days. Pay attention to your body and note how you feel at the beginning and end.

Schedule a regular meat-free day of the week, or week of the month.

Sign up for your local Community Supported Agriculture (CSA). Receive a harvest of fresh, whole produce, supporting farmers and your own health at the same time.

Prepare and serve a plant-based meal for family or friends. Make it fun and share your favorites. The gamechangersmovie.com website is full of recipes.

Consider the source of your food. Shop ethically. Join one of the emerging community-driven urban organic food schemes, such as Mumbai Organic Farmers and Consumers Association), started in 2009; the Adarsh Bio Organics in Gurgaon (Haryana), started in 2013; or Sahaja Aharam Organic Consumers and Producers Cooperative, started in 2009 in Hyderabad.

For extra credit, examine the other animal products in your life—leather goods, health and beauty products—and look for vegan alternatives when possible.

In consultation with your doctors, consider fasting for short periods to detoxify, reset, and commune with your health. Go easy on yourself, it's not necessary to level up to Gandhi.

GANDHI IN SOUTH AFRICA

Years of Fighting Discrimination All for Naught?

Most people familiar with only parts of the Gandhi "legend" can usually recount the story they say converted him into a social justice activist. It was when he got thrown off a train in South Africa for sitting in a whites-only section. The rest of the details may remain vague or unknown to them, largely unaware that Gandhi went on to spend 21 years there, from 1893 to 1914, from the formative age of almost 24 to 45. In those years he also formed and experimented with the ideas—of nonviolent resistance (satyagraha), of how to organize aligned groups (such as the Natal Indian Congress to protest oppressive treatment of the native Africans and Indians), of communal ashram-like living (Phoenix Farm near Durban) and how to endure jail (in 1909 he served a three-month jail term)—that would become the signatures of his life.

It was also in South Africa that Gandhi, under the influence of the ideas of Leo Tolstoy and John Ruskin, began to live a life of premodern simplicity, publishing his famous critique of Western modernity, *Hind Swaraj*, and adopting a simple village way of life. Finally, it was in South Africa that Gandhi took a vow of sexual abstinence, or brahmacharya, an aspect of his spiritual development that Gandhi disciples such as Nelson Mandela and

Martin Luther King Jr. chose not to follow.

He had left the country of his birth as a young barrister named Mohandas Karamchand Gandhi, traversed 5,000 miles across the Arabian Sea and the Indian Ocean to South Africa, to work for Muslim Indian traders there; and returned to India as Mahatma Gandhi, the activist standing up for the freedom of all oppressed and especially freedom from India's colonizer of about 200 years.

Mr. Gandhi, in spearheading popular resistance, had succeeded in gaining India's independence from the United Kingdom. In South Africa, not so much. In 1948, the same year that the Mahatma was assassinated in New Delhi, the National Party-led South African government passed apartheid, a political system based on institutionalized racial segregation and discrimination. Apartheid is an Afrikaans word meaning "separateness," or "the state of being apart," literally "aparthood"—basically anathema to everything Gandhi advocated. Officially, apartheid was ended in 1994, thanks to the efforts of Nelson Mandela and sanctions from multiple countries condemning the merciless policy—but not without much bloodshed. The well-respected South African Institute of Race Relations (SAIRR) reported in 1990 that 10 South Africans were being killed every day as the direct result of political violence; the death count was 8,500 from 1984 to 1990.

Through the 80s and into the 90s, I watched this insult to humanity from our side of the pond, singing with others "Free Nelson Mandela," the 1984 song by the British group The Special AKA... *"Twenty-one years in captivity. Are you so blind that you cannot see?"*

We wore Mandela t-shirts, we saw Mandela wall posters, we followed the progress of the anti-Apartheid movement, we watched TV news footage of violence in the city streets going as far back as 1960. That was the year of the so-called Sharpeville massacre, when South Africa police shot dead 69 blacks protesting the "pass laws" which controlled their every move, reminiscent of how Hitler controlled the Jews in Germany. The penalties for disobeying the pass laws were as brutal as they were for Jews of Europe.

Then, finally, almost unbelievably, after more than two decades, Mandela was released from prison. He was elected South Africa's first black president and arguably the world's most blatant example of government-approved—no, government-mandated—racism was dismantled.

Or was it?

Almost immediately upon landing at the airport in Johannesburg, I sensed that there were still two South Africas and that racism was still alive and well. Or not well, as the case may better be expressed. I'd commissioned my friend Elizabet Kurumlu, a Turkish woman who wears many hats as tour guide, field director, sometime cinematographer and all-around brilliant problem solver, to accompany me. On the way out of the airport, we passed a group of terminal employees, all black, singing a beautiful joyous song in their language, clapping hands. It could have been in Sotho, Sesotho, Swazi, Setswana or Zulu. I did not need to know what language because the message was clearly one of shared happiness. I was told they were singing happy birthday. I was tempted to chime in but I felt like I would be crashing a party to which I wasn't invited.

An hour or so later I knew I was not in Kansas anymore, or any other white-majority region of the world. As we approached our B&B in a suburban area called Hurlingham Gardens (not to be confused with Hurlingham Gardens in South West London), a 20-minute drive from downtown Joberg and Gandhi Square, I noticed all the nicely appointed homes hid behind high walls. The walls had barbed wire at the top; a small toll booth was beside the entrance gate. Inside the booth was a black man, who opened the gate if your name appeared on his guest list.

Obviously the white inhabitants of these homes feared an invasion of unwanted intruders. Our white host was charming and hospitable, but I felt uncomfortable, as though I was trapped in an insulated bubble without air.

That night we had our first meal at a Thai restaurant in Nelson Mandela Square, a retail and dining area and one of the largest open public spaces in the country. In the middle of the plaza was a majestic 20-foot high (6-meter) statue of Mandela, a popular attraction for locals and tourists. Liz took my photo hamming it up under the statue. Well-dressed whites and blacks easily comingled in the plaza and restaurant. All seemed relatively integrated and without tension.

Then next morning we met with Eric Itzkin, deputy director of Immovable Heritage as part of the city's Directorate of Arts, Culture and Heritage. He also wrote *Gandhi's Johannesburg: Birthplace of Satyagraha* (2000; Frank Connock Publication). He took us on an eye-opening tour based on his book. In the center of Gandhi Square, which is around the corner from Gandhi's humble first law office in South Africa, Eric proudly displayed a statue of Gandhi. Introduced in 2003, the statue depicts a young lawyer in his legal gown. In 2015 a protester, among a group wielding placards reading "Racist Gandhi must fall," splashed white paint on the statue and the plaque under it. Eric confided it broke his heart but that he was not unaccustomed to such anti-Gandhi sentiment, especially in the wake of the global Black Lives Matter Movement that started in about 2013, prompted by the deaths of several black Americans at the hands of the police.

The accusations that Gandhi was racist stem from derogatory comments he had made about blacks in South Africa, among them using the term "kaffir."

In *The South African Gandhi: Stretcher-Bearer of Empire* (Navayana Publishing New Delhi; and Stanford University Press, 2015), sociology professor Ashwin Desai and history professor Goolam Vahed, both South Africans, make a string case evidencing Gandhi's pattern of racist actions and writings. In reading their book, I did not want to accept that they may be right. Yet, compelled by their observations and conclusions, I felt it my duty to meet with Professor Desai when I got to Durban.

We met at Ike's Books and Collectables in a small and very hot upstairs room. It all started out quite amicably. He spoke of his childhood hero John Wayne, the man who killed Indians—and the irony of the double meaning of Indian did not escape him. Of Mahatma Gandhi, Desai said he bought the majority of what teachers and books had spoon fed him: a fighter for freedom, a hero of the downtrodden.

"You build up the idea of an all-encompassing figure," he said.

It was only when he dove into the man's background—what he wrote—that he began to see Gandhi in a wholly different light. How Gandhi tried to play both ends: as loyal to England, South Africa's colonizer; and as defender of Indian and Black rights.

How Gandhi frequently referred to natives of Africa as "savages" with whom he did not want Indians to be associated, either in public places, organizations or in such restrictive social policies as those he himself experienced in Pietermaritzburg.

Desai poo-pooed respected Indian social and political observer Ramachandra Guha regarding Gandhi's racist attitudes in his book, *Gandhi Before India* (Alfred A. Knopf, 2014).

"Guha basically writes Gandhi's racism out of the man's history," he said. "It's a shocker to me that post-1990 this chapter has been airbrushed out of the picture."

He was beginning to convince me with irrefutable facts.

In my own experience in South Africa, I felt the cloud of racism on a number of occasions. Driving from Johannesburg to Durban, pockets of poor settlements with houses of thatched roofs, peopled by only blacks, dotted the breathtaking landscape. I came to know they were communities marginalized by white South Africans. At the commune Gandhi has founded called Phoenix House, now a museum, a young dark-skinned man named Sanele, who served as our guide, took us aside to a quiet corner and confided that a rumbling of anger against whites still in power boiled under the surface and that he would not be surprised if another uprising would soon boil over. I had felt this sentiment almost palpably.

As our conversation with Professor Desai came to an end, I asked Desai the question I had asked throughout my travels: despite any objections to Gandhi's flaws and imperfections as a man, did Desai himself adhere to any of the Gandhian principles I was following. First, he clarified, they were not "Gandhi's principles." They were basic lifestyle and philosophical choices that have been out there in the air for many centuries of human existence. So I explained the ones I was following and how I was going to write about them.

At that, he let out a huge laugh and jumped from his seat, taking both me and Liz (who was videotaping the conversation) aback.

"Forgive me but this is such a typical United States take: you guys are so obsessed with the I-isms. 'I am processing and working through this. I am the moral compass.' It f***ing drives me crazy that you guys are so I-centric. All in the context of some being niceness. Go sit in an ashram and carry on with yourself. Really. For me I want to help mobilize people."

I left in a real existential crisis. Was he right? Was I even doing something of value here? Despite my world travels and my claim to be a "citizen of the Planet," was I the ugly egocentric American? Was my experiment, and my life's work as a writer all a coverup for my self aggrandizement? I thought I was also attempting to mobilize people to do the right thing—for themselves and for the world at large. Suddenly I felt more like Gandhi than ever. Those, including myself, who sensed Gandhi was selfishly driven, often leaving his roles as father and husband in the wake in the name of a righteous cause.

These thoughts stayed with me as I interviewed several more people in South Africa. My 10 weeks on the road, from Istanbul to India to South Africa, were beginning to catch up to me and despite interviews with prominent Indian South Africans—peace activist Ela Gandhi, granddaughter of the Mahatma and former Member of South Africa's Parliament; Satish Dhupelia, a media professional who was instrumental in establishing the 1860 Heritage Centre museum in Durban; and his sister Kirti Menon, an education reform activist and chairman of South Africa's

Gandhi Centenary Committee—half of my mind was on a flight back home to California and other half still chewing on Professor Desai's observations, way too close to my home.

From Durban we took a shortcut back to Joberg before our flight back to Istanbul, opting to fly rather than drive the 350 miles we'd traversed 12 days earlier. We spent two nights at the home where Gandhi had lived with his good friend, architect Hermann Kallenbach, in 1908-09, the house now a B&B called Satyagraha House, in which every room was chock-a-block with Gandhi memorabilia. Liz and I wandered through the room, marinating and absorbing the life and times of the man. It was a fitting ending. But there was one more stop.

Our very last experience was a visit to the very impressive and emotionally moving—even emotionally draining—Apartheid Museum, opened in 2001 to illustrate the rise and fall of apartheid. Exhibition photos, murals and old videos depict the atrocious conditions and treatment of Blacks after centuries of colonialism and more than 40 years of life under apartheid. A section identifies the role Gandhi played in South Africa's struggle for equality, but sensibly the major emphasis is on Mandela and others who fought for freedom. I kept returning, though, to uplifting footage of the exuberant concert in 2008 celebrating Mandela's 90th birthday at London's Hyde Park, where more than 30 top international and South African musicians performed. The video, on an endless loop, features the late Amy Winehouse leading a rousing 5-minute version of "Nelson Mandela." One could not ignore the image of this pale and skinny, painfully shy and at times physically awkward young Brit whose incandescent voice nonetheless touches anyone with a soul, singing her heart out for a black man who led the fight to free black people. The juxtaposition spoke volumes to me about the transcendent power of a cause based on the simple moral principle that we all—regardless of race, creed, religion or national origin—deserve the right to live in peace and harmony.

That song rang in my ears en route to the airport.

In the back seat of the Uber, I whispered to Liz, "We made it." I meant we made it through this trip without incident, other than that her $200 boots were stolen. But in retrospect, I meant it as more hopeful than reflective—that we as a society are trying hard to make it a just world.

7

THE LEAP OF FAITH

Gandhi the Pragmatist v Gandhi the True Believer

"He who is full of faith and zeal and has subdued his senses obtains Knowledge; having obtained Knowledge, he soon attains the Supreme Peace. But the man who is ignorant and without faith and always doubting goes to ruin. Not this world nor the world beyond nor happiness is for the doubting soul."

—*Bhagavad Gita*

"You must not lose faith in humanity. Humanity is like an ocean; if a few drops of the ocean are dirty, the ocean does not become dirty."

—Mahatma Gandhi

A joke may not be the most pious way to begin a discussion about Gandhi's faith. Nor will this one align with Gandhi's own ideas but it raises legitimate questions about exactly what is faith, who is God and what is his (or her) role in a human life. It's not really a joke as much as a spiritual parable, told in many variations depending on one's religious affiliation:

A storm overwhelms a small town. As the waters rise, the local preacher kneels in prayer on the already flooded church porch. Soon one of the townsfolk paddles toward him in a canoe.

"Better get in, Preacher. The waters are rising fast."

"Thanks," says the preacher, "but have faith in the Lord. He will save me."

Now the preacher is up on the balcony when another guy zips alongside in a motorboat: "Come on, Preacher. We need to get you out of here. The levee's gonna break any minute."

Again, the preacher defers: "I shall remain. The Lord will see me through."

The levee breaks; the preacher is now clinging to the steeple when a helicopter shows up. "Grab the ladder, Preacher," shouts a state trooper. "This is your last chance."

Once again, the preacher insists the Lord will deliver him. But he drowns. In Heaven, he beseeches The Almighty: "Lord, I had unwavering faith in you. Why didn't you deliver me from that flood?"

Bewildered, God replies: "What did you want from me? I sent you two boats and a helicopter."

At what point is faith alone not enough? When does free will become necessary?

The 19th century reclusive American poet Emily Dickinson wanted to have it both ways as a safeguard. She put it succinctly in one of her most famous 4-line poems:

"Faith" is a fine invention
For Gentlemen who see!
But Microscopes are prudent
In an Emergency!

Mahatma Gandhi acted as though he too wanted it both ways, absolute faith in his God while also going to extremes to ensure he accomplished whatever was necessary to not drown, metaphorically speaking.

Gandhi was brought up in the Hindu tradition by his devout mother, Putlibai, who was by all accounts so devoted that she would eat only after prayers (puja), attend temples regularly, maintain fasts and follow all other rituals to the letter. She imbued her children with this same rigor toward all things holy. The Gandhis were Sanatani Hindus, who incorporate teachings from the Vedas, Upanishads and other Hindu texts such as the *Ramayana* and Bhagavad Gita. As such, they follow such virtues as honesty, refraining from injuring living beings, purity, goodwill, mercy, patience, forbearance, self-restraint, generosity, and asceticism.

He was deeply impressed by the ethical and spiritual outlook of Hinduism. Gandhi said, "The chief value of Hinduism lies in holding the actual belief that all life is one i.e. all life coming from one universal source, call it Allah, God or Parameshwara."

When asked his religion, he'd say he was a Vaishnav. The largest Hindu sect, its practitioners consider the god Vishnu the sole supreme being, above all other Hindu deities. Yet Gandhi never went to a temple, nor kept idols in his house or offered sweets to the God, nor wore beads. By explanation, he said, "I am a Vaishnav by heart," and referenced such qualities as "one who feels empathy, hold no grudges, keeps a pure heart, slanders no one, never lies, and remains free of temptation..."

Of the many ways he has written about his faith, this one by him comes closest to my own attempt to define the undefinable:

"To me God is Truth and Love. God is Ethics and Morality.

God is Fearlessness. God is essence of life and light and yet He is above and beyond all these. God is conscience. He is even the atheism of the atheist. For in his boundlessness, God permits the atheist to live. He is the searcher of hearts. He is a personal God to those who need his personal presence. He is embodied to those who need his touch. He is the purest essence... He is all things to all men. He is in us and yet above and beyond us."

Despite being rooted in his family's Hindu faith, he was respectful and interested in all religions and welcomed the chance to speak with leaders in other faiths. Among the more than 400 books he read in his lifetime, a great number delved into the origins and tenets of the world's religions. I believe he incorporated what he learned into his own unique belief system.

The role of faith was central in his life; its importance cannot be overstated. The Mahatma felt that all of his thoughts and actions—the very moral principles we've explored here—were unified by the core of faith which guided his intentions. He could draw strength from his faith in times of uncertainty. His fearlessness was driven by his own certainty in God and humanity. He wrote religion "changes one's very nature, which binds one indissolubly to the truth within and which ever purifies." He relied on that faith to become a moral leader and carve an uncharted path that hundreds of thousands follow.

Here's one example of Gandhi's unswerving belief in the core goodness of his fellow human. In July 1939, as World War II loomed, the spiritual leader of India wrote a letter to Adolf Hitler, imploring him to "prevent a war which may reduce humanity to the savage state," signing the letter, "Your sincere friend, M.K. Gandhi."

Hitler did not reply.

In December 1940, with the war raging, he wrote a longer letter, imploring Hitler to end the war, pleading, "Is it too much to ask you to make an effort for peace...?" The letter is a fascinating read. He alternated between flattering—"We have no doubt about your bravery or devotion to your fatherland, nor do we believe that you are the monster described by your opponents"—and scolding the Nazi dictator—"many of your acts are monstrous and unbecoming of human dignity...You are leaving no legacy to your people of which they would feel proud. They cannot take pride in a recital of cruel deed, however skillfully planned." He referenced India's own struggles against British rule across half a century.

But the part that stands out for me are his opening lines of that second letter.

"DEAR FRIEND,

That I address you as a friend is no formality. I own no foes. My business in life has been for the past 33 years to enlist the friendship of the whole of humanity by befriending mankind, irrespective of race, colour or creed."

This letter, while critical of Hitler's methods, was still imbued with the pure faith that Gandhi could move mountains and touch the inherent goodness of anyone. Adolf Hitler was apparently unmoved. Gandhi's faith did not work a miracle that time—we all know the tragedy of the Holocaust and the six million that died—but he continued his mission undeterred.

We "take a leap of faith," goes the expression. What exactly are we talking about? Leap? Like attempting to jump across a deep canyon, a la daredevil cyclist Evel Knievel? (Note the "devil" in daredevil, as if to dare to defy faith leads to hell.) Without even measuring the distance or your own leaping ability? Comparing that leap of faith with faith in God?

The idiom—to believe in something or someone based on faith rather than evidence; an attempt to achieve something that has little chance of success—first appeared in the mid-1800s and comes from a translation of the Latin words *saltus fidei*. The Danish philosopher Søren Kierkegaard came up with this expression as a metaphor for belief in God. He argued that God was spiritual rather than physical and was completely separate from the material world of man. Therefore, God could not be understood through science or logic. One could only understand God through faith alone.

Conversations about faith and specifically faith in God become tautological.

This approach doesn't land well with people who depend on proof for their understanding of the world. Surveys have shown that scientists are roughly half as likely as the general public to believe in God or a higher power. The term "evidence-based medicine" was introduced by Canadian physician and professor Gordon Guyatt and his team in 1991 to shift the emphasis in clinical decision-making from "intuition, unsystematic clinical experience, and pathophysiologic rationale" to scientific research.

I first heard the concept when I started writing about alterative health trends, which previously often relied on anecdotal evidence and what used to be called "old wives' remedies," the kind you'd read about in magazines like *Prevention* and *Reader's Digest*.

Given this, do people still "keep the faith," as the saying goes? Less and less, at least in the United States, if religious affiliation is any indicator. According to a December 2021 Pew Research Center survey, the religiously unaffiliated share of the American public is 6 per centage points higher than it was five years ago and 10 points higher than a decade ago. The survey found that three-in-ten American adults (almost 30 per cent) are religious "nones"—people who describe themselves as atheists, agnostics or "nothing in particular." In addition, the share of United States adults who say they pray on a daily basis has been trending downward, as has the share who say religion is "very important" in their lives. A March 2021 Gallup poll revealed that membership in houses of worship continued to decline in the previous year, dropping below 50 per cent for the first time in Gallup's 80 years of watching this trend. United States church membership was 73 per cent when Gallup first measured it in 1937 and remained near 70 per cent for the next six decades, until a steady decline began at the start of the 21st century.

And yet, there is a strong and growing spiritual presence on digital platforms. Young people who are hungry for purpose and meaning may be seeking fewer teachings from their priests and rabbis, and more from social media influencers on Instagram. Sharing inspirational quotes online has become our new form of communal prayer. Meditation and mindfulness apps like Calm and Headspace each have millions of subscribers. Is this filling the void? Must faith and spirituality thrive only in a brick-and-mortar house of worship, or adhere to a specific religion, to provide people a moral foundation? I've noticed that more people feel comfortable describing themselves as spiritual, as opposed to religious.

As I pondered these trends, I was struck by how many varied and accessible opportunities there are for people to examine their faith through participation in organized religious groups. The road to faith does not require one to climb Mount Emei in China's Sichuan Province, as do Buddhists; or to circumambulate the Kaaba (most sacred site in Islam), as do Muslims; or participate in the Kumbha Mela, the Hindu festival and pilgrimage to four sacred rivers in India. There are dozens of places of worship in one's own neighborhood. To corroborate that notion, I asked Parthti to identify churches, temples, synagogues and mosques within a 2-mile radius of several cities including her own and mine:

Vadodara, also known as Baroda, Gujarat (where Prarthi lives, population 64 million): temples, 40; churches, 2; Jain temples, 8; mosques, 8.

West Orange, New Jersey (my hometown, population 48,000): churches, 44; Jewish synagogues, 5.

Like Gandhi, I do not attend temple regularly either, and my temple would not be a Hindu temple; it's a Jewish synagogue (shul in Hebrew), also called a temple. I don't belong to a synagogue, nor do I donate to Jewish community causes or to Israel, but I know the difference between lean and fatty corned beef. I'm culturally Jewish, but secular. My other Jewish credentials are that I worked for several years for a Jewish fundraising organization called the Jewish Community Federation. But it was the community, not the Jewish part that attracted me to it. That's where I learned that people like me are called "unaffiliated" Jews.

Searching for answers to the unanswerable Zen koan—"what is faith"—I looked for insight to my own local community of spiritual leaders within two miles of where I live. I started each conversation with that simple question in visits to the heads of a Catholic church, a Jewish temple, a Unitarian Universalist center, a Buddhist center, a Lutheran church, and a Baptist church. Their answers left me without answers. Here's a sampling of their responses.

The priest at Saint Joseph the Worker Roman Catholic Church, diagonally across the street from my apartment:

"The simple answer is believing in what we can't see. The most profound aspect of faith in our relationship with God. Maybe we can't see God but believing in Him, he becomes real, that God is here, not just in the heavens but here with us. I try to help people look at the blessing in their life as a sign of God, to have a grateful heart. And that God works through all that. And if you look back at your life, you may say, 'Maybe God was directing me to here or that.' I believe that God has given us free will, that we can make decisions for our own lives. He gives us the freedom but if we fall off that path, God kind of adjusts it for us. We all encounter bad things, stuff we wouldn't choose but at least in my experience they can be transformed."

The rabbi at the Modern Orthodox synagogue Congregation Beth Israel:

"Faith is not abstract. It's how one lives one's life. We should never mistake faith for science. It's like we try to take faith and analyze it in a lab. That's not what faith is. I don't look for certainty in my faith. If I mistake faith for dogma, that's not faith either. To me God is unknowable; God is surprising. I want to be surprised by God. God commands us and we take action. When Shabbat comes, we pray and are reminded of our commitment to God as the creator of the world and then we rest on the 7th day."

Two monks at the Dharma Realm Buddhist Association:

"With my Christian friends, the emphasis is on the faith aspect. If you believe in Jesus, you are saved. So is the corollary if you don't believe in Jesus, you're damned? Forever? Wow I don't know if I can really swallow that kind of belief. I find faith is something like a trust that grows over time. So for example, let's say my faith or my trust in Buddhism, or this organization, comes from trying out the practices and seeing myself little bit by little bit change, kind of becoming a little bit more open minded. So, there's a sense of like, 'Oh, I can trust that this leads to a good place, based on my own experience.' I think that's probably the deepest place I trust, is the trying out and saying, 'Okay, I think I can see this works.' As the Buddha said, 'Don't believe me, trust your own experience.' The first very important element is to establish trust in myself behind my narrative story. In fact, in Buddhism we have had three aspects of faith. It's believing in our capability that we can be free. We can be awakened. We can transform, completely, by ourselves. And we also have trust in the methods given by the Buddha. But we need to try them ourselves."

Pastor at the Lutheran Church of the Cross:

"The Lutheran perspective is that faith is a gift given by God based on the sacrifice that Jesus made on the cross, which freed all sinners. The gift of faith is given to all of us. I don't think everybody partakes in it, but I'm confident that even those that don't have faith in the same God have some faith in a higher power and higher calling. It's still that faith that's been given by God. What's wrong with having the unexplained be explained by something that's from our faith and not from empirical physical evidence? The evidence in my own life is the fact that when I pray, my day goes better."

The Reverend at the Berkeley Fellowship of Unitarian Universalists:

"Faith is being in touch with the spirit of love and life. For me, that's everything. I think it's realizing that there is an extraordinary universe out there that we didn't make. We weren't here when that seed was held in the palm of a hand and became the whole universe. From that seed, where would beauty come? Where would love? We think that we humans invented love. That's ridiculous. We see what happens with animals, not just taking care of their young, but how they connect with other species. There's so much of this life and of love that we are part of. It's a mystery but accepting it as this mystery that's taken care of so much that we think we know it exists or has existed and yet where it comes from, how it comes about, all of that is sacred mystery."

Back in 2004, in the footsteps of the Buddha for a major *National Geographic* magazine feature, I learned something about faith I had never considered before. Interviewing Buddhist practitioners from all walks of life around the world, their responses to the same question ("What is faith?") suggested a trend. It is relevant here.

I always asked what drew them to Buddhism. I especially recall meeting a Catholic nun, born and raised in India, who was principal of a Catholic school in New Delhi. Very progressive, she had introduced meditation to the students' curriculum. She took me to watch some 100 kids listening to poor-quality tapes of S.N. Goenka, the very popular and highly respected vipassana meditation teacher. Then the principal took me to her office and when I told her I'd gone on several vipassana retreats of five to 10 days, she warmed up and opened up to me.

I asked the obvious question: "Why or how did a Catholic nun get interested in Buddhist meditation?"

She told me she had been diagnosed with breast cancer and had had a mastectomy. "Why me?" she asked God, the age-old question of those who have had either bad luck or good. No satisfying answer came back. It made her question "not just God, but Jesus too. It was like I lost faith in faith itself." She was in despair. That was when someone suggested she take a 10-day vipassana. She did and it clicked. She said it helped her let go of the victim role, and enabled her to return to a life of faith and the church without attachment to the idea that things will work out the way she wanted them to simply by praying to God.

But that phrase—losing faith in faith itself—rang in my ears, and I heard it echoed in very similar words by people who told me they found their Buddhist practice by way of some event that made them doubt the existence of God—that is, a God who saves you from your troubles and adversities.

While Buddhism is categorized as one of the major religions (it *is* major in that it has 507 million follows as of 2020), Buddhism is not a religion. A religion requires a God, which Buddhism does not have. Buddhism is a philosophy; the Buddha offered a well-thought-out approach to happiness. It is not built on faith, as in faith in someone or something outside yourself.

I can trace my own inquiries into the efficacy of faith all the way back to my grandfather.

I was born into a family of Jews, on both my parents' sides and their parents and their parents and beyond. I know very little about my ancestors beyond my grandparents. My father's father was one of the founders of a small Conservative Jewish synagogue in Queens Village, New York, in 1925. Moe Garfinkel was a big macher (Yiddish for a big shot, someone who is extremely important) in that Jewish community center. When I was young, I accompanied him on the High Holy Days of Rosh Hashanah and Yom Kippur to the Queen Village Jewish Center. As we approached, on the sidewalk outside the temple, congregation members glad-handed him, shook mine and ruffled my hair, until we took our reserved seats in the front pew. When I turned 13, according to the Jewish tradition, I became a man and then Grandpa made sure I was called to the front, to the "bema" where the ark holds the Torah, for an "aliyah." The Torah is a scroll that contains the first five books of the Hebrew Bible. This was a big deal—a mitzvah (in Hebrew, meritorious act); to say the short introductory "bracha" (prayer) to each section of the reading is a great honor that I did not take lightly. By proxy, I had become a big macher. The several hours of the service, standing up and sitting down at various sections of the reading, surrounding by the elders and other machers in the front pews with Grandpa, I not only was close enough to watch the men daven, rocking back and forward and side to side, chanting the lines from the Bible, but close enough to feel their energy.

I had no idea what they were chanting, as it was all in Hebrew and anyway they mumbled. I sort of inferred the depth of the meaning by proxy.

But I wanted desperately to have the experience of transcendence. I was a nascent spiritualist. While Grandpa was a devoutly spiritual man, even while holding the position of a family man and hard worker, my father moved away from it. Oh, he made sure I attended Hebrew school and had my bar mitzvah, and attended the high holy day services on Rosh Hashanah, and of course we celebrated Hanukkah ("for the kids," he'd say, I sensed his cynicism). He'd say the high holy days had turned into a bourgeois fashion and showoff parade, with women flaunting their mink coats and men standing alongside their big-finned Cadillacs.

My own cynicism grew from his. I began to see my grandfather's passion for God as naïve in the context of an increasingly materialist world. But I had one experience that turned me away from Judaism as I entered my years of teen revolt. There were rumors that our rabbi at the West Orange Jewish Center was a bit of a drinker. I did not believe it, until the day of my bar mitzvah ceremony. After the newly minted young man finishes his reading from the Torah, traditionally the rabbi gives a short bit of advice to the kid. When the rabbi turned and learned toward me a little bit and began, "Perry...." I could smell liquor on his breath. This before noon to boot. At that moment, I was washed over with the same cynicism as my father's, throwing in hypocritical as well. Traditional Jews in that time were not big drinkers, except for Manischewitz at Passover.

That experience rocked my faith in the basic tenets of Judaism, and from that time forward, I felt disconnected from the religion of my ancestors and from my roots.

It's why I and many other Jews I knew then looked to the East for the experience of being closer to God, whose existence I could not verify with my own experience of Him.

Some 10 years after my bar mitzvah, I went to India too, looking for the Hindi guru, Ram Dass, because I sensed in this religion I would have an experience of the Higher Power, if it existed. When Ram Dass saw so many Jews drawn to Hinduism, he suggested we turn to Buddhism, because, he said, Judaism and Hinduism both had too many ornate rituals. That was why I turned to Buddhism, the practice of less.

Today I call myself a Hind-Bu-Jew, to cover all the bases and gods. So I went from the religion credited with innovating the One God theory, to the religion of the hundred thousands of gods theory, to the philosophical practice called Buddhism, of the no god theory.

Gandhi's ideas spread throughout the world, like dandelion seeds blown hither and yon in a strong wind, landing in unexpected places that might have also blown Gandhi's mind. One was in the conscience of a Harvard professor turned LSD user and proponent who was ousted from the psychology department for experimenting with the drug on graduate students. He became a student of Hinduism and then spiritual teacher whose expertise in interpreting Eastern philosophy for the Western mind gained him a worldwide audience. In the process he went from Richard Alpert, son of wealth, to Baba Ram Dass, stripped of material possessions, to simply Ram Dass, beloved by millions. He was my first spiritual leader.

His book *Be Here Now*, published in 1971, was a countercultural underground bestseller, some say the first in that category, with more than 2 million books in print. Even its design broke all the molds: sentences swirled in circles on the pages like inwardly spiraling mesmerizing serpentines.

I bought a copy upon the recommendation of a reliable source: a hippie I picked up hitchhiking down the California coast from Vancouver, British Columbia, in the summer of 1971.

I read it several times; it was why my then-wife Iris and I decided to go to India, mainly to find the guru Ram Dass had written about so glowingly, Neem Karoli Baba. We didn't find him but she did a retreat at a Sivananda ashram in Northern India and I studied classical Indian drums with a famous tabla guru in Benares. The experience of India fundamentally changed our previously narrow world view.

Two years later, now living in Cambridge, another odd coincidence led us to eventually meet Ram Dass. We invited him to teach a small group at the carriage house we rented, where he taught us how to chant, meditate and practice Bhastrika, the yoga exercise of intense breathing in and out through the nostrils. When Iris became pregnant, we asked him to be the godfather, and at least in title, he agreed. It was an important and pivotal few years in our lives. And while I had lost touch with him personally, his teachings became a touchstone by which I measure my spiritual and psychological growth.

In 1997 Ram Dass suffered a near-fatal stroke, which left him paralyzed on the right side of his body; expressive aphasia limited his ability to speak and process information at a normal speed. He had moved to Maui where a team of followers saw to his needs while he did his best to continue leading meditations and lecturing virtually. I'm not sure why I kept resisting the desire to go see him; but the more I delayed, the more guilty I felt. In the summer of 2017, assigned a story by the *New York Times* in Maui, I used the visit to Hawaii as an excuse to see Ram Dass.

I doubted he would remember me but as soon as I walked into his bedroom, which was set up to accommodate a hospital-style bed and various devices so he could communicate with the outside world, he let out a big, "Wow" of recognition. I could only imagine what thoughts and memories passed through his mind. It was as though no time had passed in our connection, a poignant enriching encounter. We reminisced for 45 minutes; I was flattered when he said he could tell I still had the inquiring mind of a reporter, my questions always probing for deeper understanding and meaning. *Why did I wait so long to see him?* Then he was pooped out. Before I left, I told him I had just started developing the idea for what became this book and asked if he might have thoughts to add. He said Gandhi was an important influence on his life. I asked if I could come back to tape a conversation just about that. He happily agreed.

Ram Dass passed away at his home on Maui in December 2019, three months after I undertook this experiment. So I lost the opportunity to see him again.

Cut to the winter of 2021. I was on a month-long writing retreat in cozy Mendocino, the coastal village 150 miles (240 kms) north of San Francisco. As is the habit of most writers, I found two local bookstores. Walking into the warm and welcoming Gallery Bookshop, I could feel the energy of true book lovers. I was not surprised by the shop's "manifesto": "We believe in surrounding ourselves with books long finished and books not yet read; in revisiting our younger selves each time we pull old favorites off the shelf... We believe that together, readers, writers, books and bookstores can work magic."

Wandering around the aisles, with no intention to buy yet another book I may not read for quite some time, I came face to face with the cover of a brand new book whose author filled the space, a face I immediately recognized. *Being Ram Dass* was his last book, published posthumously and co-authored with Rameshwar Das, a friend I knew from many years back, a close friend of R.D. and a follower of Neem Karoli (aka Maharaj-ji). By now I knew there are no coincidences: it was published by Sounds True, publisher of *Becoming Gandhi*. I called Ramesh right away, asking if there was anything in his book mentioning Gandhi. "Plenty," he said, and sent me pages where Ram Dass alludes to Gandhi.

From his first reference, I was both grateful—that his thoughts were like mine—but regretful we did not get the chance to talk.

He recounted an exchange with Neem Karoli.

"Do you know Gandhi?" Maharaj-ji asked him.

"No, but I've heard of him."

"Be like Gandhi," his guru told him.

Writes Ram Dass: "I had no idea what to make of this exchange. He was not talking about... a historical figure... (but someone) present for him in a way I could not grasp."

I've felt the same way in the last two years when talking to true followers of Gandhi's every word, as though he were alive.

Ram Dass reflected on Gandhi having said, "My life is my message."

"I think that's what Maharaj-ji was trying to tell me. His directive had to do with participating in the human condition. Our relations with one another are ultimately rooted in who we are—what all our experiences, education, and karma have made us. Life is the message."

Still later, he quotes Gandhi again:

"When you surrender completely to God as the only Truth worth having, you find yourself in the service of all that exists. It becomes your joy and recreation. You never tire of serving others."

RD used to ask us, "Do you want God or do you want to want God?"

I never have gotten all the way there. I still want to want to... Perhaps my lack of surrender completely to God is why writing has not brought me joy in the last few years, even though I am proud of the ways in which my writing about health, psychology and even spirituality have brought some insight and the surcease of suffering for readers.

I found it odd reading how meaningful Gandhi was to my first true spiritual teacher, because in the many talks and lectures I attended—in small groups of 30 at the carriage house or large arenas like the full house in the auditorium of Boston University—I cannot recall Ram Dass mentioning Mahatma Gandhi. Did he think the Western audience would have placed Gandhi in the past, like a bronze statue collecting dust? Was the message of Gandhi so deeply internalized by Ram Dass that he felt it almost obvious? Or was I not listening carefully enough because it was I who had left Gandhi in the past?

We'll never know. And it doesn't matter because whatever pieces of Gandhi were implanted into Ram Dass were expressed not by his many eloquent words but by the message of his life. At least Ram Dass made sure in his last book that no one would doubt the influence Gandhi had on him.

"How good and lovely it is for people to be together."

This line comes from the Hebrew prayer "Hinei Ma Tov" ("How Good It Is").

It jumped out at me when we chanted it recently on Yom Kippur, the holiest of Jewish holy days. I was sitting next to my daughter and granddaughter, along with about 100 or so others in Berkeley at Jewish Gateways, which practices a modern form of Judaism. My grandfather would not have recognized the service rituals, with a cantor/guitarist and most of the prayers in English, compared with the traditions practiced at Grandpa Garfinkel's conservative synagogue in Queens, New York. Jewish Gateways welcomes "wanderings Jews" and "wondering Jews," as its literature puts it. I'd call them New Age Jews.

No matter. We all follow the same Jewish values, more or less.

In Hinduism, a group worshipping together is called a *satsang*. In Buddhism it's a *sangha*. In Islam, a *cemaat*. In Judaism, simply a congregation.

This practice "to be together" is not just "good and lovely." It seems to be integral to showing faith. In fact, I realize, it's how we gain, grow and keep faith in the belief system of our choice. Surrounded by others who look to the same sources of wisdom—the Torah in Judaism, the Koran in Islam, the Bible for Christians, the Veda in Hinduism—reaffirms and reinforces their faith in that belief system. It's hard to look around at a group of people all focused on the same thing and *not* have faith that you're moving in the right direction. *"Well, if all these people schlepped all this way for this, there must be something to it."*

This may be why there are cracks in my own faith—in my own faith in faith. I'm not a joiner or follower; I am a bit of a lone wolf. Being part of a group makes me feel like a lemming. Only in moments of great self-doubt do I reluctantly turn to my own congregation—daughter, sister, family, closest friends—and let down my guard, show my vulnerability. Then and only then does faith wash over me, like a warm shower. It's faith in my fellow man, not necessarily to a Higher Power, that brings me to a greater understanding of why I am here and how I can serve others.

Gandhi's go-to source of spiritual inspiration was the Bhagavad Gita. Among the great pearls of wisdom Gandhi read and internalized: "And the man who hears this, full of faith and free from malice, even he shall attain the happy worlds of the righteous, freed from all evil."

In this I take great hope. If I remain free from malice, free from evil, faith will envelop me and lead me to happiness.

Amen.

HOW TO GANDHI: Keeping the Faith

Keep seeking, keep your heart and mind open.

Make space in your day for contemplation, gratitude, and growth.

It's not important which exact religion or ideology you choose to follow.

To believe in something outside yourself, whether you call it God, The Force, the Universe, is the heart of faith.

EPILOGUE

The Becoming Continues

Before Gandhi, chop wood, carry water. After Gandhi, chop wood, carry water.

That's my adaptation of the old Zen saying: "Before enlightenment chop wood, carry water. After enlightenment chop wood, carry water." There are several interpretations of that quote. Mine is that even after you reach your goal, you still have to maintain the discipline to wash the dishes and do the laundry and other mundane things to keep your life moving forward—but now with greater attention to the process, now with greater enjoyment and joy. But now those simple acts take on Higher Purpose, even when outsiders can't see the inner changes you've been through. One must try to stay grounded in the present moment, while flying high above everyone else in timeless bliss—with humble work effort and even more humble ego. The repetition of these daily chores remains as a reminder that there is more work to do. There is no finish line to life. In the vernacular of our time, we keep on keeping on.

If I ever thought I could become Gandhi, I was not even close. Just thinking it shows how far I still have to go. Like the 9th century Chinese Buddhist monk Linji Yixuan, one of the most prominent masters of Zen history, is attributed to telling a monk: "If you meet the Buddha on the road, kill him." He meant that if you think you know the answers, if you think you have attained Buddhahood, simply thinking you have achieved that state of consciousness shows you have not. There are always questions, there are always deeper levels to strive for, despite knowing you cannot fully know the answers nor reach that level. But, now channeling Yoda, strive we should. While Yoda famously said, "Do. Or do not. There is no try," I advocate the notion that trying, with true intention, is a very good step in the right direction.

The lessons of my experiment are still sinking in and they will continue to do so for the rest of my life.

Mahatma Gandhi was a man, a human being with flaws who made errors and missteps. Sometimes throughout this process the phrase "Do what I say, not what I do" came to mind. The moral principles he wrote about and for the most part lived will eternally be dissected by scholars and pundits—all good ways to keep them relevant.

Will I ever become Gandhi? I hope not. Being Gandhi is impossible. But becoming Gandhi—Gandhi-like—will always have possibilities.

Can you become Gandhi? No. But in these times when morals have taken a back seat to Machiavellian self-interest, there is no better time to take from this book what you find of value, what you find worth changing in yourself to recalibrate your personal moral compass. If enough people took that step, I predict a more compassionate, more peaceful world.

Do you need to go cold tofu vegetarian to achieve Gandhihood? Or could you taper down to once a week, once a month, every few months. Could you taper down from chicken and fish? Sure. I'm happy now as a pescatarian. Maybe I will eliminate fish as well.

Could you direct your mind away from thoughts of violence by watching less of it on TV and films, and in the news? Worth a try, considering the detrimental effect these impressions leave in your mind.

Can you lie less—to others, to yourself? Live with less? Examine your faith more? Limit the power of sexual desire in your life?

I hope this book sparks unexpected contemporary conversations about the teachings of Gandhi from East to West and back again, whether you agree with my thoughts or not, whether you think them sacrilege or not, quirky or enlightening or not.

After a lot of reading, a lot of thinking, and a lot of putting thoughts into action, I came to the realization that often wisdom comes "out of the mouths of babes," that phrase originally found in the Bible's Psalms 8:2.

So I turned to my brilliant granddaughter Kasey Romeiser (her intellectual prowess is not a biased appraisal; this is fact, according to me, her parents and teachers). She knew very little about Gandhi and wondered what the heck I'd been doing the last three years. In response, I asked her to review *Who Was Gandhi?* (Penguin Workshop, 2014) by Dana Meachen Rau, a short book written for middle schoolers, of which Kasey was one at the time. This was her conclusion:

"If Gandhi was still alive today, the world would be a better place. Gandhi encouraged people to protest and speak out to change the world. He fought for what was right by using satyagraha, truth force, which involved noncooperation, nonviolence, and nonpossessions. Noncooperation means breaking unfair laws in a way that isn't harmful or violent. Nonviolence simply means not being violent towards anyone. And lastly, nonpossession is not having too much stuff, and using only what one needs, never more. The main thing I learned from this book is that Gandhi made a difference in many ways, and he still inspires people to do the same."

Mouths of babes indeed. She succinctly sums up the essence of what it took me these many pages to write, and these several years to learn. May her generation and the next ones take to heart her hope that Gandhi still inspires.

Bibliography

Adams, Jad. *Gandhi: Naked Ambition.* London, England. Quercus, 2010.

Ajgaonkar, Sri Meghshyam T. *Mahatma: A Golden Treasury of Wisdom—Thoughts & Glimpses of Life.* Mumbai, India. Sri Meghshyam T. Ajgaonkar.

Boo, Katherine. *Behind the Beautiful Forevers: Life, Death, and Hope in a Mumbai Undercity.* New York, New York. Random House, 2012.

Dass, Ram with Das, Rameshwar. *Being Ram Dass.* Boulder, Colorado. Sounds True, Inc, 2021.

De Lambilly, Elisabeth. *Gandhi: his Life, his Struggles, his Words.* Brooklyn, New York. Enchanted Lion Books, 2010.

Desai, Kalpana. *The Mahatma Beyond Gandhi.* Mumbai, India. Sarvodaya International Trust, 2001.

Desai, Ashwin and Vahed, Goolam. *The South African Gandhi: Stretcher-Bearer of Empire.* Shahpur Jat, New Delhi. Navayana Publishing, 2016.

Desphande, M. S. *The Way to God.* Berkeley, California. Berkeley Hills Books, 1999.

Duhigg, Charles. *The Power of Habit: Why we do what we do in Life and Business.* New York. The Random House Publishing Group, 2012.

Duncan, Ronald. *Gandhi: Selected Writings.* London, England. Fontana/Collins, 1971.

Easwaran, Eknath. *Gandhi the Man: How One Man Changed Himself to Change the World.* Tomales, California. Nilgiri Press, 2011.

Ekman, Paul. *Telling Lies.* New York, New York. The Berkley Publishing Group, 1986.

Fischer, Louis. *Gandhi: His Life and Message for the World.* New York, New York. New American Library, 1982.

Fischer, Louis. *The Essential Gandhi: An Anthology of his Writings on his Life, Work and Ideas.* New York, New York. Vintage Books, 1962.

Gandhi, Arun. *Legacy of Love: my Education in the Path of Nonviolence.* Mattoon, Illinois. Gandhi Worldwide Education Institute, 2009.

Gandhi, Arun. *The Gift of Anger.* New York, New York. Jeter Publishing, 2017.

Gandhi, Mahatma. *A Guide to Health.* San Bernadino, California. First Rate Publishers.

Gandhi, Mahatma. *The Bhagavad Gita According to Gandhi.* Berkeley, California. North Atlantic Books, 2009.

Gandhi, M. K. *Basic Education.* Ahmedabad. Navajivan Publishing House, 1956.

Gandhi, M. K. *Hind Swaraj or Indian Home Rule.* Ahmedabad, India. Navajivan Publishing House, 2011.

Gandhi, M. K. *The Power of Nonviolent Resistance.* New Delhi. Penguin Books, 2019.

Gandhi, M. K. *The Way to God.* Albany, California. Publishers Group West, 1999.

Gandhi, Mohandas K. *Gandhi: An Autobiography.* Boston, Massachusetts. Beacon Press, 1957.

Guha, Ramachandra. *Gandhi Before India.* New York, New York. Alfred A. Knopf, 2013.

Ingram, Catherine. *In the Footsteps of Gandhi: Conversations with Spiritual Social Activists.* Berkeley, California. Parallax Press, 1990.

Kakutani, Michiko. *The Death of Truth.* New York, USA. Tim Duggan Books, 2018.

Kalia, Ravi. *Gandhinagar: Building National Identity in Postcolonial India.* Colombia, South Carolina. University of South Carolina Press, 2004.

Khilnani, Sunil. *The Idea of India.* New York, New York. Farrar Straus Giroux, 1999.

Lelyveld, Joseph. *Great Soul: Mahatma Gandhi and his Struggle with India.* New York. Alfred A. Knopf, 2011.

Meer, Fatima. *Apprenticeship of a Mahatma.* Phoenix, Arizona. Phoenix Settlement, 1994.

Merton, Thomas. *Gandhi on Non-Violence.* Canada. Penguin Books, 1965.

Metcalf, Barbara D. and Metcalf, Thomas R. *A Concise History of India.* Cambridge, United Kingdom. Cambridge University Press, 2002.

Mukherjee, Rudrangshu. *The Penguin Gandhi Reader.* India. Penguin Books, 1993.

Nagler, Michael N. *The Third Harmony: The Nonviolence and the New Story of Human Nature.* Oakland, California. Berrett-Koehler Publishers, 2020.

Nanda, B. R. *Mahatma Gandhi: A Biography.* New Delhi. Oxford University Press, 1981.

Robbin, Jeanette. *Dr. Ambedkar and his Movement.* Narayanguda, Hyderabad. Dr. Ambedkar Publications Society, 2000.

Parel, Anthony J. *Gandhi: Hind Swaraj and Other Writings.* Cambridge, United Kingdom. Cambridge University Press, 2007.

Patel, Narottambhai. *Nai Talim in Gujarat: Philosophy and Development.* India. Gujarat Nai Talim Sangh, 2002.

Patel, Raojibhai M. *The Making of the Mahatma: Based on 'Gandhiji ni Sadhna'.* Usmanpura, Ahmedabad. Ravindra R. Patel, 1990.

Rau, Dana Meachen. *Who was Gandhi?* New York. Penguin Workshop, 2014.

Sharma, Arvind. *Gandhi: A Spiritual Biography.* India. Yale University Press, 2013.

Slate, Nico. *Gandhi's Search for the Perfect Diet.* Seattle, Washington. University of Washington Press, 2019.

Senauke, Alan. *Heirs to Ambedkar—The Rebirth of Engaged Buddhism in India.* Berkeley, California. Clear View Press, 2015.

Varia, Avani. *Chalo Charkho Ramiye: A Contemporary Charka Movement.* Ahmedabad. Navajivan Publishing House, 2020.

Weber, Thomas. *On the Salt March: The Historiography of Mahatma Gandhi's March to Dandi.* Daryaganj, New Delhi. Rupa Publications, 2009.

Wolpert, Stanley. *Gandhi's Passions: The Life and Legacies of Mahatma Gandhi.* New York, New York. Oxford University Press, 2001.

Acknowledgements

This book has been almost 15 years in the making.

In those years many friends and colleagues continued to encourage me, challenge me, inspire me, feed me, house me, support me financially, spiritually and emotionally. I thank these people for being part of my experiment with Truth.

My previous agent, Candice Fuhrman, first planted the seed when she recommended I “do the same thing with Gandhi” that I did with the Buddha in my last book, “Buddha or Bust.” Six years later I picked up on the idea when I met Jayapriya Vasudevan of Jacaranda Literary Agency in Bangalore (Bengaluru), India, who recognized its potential and sold it to Simon & Schuster India. Helen Mangham, her colleague in the United Kingdom, has also been instrumental in offering it to European publishers. Jayapriya introduced me to her co-agent Susan Raihofer, of the David Black Agency in New York. Susan was dogged in finding Sounds True, the perfect United States publisher for this book. David Black co-agents Mohrbooks sold it to Random House Germany/Integral.

Haven Iverson, of Sounds True, has been the perfect editor any writer could hope for: enthusiastic champion of this book from acquiring it to the end and then some, supportive, patient beyond belief. If this book holds together well, it is thanks to her.

Elizabet Kurumlu of Istanbul, holder of many hats

including travel guide, film director, sometime cinematographer, accompanied me to South Africa after a rocky start, helped me recover a lost cellphone and a laptop mistakenly left at the airport in Mumbai. Her film work of my interviews and adventures with me in South Africa is part of a short video that accompanies this book.

Nestor Serrano, then chief concierge at the Intercontinental Hotel Marine Drive in Mumbai, put in the extra hours to help recover the aforementioned laptop from his end.

Prarthi Shah, of Baroda, Gujarat, India, worked into all hours of the night as my chief researcher, off of whom I bounced endless questions.

There were a handful of hotels that at one point or another gave me shelter: the SilverCloud Hotel in Ahmedabad, Gujarat; the Intercontinental Marine Drive, Mumbai; the Rosewood Hotel, London; the Mount View Hotel, Calistoga, California; the Four Seasons Hotel, Mumbai; the Richmond Istanbul and the Richmond Nua Wellness Spa, Sapanca, both in Turkey.

Wes Nisker, author, radio newsman, Buddhism teacher, raconteur and most importantly the devoted friend who called all too frequently with the burning question, "Are you done yet?" He's been there for me even when I was not there for me for some 30+ years.

Thanks also to these friends who have been inspiring each in his and her own way: Padmaja Kumari Parmar, Mudita Nisker and Dan Clurman, Jeff Greenwald, Chris Barnett, Mark Mazer, Belgin Aksoy, Mikkel Aaland, Daniel Ben-Horin, Daniel Shiner, Rahul Akerkar, Margaret Fox.

Special thanks to my rock-solid son-in-law, Ryan Romeiser, always there through thick and thin.

Kasey Romeiser, so much more to me than my one and only granddaughter, applied her nascent editorial skills and great writing potential by organizing and typing up the bibliography at the end of this book.

There is a cliché in book acknowledgments that goes, "This book could not have been written without the help of..." This is more than a cliché in the case of my daughter Ariana Garfinkel, without whom literally I would not have finished writing this book. Award-winning independent documentary film producer, she has been the one in the room holding it together for many a creative filmmaker and I had the fatherly privilege of watching her in action as she demonstrated her considerable organizational skills and gentle editorial diplomacy in the final stages here.